Tyrants on Twitter

STANFORD STUDIES IN LAW AND POLITICS

Edited by Keith J. Bybee

TYRANTS ON TWITTER

Protecting Democracies from Information Warfare

David L. Sloss

STANFORD UNIVERSITY PRESS | STANFORD, CALIFORNIA

STANFORD UNIVERSITY PRESS
Stanford, California

Printed in the United States of America on acid-free, archival-quality paper

Library of Congress Cataloging-in-Publication Data

Names: Sloss, David, author.
Title: Tyrants on Twitter : protecting democracies from information warfare / David L. Sloss.
Other titles: Stanford studies in law and politics.
Description: Stanford, California : Stanford University Press, 2022. | Series: Stanford studies in law and politics | Includes bibliographical references and index.
Identifiers: LCCN 2021049970 (print) | LCCN 2021049971 (ebook) | ISBN 9781503628441 (cloth) | ISBN 9781503631151 (epub)
Subjects: LCSH: Social media—Political aspects—Western countries. | Social media—Government policy—Western countries. | Social media—Law and legislation—Western countries. | Information warfare—Political aspects. | Information warfare—Russia (Federation) | Information warfare—China. | Democracy—Western countries.
Classification: LCC HM742 .S588 2022 (print) | LCC HM742 (ebook) | DDC 302.23/1091821—dc23/eng/20211108
LC record available at https://lccn.loc.gov/2021049970
LC ebook record available at https://lccn.loc.gov/2021049971

Typeset by Newgen North America in 10/15 Galliard

CONTENTS

TABLES AND FIGURES

THIS BOOK ADDRESSES the problem of Chinese and Russian information warfare. I define the term "information warfare" as the use of social media by state agents to conduct foreign influence operations. The book proposes a new Alliance for Democracy so that democratic states can develop a coordinated, transnational approach to regulating social media to protect the integrity of their democratic political systems from the threat posed by Chinese and Russian information warfare.

I completed work on the initial manuscript for this project in November 2020. Then, on January 6, 2021, there was a riot at the Capitol in Washington, DC, unlike anything the United States had experienced since the Civil War.[1] The insurrectionists were not Chinese or Russian agents; they were U.S. citizens. Most of them came to the Capitol because they believed the Big Lie: the claim that Democrats engaged in massive electoral fraud to steal the 2020 presidential election from the rightful winner, Donald Trump. Social media clearly played a role in disseminating the Big Lie, but so did several legacy media networks, such as Fox News, Newsmax TV, and One America News Network (OANN). Given available data, it is impossible to measure the relative influence of social media versus legacy media in spreading the Big Lie. Nevertheless, one thing seems clear: the people primarily responsible for spreading the Big Lie were U.S. citizens, not Chinese or Russian agents. There is some evidence that foreign agents helped amplify the main narrative, but their contribution appears to have been fairly minor.[2]

In light of the insurrection at the Capitol on January 6, one might legitimately ask whether the book's focus on Chinese and Russian information warfare is misplaced. One could argue that the primary threat to American democracy comes not from foreign influence operations but from domestic disinformation campaigns. Indeed, after the events of January 6, if someone asked me to rank the significance of various threats to American democracy, I would rank domestic disinformation higher, and foreign interference correspondingly lower, than I would have before January 6. Even so, there are two primary reasons why a book focusing on Chinese and Russian information warfare is still timely and important.

First, Chinese and Russian information warfare poses a threat to democracies around the world, not just in the United States. The book's central argument is framed in terms of the global threat to democracy. Chapter 1 demonstrates that, on a global basis, democracy has been declining and authoritarianism has been gaining momentum since about 2010. Moreover, chapter 3 notes that, since 2014, Russia has conducted foreign influence operations in at least twenty-one countries that are members of NATO, the European Union (EU), or both. Meanwhile, as documented in chapter 4, Chinese technology companies are helping to strengthen autocratic control in several countries by exporting "digital authoritarianism," and China is exploiting social media to conduct foreign influence operations in Australia, Canada, the United Kingdom, and Taiwan, to name but a few states. Furthermore, as of this writing (in May 2021), there is no evidence that domestic sources of disinformation have been sufficiently influential to spark events comparable to the January 6 riots in other leading Western democracies. Thus, from the perspective of the global struggle between democracy and autocracy, Chinese and Russian information warfare remains a topic of vital concern.

Second, from a U.S. perspective, the First Amendment imposes significant limitations on the government's power to regulate domestic sources of disinformation.[3] Hence, the Constitution severely constrains the range of potential regulatory responses to the problem of domestic disinformation on social media. In contrast, Russian and Chinese agents who conduct information warfare activities on U.S. social media platforms—and who are physically located in Russia and China, respectively—are not entitled to any First Amendment protections.[4] Granted, the First Amendment imposes some limits on the government's power to regulate speech on social media by Chinese and Russian agents, because the Constitution protects the right of U.S. listeners to receive that speech.[5] Even so, the government has much greater leeway to regulate speech by foreign agents on U.S. social media platforms than it does to regulate speech by U.S. citizens on those same platforms. Part Two explains and defends a proposal for democratic states that are members of the proposed Alliance for Democracy to develop and implement a transnational regulatory system that would ban Chinese and Russian agents from U.S. social media platforms. (As explained in chapter 6, the proposed ban is subject to an exemption for benign state agents to protect the First Amendment rights of U.S. listeners to receive foreign speech.) Such a ban, if applied to domestic sources of disinformation in the United States, would clearly violate the First Amendment. However, as shown in chapter 8, the proposed ban is constitutionally defensible when applied to Chinese and Russian agents.

Two very different aspects of my own professional background shaped my thinking about the proposed transnational regulatory system. First, during the Cold War—before I became a law professor—I spent almost a decade in the U.S. government, where I worked on East-West arms control negotiations. During that time period, I developed substantial expertise in designing arms control verification systems. The proposed system for defending Western democracies from Chinese and Russian information warfare draws on my expertise in arms control verification systems. Second, during my academic career, I have developed substantial expertise in U.S. constitutional law. Accordingly, I designed the proposed transnational regulatory system to be consistent (or arguably consistent) with constitutional limitations on the government's power to regulate speech.

Critics may argue that the proposed transnational regulatory system is flawed because it does not solve the "useful idiot" problem. Russian strategists refer to foreigners who unwittingly help advance Russia's foreign policy goals as "useful idiots." Donald Trump is a classic example of a useful idiot. By spreading the message that the 2020 presidential election was tainted by fraud, Trump helped advance Russia's goal of undermining the faith of U.S. citizens in the integrity of American democracy. There is no credible evidence to support the fraud allegation. Nevertheless, a CBS News poll in December 2020 found that 82 percent of Trump's supporters believed that Biden's victory was illegitimate and tainted by fraud.[6] That widespread belief clearly serves Russia's foreign policy interests. However, neither Vladimir Putin nor his legions of cyber troops can claim primary credit for the successful disinformation campaign. To the contrary, Donald Trump, more than any other single individual, deserves the blame for persuading millions of Americans that the 2020 election was fraudulent.[7]

The useful idiot problem is a serious problem that merits a thoughtful policy response. My proposed transnational regulatory system does not solve that problem. However, it bears emphasis that no regulatory proposal can solve every problem. This book focuses on information warfare conducted by foreign cyber troops, not domestic disinformation. The useful idiot problem—as illustrated by Donald Trump's effort to promote the Big Lie—falls outside the scope of my proposal because it fits in the category of domestic disinformation, not information warfare.

Implementation of the proposed ban on Chinese and Russian agents is not cost-free. The primary cost is that—to make the ban effective—members of the Alliance for Democracy would need to implement a social media registration system requiring citizens and nationals of Alliance member states to register their social media accounts with their home governments if they want to engage in public communication on social media.[8] Reasonable people may disagree as to whether the benefits of the proposed transnational regulatory system outweigh the costs. The January 6 insurrection clearly alters that cost-benefit calculus by strengthening the argument in favor of the view that domestic disinformation is a much bigger threat to American democracy than foreign interference. People who believe that domestic disinformation is a major threat to American democracy, and that foreign interference is a minor threat, might well conclude that the costs of the proposed transnational regulatory system outweigh the benefits, because the proposed ban and registration system would do very little to address the problem of domestic disinformation. (The proposed registration system may provide a useful building block for designing a regulatory system that could help alleviate the threat of domestic disinformation, but the proposal developed in chapter 6 focuses primarily on the threat of information warfare.)

Chapter 7 presents a detailed analysis of the costs and benefits of the proposed transnational regulatory system. The key point here is this: Given First Amendment constraints on regulating domestic sources of disinformation, and given that Chinese and Russian information warfare poses a threat to democracies around the world, it makes sense from a public policy perspective to think about Chinese and Russian information warfare as a problem that is distinct from the problem of domestic disinformation, and that warrants a different type of policy response. The fact that foreign agents often amplify narratives disseminated by domestic sources of disinformation[9] does not alter the conclusion that domestic disinformation and foreign information warfare are analytically distinct problems that, although related, warrant separate treatment.

This book contributes to the scholarly and public policy debate by analyzing Chinese and Russian information warfare as a distinct threat to democratic governments, and by proposing and evaluating policy solutions tailored to that threat. Many readers will not be persuaded that my proposed policy solutions are the best possible solutions. Regardless, I hope that the book will help readers gain a better understanding of the threat posed by Chinese and Russian information warfare, and that it may prompt readers to develop their own ideas about how Western democracies can and should defend themselves against that threat.

ACKNOWLEDGMENTS

NO PERSON IS AN ISLAND. I could not have written this book without the assistance of many helping hands. As an author, it is a pleasure to take this opportunity to thank the many people who contributed to the successful completion of this project. I can only hope that I am not offending anyone by failing to mention his/her name in this brief expression of thanks.

First, I want to thank Santa Clara University School of Law—especially Deans Lisa Kloppenberg and Anna Han—for providing financial support for my research, and also for nurturing an intellectual environment that encourages scholars to pursue serious research projects. I wrote large portions of the book while I was on sabbatical leave in fall 2020, generously funded by Santa Clara University.

I thank Elizabeth Edwards and Ellen Platt—both of whom are research librarians at the Law School—for superior research assistance. I am also indebted to several students who provided excellent research assistance over the course of this project: Katherine Blake, Jonathan Greene, Rory Hayes, Patrick Malone, and Sydney Yang. Additionally, I am grateful to my many colleagues at the Law School who have helped make Santa Clara such a stimulating intellectual environment, especially David Ball, Colleen Chien, Eric Goldman, Pratheepan Gulasekaram, Brad Joondeph, Michelle Oberman, Gary Spitko, and David Yosifon.

In 2019, when the book was still in its early stages of development, I published two blog posts that helped me work out ideas that were later incorporated into the book: "Could Russia Swing the Next Presidential Election?", *The Hill*, May 31, and "Corporate Defenses to Information

Warfare," *Just Security*, August 20. I thank the editors of those publications for helping me sharpen certain arguments, and for giving me the opportunity to disseminate ideas in a form that generated helpful feedback.

Numerous scholars provided valuable feedback on early drafts of certain chapters; in particular, I want to thank Ashutosh Bhagwat, Erica Frantz, Kyle Langvardt, Helen Norton, Jeremy Rabkin, Wayne Sandholtz, Joseph Thai, Alexander Tsesis, and Andrew Woods. The book is undoubtedly better than it would have been if I had not benefited from their constructive criticism. I also owe thanks to several scholars who generously took time to discuss ideas with me in a series of ongoing conversations, including Rohit Chopra, Rebecca Hamilton, Herb Lin, and Irina Raicu. I gained a more nuanced understanding of various problems as a result of those conversations.

I was fortunate to be able to present portions of the book at various conferences and workshops both before and during the pandemic. When the project was still in its earliest phase, and had not yet fully taken shape, I presented a draft at the Internet Law Works in Progress conference at Santa Clara University in spring 2019. I thank my colleague Eric Goldman for inviting me to present at that conference, and to all the scholars in attendance who provided me with valuable feedback. During that same time period, I also gave presentations for a workshop at Fordham University School of Law (hosted by my friend Martin Flaherty) and for a faculty workshop at Santa Clara Law. I received very helpful feedback from participants in both those workshops. These early presentations helped me refine my thinking and helped shape the future direction of my research.

As the book was nearing completion (in the midst of the pandemic), I was fortunate to be able to give presentations via Zoom to the Technology and Ethics Group at the Markkula Center for Applied Ethics at Santa Clara University; the ACS Constitutional Law Scholars Forum (hosted by Eang Ngov, at Barry University); and a conference on Democracy and Information Warfare (hosted by Antje von Ungern-Sternberg at Trier University, and Thomas Burri at University of St. Gallen). In all cases, I received valuable comments from participants that helped me refine and sharpen my arguments.

I owe special thanks to my editors at Stanford University Press (SUP). Marcela Cristina Maxfield has supported the project since I first submitted a book proposal in spring 2020. Sunna Juhn, Gigi Mark, and Paul Tyler also provided excellent editorial assistance in later phases of the project. I am also very grateful to the two blind reviewers who—at SUP's invitation—reviewed and commented on the entire manuscript. The final product is undoubtedly much improved, thanks to their very constructive comments.

I never would have launched this project without the encouragement and assistance of Dominic Booth. In summer 2018, Dominic was taking a break before starting his first year of law school. He asked me whether I was working on any research projects that might benefit from his assistance. I was very interested in learning more about Russia's use of social media to interfere in the 2016 U.S. presidential election. At that time, I knew a lot about U.S.-Russian relations (based partly on my prior government experience), but I knew nothing about social media. In summer 2018, Dominic educated me about social media technology. That education provided a springboard that enabled me to pursue the rest of the project. Dominic also helped me think through my ideas about social media regulation, which ultimately developed into the proposal in chapter 6. I am extremely grateful for his substantial intellectual contribution to this project.

Finally, I owe special thanks to my beloved wife, Heidi Sloss. She is an ongoing source of support and encouragement for all of my professional endeavors. Writing a book is a long, slow, laborious process. Heidi has been with me on every step of that journey. She makes me a better person, which hopefully also makes me a better scholar. Thank you.

Tyrants on Twitter

PART ONE

DIAGNOSIS

CHAPTER ONE

INFORMATION WARFARE
AND DEMOCRATIC DECAY

"ETERNAL VIGILANCE IS the price of liberty." These famous words, often incorrectly attributed to Thomas Jefferson, may seem appropriate in the midst of the Covid-19 pandemic.[1] But they are equally appropriate for a book about information warfare and social media. In the midst of the pandemic, many people mistakenly believed that a mandate to wear masks was an unwarranted infringement of individual liberty. In fact, such a mandate is an example of the vigilance that is necessary to preserve our lives, without which there can be no liberty.

Similarly, in the modern era of social media, many techno-utopians mistakenly believe that any government regulation of social media is an unwarranted infringement of individual liberty. In fact, such regulation is necessary to protect our body politic from the threat posed by Russian and Chinese information warfare. Let us be clear: Liberal democracy is under attack, not just in the United States but around the world. As of 2019: "For the first time since 2001, there are more autocracies than democracies in the world."[2] To protect our cherished liberties, we need to protect democracies from Chinese and Russian cyber troops because democratic self-government is the foundation of individual liberty. The big technology companies are not up to the task. We need government regulation so that Facebook, Twitter, and other social media companies do not continue to function as Trojan horses, allowing the virus of information warfare to infect and ultimately subvert liberal democracy.

In the current geopolitical and technological environment, proponents of liberal democracy and liberal internationalism—and I openly declare myself a proponent of both—confront a difficult choice. Advocates of liberal democracy are committed to freedom of expression, with minimal government controls. Advocates of liberal internationalism are committed to reducing barriers to transnational flows of people, goods, and information. Russia and China are working "to upend the Western liberal order by turning Western virtues of openness . . . into vulnerabilities to be exploited."[3] Unfortunately, their strategy is working because democratic governments have failed to regulate social media to protect democracy. If we want to preserve both liberal democracy and liberal internationalism, Western democracies must restrict the ability of Chinese and Russian cyber troops to exploit social media to conduct information warfare.

Until now, democratic governments have given social media companies carte blanche to decide who is entitled to create and operate accounts on their platforms. The companies have adopted open-door policies, allowing almost all people from all countries to create social media accounts. Consequently, Chinese and Russian cyber troops have developed an active presence on U.S. social media platforms. Russia has taken advantage of U.S. social media platforms to interfere with democratic elections and to erode faith in democratic institutions.[4] China has exploited U.S. social media platforms to disseminate foreign propaganda extolling the virtues of its authoritarian system and highlighting the flaws of liberal democracy.[5] By granting Chinese and Russian agents unrestricted access to U.S. social media platforms, democratic governments are inadvertently making a significant, albeit indirect, contribution to the worldwide erosion of liberal democratic norms.

For the foreseeable future, the world will be divided between democratic and authoritarian states. The United States will continue to be the most powerful country in the democratic camp. China and Russia will be the most powerful countries in the authoritarian camp. The United States and its allies will engage in geopolitical competition with China and Russia in both military and economic domains. However, the present era differs from the Cold War in several respects. Most importantly, for the purposes of this book, due to the spread of information technology, the domain of information operations has become a much more significant battleground in the broader geopolitical landscape. As one commentator noted: "The new great-power competition won't necessarily take place on battlefields . . . it will happen on smartphones, computers, and other connected devices and on the digital infrastructure that supports them."[6]

Currently, U.S. social media platforms—primarily Facebook, Twitter, YouTube, and Instagram—are critical battlefields in the ongoing competition between democratic and authoritarian states. Russian citizens use VK to communicate with each other via social media, but Russian agents exploit U.S. social media platforms to conduct information warfare in foreign countries. Chinese citizens use Sina Weibo and other platforms to communicate with each other, but Chinese cyber troops often use U.S. social media platforms to disseminate foreign propaganda. (Chinese agents also use WeChat, a Chinese platform, for this purpose.[7]) The power of democratic governments to regulate social media could potentially give liberal democracies a major strategic advantage in the information warfare domain. Until now, Western democracies have squandered that advantage by granting Chinese and Russian agents unrestricted access to U.S. social media platforms. Those platforms are some of the most powerful weapons available in the modern information warfare arsenal. Chinese and Russian cyber troops are deploying those weapons with great effect to undermine liberal democratic norms. U.S. technology companies are effectively subsidizing their information warfare activities by granting them access to U.S. social media platforms.

Aside from the development of information technology, there is an additional reason why information operations have greater strategic significance today than during the Cold War. The West will not defeat China militarily for the same reasons that we did not defeat the Soviet Union militarily: armed conflict is too dangerous and costly. The United States and its allies won the Cold War economically because it became painfully obvious to people and governments throughout the world—including people and governments within the Warsaw Pact—that the Soviet system was an economic disaster. In contrast, China is an economic success story.

Between 2000 and 2018, China's share of global GDP increased from about 3 percent to about 14 percent. During that same period, the U.S. share of global GDP decreased from about 26 percent to about 21 percent.[8] Hence, the United States is unlikely to outperform China economically for the foreseeable future.

Since Western democracies cannot defeat China or Russia militarily, or outperform China economically, we must compete effectively in the information operations domain to score geopolitical gains. To reiterate, the global dominance of U.S. social media platforms and the power of democratic governments to regulate those platforms could potentially give democratic states a major strategic advantage in information warfare. This book contends that the United States and its allies should exploit that advantage by banning Chinese and Russian agents from U.S. social media platforms. (The proposed ban would be subject to an exemption for benign state agents.) An effective ban would help protect liberal democracies and liberal internationalism from the threat posed by information warfare. In short, although my proposal is somewhat paradoxical, I contend that we should adopt seemingly illiberal policies to preserve the values of liberalism.

The current laissez-faire approach to regulating social media is not working. The policy of permitting Chinese and Russian agents to maintain an active presence on U.S. social media platforms creates substantial costs that far outweigh any purported benefits. The primary costs are the erosion of faith in democratic institutions in established democracies and the steady spread of authoritarian governance models to an increasing number of countries. The primary ostensible benefit of the laissez-faire approach relates to a utopian dream of an unregulated internet. That utopian dream may have seemed plausible in the 1990s.[9] Indeed, as recently as 2011, when political protests fueled by social media unseated several Arab dictators, many people believed that social media would contribute to increasing democratization.[10] Today, however, it has become clear that the failure to regulate social media is creating a nightmare that is starkly at odds with libertarian ideals. Internet libertarians envision a world in which an unregulated internet expands the sphere of individual freedom. Unfortunately, though, the laissez-faire approach makes the world less free.[11]

The laissez-faire approach is also inconsistent with foundational principles of democratic self-governance. The constitutions of modern liberal democracies establish a system of representative democracy. The core idea of representative democracy is that We the People govern ourselves by electing legislators who enact the laws that regulate our conduct. In the modern era, many citizens of democratic countries spend a significant portion of their waking hours on social media. Insofar as we live our lives on social media, we are *not* governed by laws enacted by our elected representatives. To the contrary, we are governed by rules—which are functionally equivalent to laws—promulgated by the private companies that effectively govern social media platforms.[12] As one commentator observed, "An enormous amount of political speech now transpires on a platform used by 1.73 billion people a day, and whose rules about speech are ultimately decided and enforced by a single person: Facebook's CEO, Mark Zuckerberg."[13] Private social media companies are not accountable to the people; we did not elect Mark Zuckerberg or Twitter's Jack Dorsey to enact the laws regulating our conduct on social media. If the citizens of Western democracies want a governance system for social media that is consistent with the core principles of representative democracy, we need laws enacted by our elected representatives to supplement the rules promulgated by private companies.

THE PROBLEM OF DEMOCRATIC DECAY

For many years, political scientists have debated about how best to classify countries into "regime types." One very helpful classification system—the "regimes of the world," or RoW system—divides countries into four groups: liberal democracies, electoral democracies, electoral autocracies, and closed autocracies.[14] "In *closed autocracies*, the chief executive is either not subjected to elections or there is no meaningful, *de-facto* competition in elections." In contrast, "*electoral autocracies* hold *de-facto* multiparty elections . . . but they fall short of democratic standards due to significant

TABLE I. Democratization during the Cold War. Source: V-Dem database.

	1960	1970	1980	1990
Countries that are liberal democracies	10%	13%	15%	17%
Countries that are democracies (total)	19%	24%	26%	34%
Countries that are autocracies (total)	81%	76%	74%	66%
Countries that are closed autocracies	52%	54%	48%	36%

irregularities, limitations on party competition or other violations of . . . institutional requisites for democracies." *Electoral democracies* are countries that not only "hold *de-facto* free and fair multiparty elections, but also . . . achieve a sufficient level of institutional guarantees of democracy such as freedom of association, suffrage, clean elections, an elected executive, and freedom of expression." Finally, under the RoW system, "a *liberal democracy* is, in addition, characterized by its having effective legislative and judicial oversight of the executive as well as protection of individual liberties and the rule of law."[15]

Classification of countries in accordance with the RoW system is codified in the Varieties of Democracy (V-Dem) database with the "v2x_regime" variable.[16] The data in table 1 is derived from the V-Dem database. Table 1 shows that there was a strong trend of democratization during the Cold War, especially between 1980 and 1990. Between 1960 and 1990, the percentage of countries in the world that qualified as democracies (including both liberal and electoral democracies) increased from 19 to 34 percent, while the percentage of autocracies (including both closed and electoral autocracies) decreased from 81 to 66 percent. During the same period, the percentage of liberal democracies increased from 10 to 17 percent, while the percentage of closed autocracies decreased from 52 to 36 percent. In short, during the Cold War, democracy was on the rise and autocracy was in decline.

These trends accelerated during the early years of the post–Cold War period. As illustrated in figure 1, the percentage of democracies in the world increased from 38 percent in 1991 to 54 percent in 2007, while the percentage of autocracies decreased from 62 percent in 1991 to 46 percent in 2007. Similarly, the percentage of liberal democracies increased from 18 percent in 1991 to 25 percent in 2007, and the percentage of closed autocracies declined from 34 percent in 1991 to just 12 percent in 2011. For more than a decade, Francis Fukuyama's optimistic prediction that all states would become democracies appeared to be prophetic.[17]

Unfortunately, we have witnessed a trend of increasing autocratization over the past decade. As shown in figure 1, the percentage of liberal democracies has been declining since 2011 and the percentage of closed autocracies has been growing since 2015. The total percentage of democracies in the world dropped sharply between 2017 and 2019, while the percentage of autocracies registered a sharp increase during that period.

Figure 2 depicts the number of states that shifted between categories in the period from 2010 to 2019. Overall, 33 states experienced democratic decay during this period, including 10 states that dropped from liberal to electoral democracies, 18 states that dropped from electoral democracies to electoral autocracies, and 5 states that dropped from electoral to closed autocracies. During the same period, only 13 states registered democratic

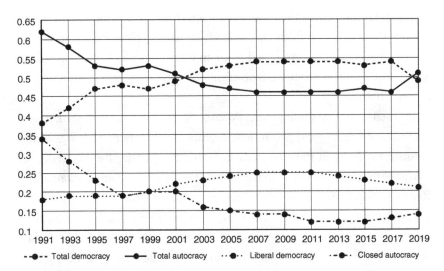

FIGURE 1. Democracy vs. autocracy after the Cold War. Source: V-Dem database.

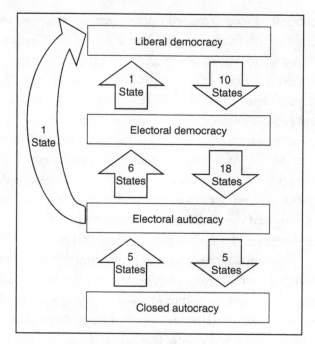

FIGURE 2. Democratic decay from 2010 to 2019. Source: V-Dem database.

gains, including 5 states that improved from closed to electoral autocracies, 6 states that improved from electoral autocracies to electoral democracies, 1 state (Barbados) that improved from an electoral to a liberal democracy, and 1 state (Tunisia) that was transformed from an electoral autocracy to a liberal democracy.

Hungary, India, Philippines, Poland, South Africa, and Turkey—to name some of the most prominent examples—all experienced significant democratic decay in the past decade.[18] Hungary, under the leadership of Viktor Orbán, is now firmly in the authoritarian camp, as are Turkey under Recep Tayyip Erdoğan and the Philippines under Rodrigo Duterte. In its most recent report, published in 2021, V-Dem downgraded India from an electoral democracy to an electoral autocracy.[19] Brazil, under Jair Bolsonaro, is moving dangerously in that direction. The quality of democratic governance has degraded significantly in numerous other countries as well.

The stakes in the geopolitical competition between autocracy and democracy are exceptionally high. This is not a contest about which country can claim the title of the most powerful nation in the world. The fundamental question is whether the citizens of Brazil, Hungary, India, and dozens of other states will have the opportunity to participate in democratic governments that respect individual freedom. The phenomenon of democratic decay means that hundreds of millions of people around the world are living in countries where the political space available for individual freedom is steadily shrinking, and governments are committing ever more egregious violations of fundamental human rights.

THE PROBLEM OF INFORMATION WARFARE

This book is concerned with threats to liberal democracy. Broadly speaking, we can divide those threats into foreign and domestic threats. Although chapter 5 touches upon domestic threats, the book as a whole focuses primarily on foreign threats. My choice to focus on foreign threats is not meant to imply that domestic threats are less important. To the contrary, I generally agree with those who argue that the project of saving liberal democracy must begin at home.[20] Nevertheless, foreign threats present a distinct set of problems that merit separate treatment.

With respect to social media, in particular, there are two reasons to focus on foreign threats to democracy rather than domestic threats. First, foreigners do not have the same rights as citizens to participate in democratic self-government because they are not members of our political community. Second, the First Amendment imposes strict constraints on the government's power to regulate speech on social media by U.S. citizens, but foreigners outside the United States do not enjoy the same First Amendment protections.[21] Therefore, with respect to social media, the government has greater power to regulate foreign threats compared to domestic threats.

Many factors contribute to the problem of democratic decay. This section highlights two such factors: foreign influence operations and organized social media manipulation. Foreign influence operations (FIOs) are activities conducted by government agents that are designed to influence domestic electoral, political, or policy processes in foreign countries, or to influence deliberative processes in international organizations. Here, the term "government agent" should be understood to include agents of political parties, such as the Chinese Communist Party (CCP). Governments have been conducting FIOs for decades, if not centuries.[22] Traditional FIOs include both covert operations (espionage) and overt operations (public diplomacy). Exploitation of social media to conduct FIOs is a relatively new phenomenon. In this book, the term "information warfare" refers to the exploitation of social media to conduct foreign influence operations. Information warfare includes both covert and overt uses of social media to conduct FIOs.

"Organized social media manipulation" (OSM) has become a feature of political communication in many states, including both autocracies and liberal democracies. OSM involves the use of government or political party employees or contractors, often called cyber troops, to manipulate public opinion online for political purposes.[23] The political goals of cyber troops might involve either domestic affairs or foreign affairs. In this book, the term "information warfare" refers to OSM that is directed toward a foreign audience or foreign policy objective. Thus, as illustrated in figure 3, information warfare lies at the intersection of FIOs and OSM.

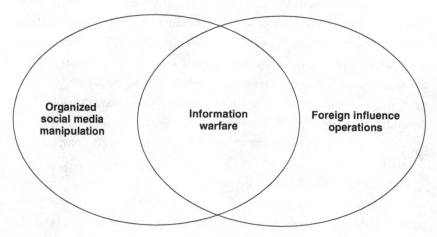

FIGURE 3. Information warfare Venn diagram. Created by author.

Some scholars have written about the threat that OSM poses to liberal democracy.[24] Others have written about the threat to liberal democracy from FIOs.[25] Each phenomenon, by itself, is sufficiently important to warrant book-length treatment. Even so, there are benefits to be gained from a sustained analysis of the overlap between the two phenomena, especially if one's goal is to develop appropriate policy responses. Both China and Russia have engaged in covert financing of political parties and political candidates in democratic countries.[26] Covert financing is an important category of FIOs, but policy solutions for that problem differ markedly from potential policy solutions for information warfare. Similarly, potential policy responses to information warfare differ from policy responses to domestic OSM because of the First Amendment concerns noted above, which severely constrain the range of options for countering domestic OSM. Thus, my choice to focus on the overlap between OSM and FIOs is guided largely by the goal of developing pragmatic policy responses to the threat of information warfare.

The problem of information warfare is closely related to, but distinct from, the problem of disinformation on social media. "Disinformation" can be defined as false or misleading information that is purposefully crafted and strategically placed to achieve a political goal.[27] False and misleading messages that are transmitted as part of an information warfare campaign clearly constitute disinformation. However, information warfare may also include the dissemination of messages that are calculated to evoke a particular emotional response, but that are neither false nor misleading. For example, during the 2016 U.S. presidential election campaign, WikiLeaks released a set of emails stolen by Russian intelligence operatives. Many of those emails were arguably neither false nor misleading. Regardless, commentators on social media—including Russian cyber troops—exploited the emails to paint a picture of Hillary Clinton as a person who is not trustworthy.[28]

Russia and China are not the only authoritarian states that practice information warfare. A report from the Oxford Internet Institute notes that China, India, Iran, Pakistan, Russia, Saudi Arabia, and Venezuela have all exploited U.S. social media platforms to conduct foreign influence operations.[29] This book focuses on Russia and China for two main reasons. First, they are the two most powerful adversaries that Western democracies will confront for at least the next two or three decades. Second, the focus on Russia and China is helpful for analyzing potential policy solutions. After policies have been implemented effectively with respect to Russia and China, they could potentially be extended to other states.

Some commentators who recognize that information warfare presents a serious threat nevertheless object to the use of military terminology to describe that threat.[30] Clearly, "information warfare," as I have defined the term, does not entail armed conflict. (Under international law, "armed conflict" involves the use of military force to cause loss of life or significant property damage.[31]) Moreover, the use of military terminology presents a danger: all too often, governments invoke threats to national security to justify unwarranted restrictions on civil liberties. For example, after the terrorist attacks in September 2001, the Bush administration invoked the threat of Islamic terrorism to justify draconian restrictions on innocent Muslims.[32]

Thus, there is a danger that militarized language—such as "information warfare" and "cyber troops"—could become a convenient excuse for the government to impose draconian restrictions on free speech on social media. Even so, there are two main reasons why militarized language is appropriate in this context. First, and most importantly, information warfare poses a significant threat to liberal democracies and to the liberal international order. The "warfare" terminology highlights the magnitude of the threat.

Second, Clausewitz famously declared that "war is a continuation of politics by other means." Chinese and Russian strategists have effectively turned Clausewitz's aphorism on its head by embracing the view that information warfare is an effective, low-cost tool for conducting warfare by political means. Subsequent chapters will highlight key differences between Chinese and Russian information warfare strategies, but for present purposes the similarities are more important than the differences. Both China and Russia engage in foreign influence operations generally—and information warfare specifically—to undermine liberal democracies from within, and to transform the liberal international order into a system that is more hospitable to illiberal, authoritarian regimes.[33] If Western democracies are going to develop an effective response, we must begin with a clear recognition of Chinese and Russian strategies. Using the term "information warfare" promotes that objective.

Finally, readers may question my choice to focus on social media. In an important book, Yochai Benkler and his coauthors argue that—in the U.S. context—traditional media plays a more significant role than social media in disseminating political disinformation.[34] In particular, they emphasize the importance of Fox News, Rush Limbaugh, and Breitbart in creating a "right-wing media ecosystem" that effectively occupies a different factual universe than mainstream media. In their view, the right-wing media ecosystem undermines democracy because the roughly 30 percent of Americans who rely primarily on Fox News and related sources for their news and information cling to demonstrably false views that are impervious to fact-checking by mainstream sources.

I find Benkler's account very persuasive as it applies to the United States. However, this book focuses on the worldwide threat to liberal democracy and liberal internationalism. Fox News and Breitbart reach very few people outside the United States, and there are few comparable media organizations in other Western democracies. In contrast, Facebook reportedly has more than 2.7 billion monthly active users around the globe.[35] Therefore, if one views threats to liberal democracy on a global basis, Facebook and other large social media organizations occupy a more central role than do U.S.-based right-wing media outlets.

Polling data from 2019 indicated that 53 percent of Americans believed that foreign interference in American elections constituted a "critical threat to the vital interest of the United States."[36] Among Democrats, that figure was 69 percent. Indeed, Democrats ranked foreign electoral interference as a greater threat than either international terrorism or North Korea's nuclear program.[37] Foreign electoral interference is not precisely the same thing as information warfare, because foreign agents can use tools other than social media to engage in electoral interference, and they can use information warfare to pursue political objectives that do not involve elections. Nevertheless, the two phenomena are closely related.

This book is written for citizens of the United States and other liberal democracies who believe that information warfare presents a serious threat to the future of democratic governance. If you are firmly convinced that information warfare is not a serious threat to democracy, this book is not for you. If you are unsure whether Chinese and Russian information warfare presents a significant threat to liberal democracy, the book will (hopefully) persuade you that the threat is both real and serious. If you are already convinced that information warfare poses a significant threat to liberal democracy, the book will help you gain a more nuanced understanding of the problem.

A PROPOSAL FOR TRANSNATIONAL REGULATION

Part Two presents a detailed proposal for a transnational regulatory system designed to protect democracies from Chinese and Russian information warfare. The proposed system includes seven central elements:

(1) A new alliance of democratic states from around the world (the "Alliance for Democracy") that will cooperate with each other to counter Russian and Chinese information warfare.

(2) Rules guaranteeing robust protection for free speech on social media by citizens and nationals of Alliance member states.

(3) A rule prohibiting Chinese and Russian agents from creating or operating accounts on regulated social media platforms, which will be implemented by appropriate legislation and/or regulations in all Alliance member states (the "ban"). The ban would be subject to an exemption for benign state agents to protect the First Amendment right of U.S. listeners to receive their speech.

(4) A disclaimer regime that will provide warnings for domestic audiences in Alliance member states whenever foreigners from non-democratic countries transmit election-related messages via social media.

(5) A registration system that will require social media users to register their accounts and declare their nationalities, including a verification system enabling governments of Alliance member states to verify that social media users who claim to be nationals of member states are, in fact, nationals of those states.

(6) Rigorous safeguards to protect informational privacy and data security.

(7) An exemption from the registration system for social media users who choose to maintain private accounts rather than public accounts.

In the past few years, revelations about harmful content on social media have sparked several proposals for increased government regulation of social media companies.[38] Additionally, the companies themselves have adopted a series of internal policy reforms to limit harmful content on their platforms.[39] Until now, most legislative proposals and most of the companies' internal policy reforms have focused on the *content of harmful speech*. In contrast, this book adopts a different approach, focusing on the *identity of dangerous speakers*. The book recommends a simple, straightforward solution: Democratic governments should enact legislation and regulations to prohibit Chinese and Russian agents from creating or operating accounts on regulated social media platforms, subject to an exception for benign state agents. Legislation that targets Chinese and Russian agents, rather than harmful content, avoids many of the First Amendment problems associated with congressional attempts to regulate speech on the basis of content. Moreover, a system that targets dangerous speakers is more administratively efficient than a system that targets harmful content because administrators (whether employed by private companies or the government) can focus on a single decision—is this person in or out?—instead of making thousands of separate decisions about thousands of individual messages.

One controversial aspect of the proposed transnational regulatory scheme is the proposal to establish a social media registration system. For some people, the very idea of a social media registration system conjures

Orwellian images of Big Brother rooted in a fear of government surveillance. That objection manifests a failure to recognize the degree to which government surveillance pervades the current system, and the ways in which a registration system could actually help alleviate that problem.[40] Moreover, for the reasons explained below, there is no practical way to provide an effective defense against information warfare without a social media registration system.

The registration system is designed to detect and block "fictitious user accounts"—social media accounts created in the name of a nonexistent person who pretends to be a citizen or national of a democratic state. The basic idea is simple. The best way to find a needle in a haystack is to confirm systematically that each piece of hay is not a needle. Similarly, the best way to identify Chinese and Russian agents who create fictitious user accounts is to confirm systematically that each innocent social media user is not a Chinese or Russian agent. Hence, prospective social media users who claim to be citizens or nationals of Alliance member states would have to be vetted at the account creation stage by the appropriate government to confirm that they are providing truthful information about their nationality. An individual who claims to be a U.S. citizen would be vetted by the U.S. government to confirm that he or she is actually a U.S. citizen. Similarly, a prospective user who claims to be a French citizen would be vetted by the French government. Vetting by national governments is essential to prevent Chinese and Russian agents from creating fictitious user accounts. An alliance of democracies is necessary so that democratic governments can cooperate to implement an effective registration system.

Part Two will address the details of the proposed registration system. Here, let us consider the core rationale for such a system. As explained in later chapters, both China and Russia are actively engaged in information warfare. Fictitious user accounts are some of the most potent weapons in their information warfare arsenals. To understand why fictitious user accounts are powerful weapons, and why we need a social media registration system to defend against those weapons, consider an analogy to traditional weapons systems.

Assume that attacking country A uses weapon X to attack defending country D, and country D uses weapon Y to block weapon X. We want to know the cost and time involved in weapons production. If country A can produce fifty copies of weapon X at roughly the same cost and in roughly the same time frame that country D needs to produce ten copies of weapon Y, then country D does not have an effective defense, because the attacker can easily overwhelm D's defenses by producing more copies of weapon X.

This stylized example is roughly analogous to the current situation with fictitious user accounts on social media. The attackers (Russia and China) can overwhelm the defense provided by social media companies because the attackers can generate fictitious user accounts more quickly, and at lower cost, than the time and expense required for social media companies to detect and block those accounts. Commentators refer to this problem as the "whack-a-troll" problem. Some data helps illustrate the scope of the whack-a-troll problem and the failure of companies to address that problem. In June 2020, Twitter discovered a network of 23,750 fake accounts that had previously evaded detection and that had all been created by Chinese cyber troops over a period of two or three months in late 2019 and early 2020.[41] A 2017 study of OSM in Poland identified a private communications firm in Poland that had "created more than 40 thousand unique identities, each with multiple accounts on various social media platforms . . . forming a universe of several hundred thousand specific fake accounts that have been used in Polish politics and multiple elections."[42]

Facebook tacitly concedes that it does not have a good solution for the whack-a-troll problem. According to Facebook's own data: "We estimate that fake accounts represented approximately 5% of our worldwide monthly active users (MAU) on Facebook during Q2 2020."[43] Five percent of 2.7 billion monthly active users would be 135 million fake accounts. It is fair to assume that the vast majority of those 135 million "fake accounts" are what I call "fictitious user accounts" because, under the current system, it is essentially cost-free for cyber troops to create fictitious user accounts. Moreover, it bears emphasis that Facebook is probably better at detecting and blocking fictitious user accounts than any other major social media company.

The social media registration system described in Part Two would make it practically impossible for foreign cyber troops to create fictitious user accounts. Chinese and Russian cyber troops could try to circumvent that system by creating other types of fake accounts. (I distinguish in Part Two among five different types of fake accounts.) However, it is more costly and time-consuming to create other types of fake accounts than it is to create fictitious user accounts. Thus, and this point bears emphasis, *the social media registration system could alter the attack-defense ratio by creating a situation in which it is more costly and time-consuming for attackers to create new fake accounts than it is for defenders to detect and block those accounts.* In contrast, absent a social media registration system, the whack-a-troll problem is insoluble, because attackers will continue to overwhelm the defenses available to social media companies.

Subsequent chapters will explain how the proposed registration system shifts the attack-defense ratio in favor of defenders. Here, let me briefly address four objections to the proposed transnational regulatory system. First, some argue that the system would, in practice, lead to massive invasions of user privacy. In fact, a well-designed and properly implemented social media registration system would enhance protection for both informational privacy and data security. However, even with rigorous safeguards to protect user privacy, people who are especially distrustful of governments might choose to close their social media accounts rather than voluntarily subject themselves to a government registration system. Thus, the registration system would almost certainly have a chilling effect on free speech on social media, although the magnitude of that chilling effect is hard to predict. My proposal would mitigate the chilling effect by specifically authorizing people to create private accounts that are exempt from the registration system. Social media users with private accounts could use social media for private communication but not for public communication. (See the appendix for a proposed definition of "public communication.") Moreover, as discussed in chapter 8, the government and social media companies could minimize the chilling effect by adopting a thoughtful public communication strategy to accompany the rollout of the registration system.

Second, some argue that the system would violate the First Amendment. The final chapter of this book analyzes the First Amendment issues based on the assumption that Congress will enact a statute to implement the proposed transnational regulatory system. The First Amendment analysis focuses on three key aspects of that hypothetical statute: (1) the requirement for social media companies to attach disclaimers to election-related messages to warn users when foreigners from nondemocratic states transmit election-related messages via social media; (2) the registration system that requires social media users to register their accounts and declare their nationalities; and (3) the ban that prohibits Chinese and Russian agents from creating or operating accounts on regulated social media platforms. The chapter demonstrates that the Supreme Court would almost certainly uphold the validity of the disclaimer requirements and would probably also uphold the registration system.[44] Finally, there are sound constitutional arguments that might, or might not, persuade a majority of current Supreme Court justices that the ban is constitutionally valid.

Third, one could argue that the proposed ban on Chinese and Russian agents is overkill: it restricts more speech than necessary because a well-designed system of disclosures and disclaimers could accomplish essentially the same goal in a way that restricts far less speech. I address this objection in detail in chapter 8.[45] Here, it is worth noting that my initial inclination when I began thinking about this topic was to design a disclosure-and-disclaimer regime, not a ban, to minimize restrictions on free speech. However, the more I analyzed the problem, the more I became convinced that it is simply not possible to create a disclosure-and-disclaimer regime (without a ban) that would be even minimally effective in shifting the attack-defense ratio in favor of defenders. Hence, I propose a ban on Chinese and Russian agents, subject to an exemption for benign state agents.

Finally, the proposed registration system would impose a significant administrative burden, and additional costs, on social media companies. Are the benefits worth the costs? The answer depends partly on one other variable that is difficult to assess. Ultimately, information warfare is dangerous because it contributes to democratic decay. However, many other factors also contribute to democratic decay. If Chinese and Russian information warfare is responsible for 1 percent of democratic decay and other causal factors are responsible for the other 99 percent, then the costs of the proposed transnational regulatory system probably outweigh the benefits. If Chinese and Russian information warfare is responsible for 50 percent of democratic decay, then the benefits of the proposed system would clearly outweigh the costs. The true figure almost certainly lies somewhere between 1 percent and 50 percent, but it is impossible to quantify the contribution of information warfare to democratic decay.

Even so, the benefits of the proposed transnational regulatory system extend beyond the problem of information warfare. Recall that information warfare lies at the intersection of foreign influence operations (FIOs) and organized social media manipulation (OSM), as illustrated in figure 3. The proposed Alliance for Democracy would provide a valuable institutional framework for democratic states to cooperate to address other types of foreign influence operations. Similarly, the proposed social media registration system would provide a valuable administrative foundation for governments to address the problem of domestic OSM. Moreover, the trifecta of domestic OSM, FIOs, and information warfare—viewed in the aggregate—clearly makes a significant contribution to the problem of democratic decay. Thus, the benefits of the proposed transnational regulatory system arguably outweigh the costs because the system as a whole would provide the building blocks for tackling the OSM, FIO, and information warfare trifecta.

Part Two explains and defends the proposed transnational regulatory system. For now, four points merit emphasis. First, enforcing a ban on Chinese and Russian agents will be costly and administratively difficult. Second, such a ban will never operate perfectly: Chinese and Russian cyber troops will find ways to circumvent the ban. Third, assuming that we can enforce the ban effectively (but not perfectly), Chinese and Russian agents will continue to engage in other types of foreign influence operations that do not rely on social media. Finally, despite these caveats, the

United States and other liberal democracies should ban Chinese and Russian agents from regulated social media platforms because the benefits of such a ban far outweigh the costs. Ultimately, those benefits must be measured in terms of enhanced protection for human rights and fundamental freedoms for millions of people across the globe who—if current trends continue—will be subjected to increasingly repressive policies of increasingly autocratic governments.

This book is divided into two parts. Part One presents a diagnosis of the problem and Part Two presents a detailed policy prescription. Part One includes two chapters on Russia and one chapter on China. The end of the book contains a glossary with definitions of key terms used throughout the book. The appendix presents draft text for a few crucial provisions to be included in a federal statute implementing the proposed transnational regulatory system.

CHAPTER TWO

RUSSIAN INFORMATION WARFARE AND U.S. ELECTIONS

THE DATE IS NOVEMBER 6, 2016, two days before Election Day. You are scrolling through Instagram and notice a friend's photo. You expand the caption and see these words:

> I say it as it is. When you decide to choose between two evil [*sic*], you are somehow condoning to whatever comes afterwards. The excuse that a lost Black vote for Hillary is a Trump win is bs. It could be late, but y'all might want to support Jill Stein instead. . . . Should you decide to sit out the election, well done for the boycott. However if you decide you are still going to vote, then don't choose any of the major ones. . . . We are on our own, esp. after Obama. Wise up my people![1]

Your friend did not write this message; it was actually posted by @woke_blacks, an Instagram account controlled by Russian cyber troops in St. Petersburg. Even so, the average reader would likely assume that an African American person wrote the message. This example shows how Russian agents developed sophisticated false personas to influence American political conversations in the 2016 presidential election cycle. Russian agents operated thousands of such fictitious user accounts that targeted different segments of the American electorate.

In the final report after completing his investigation (the "Mueller Report"), Special Counsel Robert Mueller stated: "The Russian government interfered in the 2016 presidential election in sweeping and systematic fashion."[2] During his congressional testimony in July 2019, Mueller noted: "They're doing it as we sit here."[3] Russia has meddled in U.S. elections for many years, dating back to the Soviet era.[4] Interference in foreign elections has proven to be an effective way for Russia to attain its foreign policy goals inexpensively, without resorting to war.[5] However, Russia's actions during the 2016 presidential election constituted a dramatic intensification of its attempts to undermine American democracy. An intelligence community assessment prepared jointly by the Central Intelligence Agency (CIA), the Federal Bureau of Investigation (FBI), and the National Security Agency (NSA) (the "ICA Report") characterized Russia's election interference as a "significant escalation in directness, level of activity, and scope of effort."[6]

The ICA Report concluded that Russia's key objectives included a "desire to undermine the US-led liberal democratic order" and "to undermine public faith in the US democratic process."[7] Other reports by independent experts bolster the intelligence community's assessment. For example, an independent report delivered to the Senate Intelligence Committee in December 2018 said that Russia conducted "a sweeping and sustained social influence operation . . . designed to exert political influence and exacerbate social divisions in US culture."[8] Similarly, a report from a team of scholars at Oxford University (the "Oxford Report") concluded that Russia "launched an extended attack on the United States by using computational propaganda to misinform and polarize US voters."[9]

Russian agents used the term "information warfare" to describe their activities.[10] The Mueller Report notes that Russia's 2016 information warfare campaign consisted of two main elements: a hacking and dumping operation and a social media influence operation. In the hacking and dumping operation, "a Russian intelligence service conducted computer-intrusion operations against entities, employees, and volunteers working on the Clinton Campaign and then released stolen documents."[11] The release of stolen documents was strategically timed to influence developments in the presidential election campaign.

Russian cyber troops who worked for the Internet Research Agency (IRA) exploited U.S. social media platforms—especially Facebook, You-Tube, Instagram, and Twitter—as weapons in their ongoing information warfare campaign. Twitter identified 3,814 Twitter accounts controlled by Russian agents. Facebook "identified 470 IRA-controlled Facebook accounts that collectively made 80,000 posts between January 2015 and August 2017." Facebook's general counsel estimated that "approximately 126 million people may have been served content from a [Facebook] Page" created by Russian cyber troops.[12]

Russia's information warfare activities continue to this day. Despite on-going activities, the bulk of this chapter focuses on Russian information warfare during the 2016 presidential election cycle because those activities have been very well documented. The chapter first analyzes Russia's broader strategic objectives and then briefly describes the hacking and dumping operation. I then present a detailed analysis of Russia's social media influence operation and assess the likely impact of Russian information warfare on the 2016 presidential election. The final section of the chapter (written before the 2020 election) discusses significant new developments related to the 2020 presidential election. For the reasons elaborated below, an impartial analyst weighing all of the available evidence could reasonably conclude there is a significant likelihood that—absent Russian information warfare—Hillary Clinton would have won the 2016 presidential election.

RUSSIA'S STRATEGIC OBJECTIVES

Robert Mueller's indictment of Elena Khusyaynova states: "The Conspiracy has a strategic goal, which continues to this day, to sow division and discord in the U.S. political system, including by creating social and political polarization, undermining faith in democratic institutions, and influencing U.S. elections, including the upcoming 2018 midterm election."[13] In his final report after concluding the investigation, Mueller noted that Russia's "campaign evolved from a generalized program designed in 2014 and 2015 to undermine the U.S. electoral system, to a targeted operation that by early 2016 favored candidate Trump and disparaged candidate Clinton."[14]

U.S. intelligence agencies concluded with "high confidence" that Vladimir Putin ordered the influence campaign to affect the 2016 U.S. election.[15] The ICA Report identified three specific Russian goals. First, Russia sought to undermine public faith in U.S. democracy and the electoral process. One expert told the Senate that Russia's ability to cause a "major political disruption in the United States" and harm the United States' standing in the world qualifies as a success from Russia's perspective.[16]

Second, Russia sought to weaken Hillary Clinton's candidacy. The ICA Report notes that Putin had maintained a vendetta against Clinton since 2011, because Putin blamed her for inciting protests in Russia and for stating publicly that Russian elections were "neither free nor fair."[17] Russia's Main Intelligence Directorate (the GRU) hacked into Democratic National Committee (DNC) computers, stole documents, and leaked stolen documents that undermined the Democratic Party and its officials. The stolen documents contained information harmful to the Democratic Party and to Clinton's election campaign.[18] Russian cyber troops often mentioned Clinton in their social media posts. They generated more than 1,700 Facebook posts regarding Clinton, all of which were negative.[19]

Russia's third primary objective was to support the candidacy of Donald Trump. During the 2016 election cycle, the Russian government "developed a clear preference" for Trump over Clinton.[20] Russia conducted information warfare to support this preference. Russia strategically timed its releases of hacked information to bolster Trump's campaign. Russian posts on social media mentioned Trump about twice as often as they mentioned Clinton. Posts that mentioned Trump were typically positive.[21]

HACKING AND DUMPING
The Russian campaign involved both a hacking operation and a social media operation. The Mueller Report describes the hacking operation as follows:

Beginning in March 2016, units of the Russian Federation's Main Intelligence Directorate of the General Staff (GRU) hacked the computers and email accounts of organizations, employees, and volunteers supporting the Clinton Campaign, including the email account of campaign chairman John Podesta. Starting in April 2016, the GRU hacked into the computer networks of the Democratic Congressional Campaign Committee (DCCC) and the Democratic National Committee (DNC). . . . In total, the GRU stole hundreds of thousands of documents from the compromised email accounts and networks. The GRU later released stolen . . . documents through online personas, "DCLeaks" and "Guccifer 2.0," and later through the organization Wikileaks. The release of the documents was designed and timed to . . . undermine the Clinton Campaign.[22]

Two units within the GRU, military units 26165 and 74455, "carried out the computer intrusions into the Clinton Campaign, DNC, and DCCC." Unit 26165 "is a GRU cyber unit dedicated to targeting military, political, governmental, and non-governmental organizations outside of Russia, including in the United States." Unit 74455 "is a related GRU unit with multiple departments that engaged in cyber operations. Unit 74455 assisted in the release of documents stolen by Unit 26165, the promotion of those releases, and the publication of anti-Clinton content on social media accounts operated by the GRU."[23]

Beginning in June 2016, "the GRU posted stolen documents onto the website dcleaks.com, including documents stolen from a number of individuals associated with the Clinton Campaign." The GRU posted thousands of documents on dcleaks.com, "including personal identifying and financial information, internal correspondence related to the Clinton Campaign . . . and fundraising files and information." GRU officers also "operated a Facebook page under the DCLeaks moniker, which they primarily used to promote releases of materials." They also "used the DCLeaks Facebook account, the Twitter account @dcleaks_, and the email account dcleaksproject@gmail.com to communicate privately with reporters and other U.S. persons." They "gave certain reporters early access to archives of leaked files by sending them links and passwords to pages on the dcleaks.com website that had not yet become public."[24]

On June 14, 2016, the Democratic National Committee "publicly announced that it had been hacked by Russian government actors."[25] In response, the GRU "created the online persona Guccifer 2.0 [which] falsely claimed to be a lone Romanian hacker." On June 15, Guccifer 2.0 published its first blog post. Between June and October, the GRU "used Guccifer 2.0 to release documents . . . that they had stolen from the DCCC and DNC." Guccifer 2.0 "also shared stolen documents with certain individuals." For example, in June 2016, Guccifer 2.0 "contacted a U.S. reporter with an offer to provide stolen emails from Hillary Clinton's staff." In August, Guccifer 2.0 "transferred approximately 2.5 gigabytes of data stolen from the DCCC to a then-registered state lobbyist and online source of political news."[26] Guccifer 2.0 "ultimately released thousands of documents stolen from the DNC and DCCC in a series of blog posts between June 15, 2016 and October 18, 2016."[27]

"In order to expand its interference in the 2016 U.S. presidential election, the GRU . . . transferred many of the documents they stole from the DNC and the chairman of the Clinton Campaign to WikiLeaks."[28] The Mueller Report documents extensive, close coordination between the GRU and WikiLeaks. "GRU officers used both the DCLeaks and Guccifer 2.0 personas to communicate with WikiLeaks through Twitter private messaging and through encrypted channels." The GRU chose WikiLeaks as a partner because WikiLeaks had the capacity to reach a very large audience and because "its founder, Julian Assange, privately expressed opposition to candidate Clinton well before the first release of stolen documents."[29]

The most significant documents released through WikiLeaks were emails stolen from the account of John Podesta, Clinton's campaign chairman. "On October 7, 2016, WikiLeaks released the first emails stolen from the Podesta email account. In total, WikiLeaks released 33 tranches of stolen emails" between October 7 and Election Day. "The releases included private speeches given by Clinton; internal communications between Podesta and other high-ranking members of the Clinton Campaign; and correspondence related to the Clinton Foundation. In total, WikiLeaks released over 50,000 documents stolen from Podesta's personal email account."[30] As discussed later in this chapter, emails stolen from the Podesta account and released through WikiLeaks had a significant impact in framing the media agenda in the final weeks before the 2016 presidential election.

THE SOCIAL MEDIA INFLUENCE OPERATION

The Internet Research Agency (IRA), a Russian company run by Yevgeniy Prigozhin, had primary responsibility for Russian social media operations.[31] The IRA is officially unconnected to the Russian government, but Prigozhin is a close ally of Vladimir Putin and his companies have earned billions of dollars in contracts from the Russian government in recent years. "The IRA began its operations in mid-2013 in St. Petersburg, Russia. Run like a sophisticated marketing agency in a centralized office environment, the IRA employed and trained over a thousand people to engage in round-the-clock" information warfare. The IRA "had a budget that exceeded $25 million USD . . . . IRA documents indicate the 2017 operational budget alone was $12.2 million US dollars."[32] A former IRA employee whose informal title was "Internet Troll" said that his job included creating fake accounts, authoring blog posts, and posting comments on social media sites.[33] In February 2018, Robert Mueller indicted the IRA and some of its employees for their role in the 2016 election.[34]

Before beginning large-scale operations, the IRA gathered intelligence about the U.S. political system to determine how best to focus its information warfare activities. In 2014, three Russian operatives visited the United States. They traveled to at least ten states to perform reconnaissance on American politics.[35] The IRA indictment stated: "In order to collect additional intelligence, Defendants and their co-conspirators posed as U.S. persons and contacted U.S. political and social activists. . . . Defendants and their co-conspirators learned . . . that they should focus their activities on 'purple states'. . . . After that exchange, Defendants and their co-conspirators commonly referred to targeting 'purple states' in directing their efforts."[36] The intelligence-gathering phase of Russian operations developed an effective foundation for subsequent information warfare activities.

During the 2016 election campaign, the IRA targeted major online platforms such as Facebook, Instagram, Twitter, and YouTube. Much of the commentary on the IRA's social media operation has focused on paid political advertisements. However, such ads constitute a relatively small piece of a much bigger operation. The Oxford Report concluded: "The most far reaching IRA activity is in organic posting, not advertisements."[37] The report defines "organic post" as "a crafted message from an IRA-managed fake page or user account pretending to be a concerned citizen."[38]

The overall scope of the IRA's social media campaign is astounding. "The IRA developed a collection of over 3841 persona accounts on Twitter," eighty-one unique Pages on Facebook, seventeen YouTube channels that produced 1,107 videos, and numerous Instagram accounts, including twelve Instagram accounts that each had over 100,000 followers.[39] In the aggregate, IRA accounts had more than three million followers on Facebook and more than three million followers on Instagram.[40] The IRA generated 67,502 organic posts on Facebook, 116,205 organic posts on Instagram, and more than eight million posts on Twitter. Facebook users shared IRA posts almost 31 million times and liked IRA posts almost 39 million times. IRA posts on Instagram "garnered almost 185 million likes."[41] Overall, "the IRA reached as many as 126 million persons through its Facebook accounts."[42]

Operating Fake Accounts

It is helpful at this point to distinguish among different types of social media accounts that are often called "fake accounts." *Bots* are automated accounts that are programmed to disseminate messages via social media without the need for human intervention. Other types of fake accounts are all operated by actual human beings. *Fictitious user accounts* are accounts in which cyber troops adopt the identity of a fictitious, nonexisting person. *Impostor accounts* are accounts in which cyber troops create a new account and misappropriate the identity of a real person without that person's knowledge or consent. *Stolen accounts* and *hacked accounts* are accounts in which cyber troops take over the operation of an existing social media account belonging to a real person without that person's knowledge or consent. *Rental accounts* are accounts in which cyber troops pay a bribe to a real person to induce that person to permit a foreign agent to operate a social media account using the identity of the person who received the bribe. During the 2016 election cycle, Russian cyber troops made extensive use of bots, impostor accounts, and fictitious user accounts. (See the glossary at the end of the book for definitions of terms.)

Russia's primary social media strategy involved the creation and operation of fictitious user accounts. During the 2016 election cycle, the IRA created thousands of fictitious user accounts designed to become "leader[s] of public opinion" in the United States.[43] Russian agents who operated those accounts portrayed themselves as concerned American citizens. For example, the IRA operated a Twitter account in the name of "@Crystal1Johnson," which adopted the persona of a black woman. It operated a Facebook account in the name of "Matt Skiber," who presented himself as a Trump supporter.[44] The IRA also created numerous accounts with names of fictitious organizations, such as "LGBT United," "Being Patriotic," and "BM (Black Matters)." These pages received significant attention. For example, the "Being Patriotic" Facebook page received a total of over six million "likes" and over 300,000 comments on its posts.[45] The "Blackstagram" account on Instagram had more than 300,000 followers and more than 27 million likes.[46]

The IRA's fictitious user accounts appealed to U.S. audiences by using language that made them appear to be American. For example, one post on the @Crystal1Johnson account posted a Tweet with verbatim text from a Los Angeles news station; the post "received 2497 retweets and 1365 likes." The tactic of stealing text from native English speakers allowed Russian agents to disguise English language deficiencies and masquerade more convincingly as American citizens.[47] The IRA's fictitious user accounts deliberately targeted particular demographic groups, frequently referencing "Clinton" or "Trump" explicitly. In other cases, IRA posts referred to sensitive issues in U.S. culture, such as youth killed by police and police brutality.[48]

The creation and operation of fictitious user accounts was the linchpin of Russia's information warfare strategy.[49] Social media platforms provided an ideal tool for Russian agents to disseminate opinions and disinformation because Russian cyber troops could disguise themselves as concerned

American citizens and use those platforms to reach millions of people. Russian agents employed fictitious user accounts to carry out all of the different messaging strategies described later in this chapter.

Russian cyber troops also operated some impostor accounts. For example, a Twitter account called @TEN_GOP claimed to be the unofficial Twitter account of the Tennessee Republican Party.[50] @TEN_GOP generated a tremendous amount of engagement. Posts from @TEN_GOP "were cited or retweeted by multiple Trump Campaign officials and surrogates, including Donald J. Trump Jr., Eric Trump, Kellyanne Conway, Brad Parscale, and Michael T. Flynn. These posts included allegations of voter fraud, as well as allegations that Secretary Clinton had mishandled classified information."[51]

On November 5, 2016, three days before the election, "TEN_GOP dominated in engagement, with 9296 [retweets] and 8800 favorites across its 12 tweets. The account tweeted claims that . . . Hillary Clinton would go to prison for 5 years, and that Hillary is the first candidate in American history to be labeled a threat by American troops."[52] The next day, November 6, "TEN_GOP repeatedly attacked James Comey's investigation into Hillary Clinton's emails, earning 38,000 engagements across the collection of tweets."[53] On November 7, "@TEN_GOP tweeted 22 times, talking about patriotism and arguing that Hillary Clinton was receiving special treatment . . . and should not be above the law; the tweets received 12,383 favorites and 16,058 retweets."[54] Finally, on Election Day, "the highest engagement account was @TEN_GOP, which . . . tweeted inspirational quotes about Donald Trump (and against Hillary Clinton) by other political figures such as Rudy Giuliani, Marine LePen, etc. @TEN_GOP earned 65,671 retweets and 56,906 favorites."[55]

Russian cyber troops also operated numerous bots. According to one source, "half of Russian Twitter conversations involve highly automated accounts that actively shape online discourses."[56] Russian cyber troops used bots to post information simultaneously from a multitude of separate, automated accounts, thereby creating the impression of widespread discussion of a topic.[57] Twitter expressly allows the use of bots. Twitter also has a "trending" feature, which causes certain phrases preceded by a hashtag to feature on the platform if enough accounts make posts with that phrase.[58] Russian operatives exploited these features. For example, although Twitter has a policy to prevent trending of hashtags promoted by bots,[59] Twitter's filters did not always work properly. Hence, Russian bots were able to induce certain hashtags, such as #HillaryDown, to begin trending.[60]

Russian agents have made some use of rental accounts, but such accounts did not feature prominently in the 2016 election.[61] Russian cyber troops did operate some stolen accounts in 2016. A Russian website, Buy accs.com, allowed IRA employees to buy real Facebook accounts and repurpose them; older ones were more expensive because they seemed to be more authentic.[62] In one case, Rachel Usedom, a young American, learned that her Twitter account had been used to promote the hashtag #ClintonCorruption.[63] Russian agents also stole the identity of several Americans, using their Social Security numbers and birth dates to open banking and PayPal accounts. In one case of identity theft, Russian agents appropriated the identity of an actual U.S. person whose initials are "T. W." and sent emails in his name promoting Donald Trump's campaign.[64]

Messaging Strategies

Russian cyber troops used bots, fictitious user accounts, and impostor accounts to generate support for Donald Trump, undermine Hillary Clinton's campaign, and increase political polarization. They played a central role in creating and disseminating disinformation during the 2016 election cycle. For example, Russian agents spread the idea that the original Statue of Liberty depicted a black woman and that the U.S. government rejected the statue, asking France to send a "whiter-looking replacement." Although this claim seems implausible on its face, posts of this type "generated enough audience engagement that they were reposted multiple times by the same accounts."[65] A BuzzFeed News analysis found that Facebook users spent more time viewing disinformation about the 2016 election than authentic news stories.[66] On Twitter, disinformation spread faster than authentic news, perhaps because the sensationalized stories motivated people to share the content.[67] In the aggregate, between 2015 and 2017, more than 30 million users "shared the IRA's Facebook and Instagram posts with their friends and family, liking, reacting to, and commenting on them along the way."[68]

One key Russian goal was to increase political polarization in the United States. Russia's cyber troops "used a variety of fake accounts to infiltrate political discussion communities on the right and left . . . in order to exacerbate social divisions."[69] They purposefully selected page names—such as "LGBT United," "Black Matters," and "Secured Borders"—to appeal to specific ideological groups. Right-targeted Facebook Pages that generated high levels of engagement included Being Patriotic (6.4 million likes and 4.4 million shares), Stop All Immigrants (6 million likes and 5.2 million shares), and Heart of Texas (5.5 million likes and 5 million shares). Left-targeted Facebook Pages that generated high levels of engagement included Blacktivist (4.6 million likes and 4.8 million shares) and Brown Power (2.1 million likes and 1.3 million shares).[70]

Russian operatives targeted "the most extreme conservatives and those with particular sensitivities to race and immigration."[71] Key tactics utilized to exacerbate political polarization included "encouraging extreme right-wing voters to be more confrontational" and "spreading sensationalist, conspiratorial, and other forms of . . . misinformation to voters across the political spectrum."[72] For example, on November 7, 2016, the day before Election Day, Secured Borders posted: "Our so-called President, Kenyan illegal bastard Barack Hussein Obama encourages illegal aliens to vote—because as you know law breaking comes naturally to both Democrats and illegal aliens . . . President Obama . . . himself is illegal and cares nothing for this country."[73] That post secured 4,891 engagements, including 1,478 shares. (The report from which this information is drawn measured four types of engagements: likes, shares, comments, and reactions.[74])

Russian agents also disseminated messages designed to impede the exercise of voting rights by conveying false or misleading information about how to vote. One Russian Twitter account tried to persuade people to post the message: "Heads Up: If you voted for Bernie in the Primaries, the Election Board will NOT let you vote for Hillary on Nov 8."[75] Another account pretended to be the online presence of a liberal gay man. He encouraged Clinton supporters to "SKIP THE LINE" and supplied a seemingly genuine link to allow people to "vote ONLINE."[76] These messages were targeted at likely Clinton voters; they were designed to suppress voter turnout by creating "confusion about voting rules."[77]

"In the days leading up to the election, the IRA began to deploy voter suppression tactics on the Black-community targeted accounts."[78] For example, an account called @afrokingdom advocated that black people not vote. One post suggested that Hillary is not the best candidate, but black people think "they have to settle for Clinton! But I say that this is the BIG mistake! Black people don't have to vote for Hillary because she is liar! Black people are smart enough to understand that Hillary doesn't deserve our votes! DON'T VOTE!"[79] Russian accounts also posted numerous images related to the election. One such image that featured pictures of both Clinton and Trump said: "Do not vote for oppressors!" Another depicted a black man standing beneath an American flag and stated: "I won't vote. Will you?"[80] A popular Instagram account insisted that people refuse to vote for "Killary" and instead not vote at all.[81] These messages were part of a concerted Russian campaign to persuade African Americans not to vote.

Finally, some Russian posts tried to drain support from Clinton by encouraging liberal voters to vote for Jill Stein or Bernie Sanders. Russian cyber troops "developed Left-wing Twitter personas . . . [that] expressed pro-Bernie Sanders and pro-Jill Stein sentiments."[82] The IRA "purchased an advertisement to promote a post on [an IRA-]controlled Instagram account "Blacktivist" that read in part: 'Choose peace and vote for Jill Stein. Trust me, it's not a wasted vote.'"[83] One Russian YouTube video encouraged "Black voters [to] stay home, or vote for Jill Stein."[84] A black-focused Instagram account said: "The excuse that a lost Black vote for Hillary is a Trump win is bs. It could be late, but y'all might want to support Jill Stein instead."[85]

The Oxford Report notes that "[s]ocial media are particularly effective at directly reaching large numbers of people, while simultaneously microtargeting individuals with personalized messages." The fact that social media permits such "fine-grained control over who receives which messages . . . makes social media platforms" a wonderful tool for advertisers. Unfortunately, though, "there is mounting evidence that social media are being used to manipulate and deceive the voting public—and to undermine democracies and degrade public life."[86]

Organizing Political Rallies

The Mueller Report states: "The IRA organized and promoted political rallies inside the United States while posing as U.S. grassroots activists." The IRA typically "used one of its preexisting social media personas . . . to announce and promote the event." IRA operatives "sought a U.S. person to serve as the event's coordinator. . . . The IRA then further promoted the event by contacting U.S. media about the event and directing them to speak with the coordinator." After the rallies, "the IRA posted videos and photographs of the event to the IRA's social media accounts." The IRA organized dozens of rallies in the United States. "Pro-Trump rallies included three in New York; a series of pro-Trump rallies in Florida in August 2016; and a series of pro-Trump rallies in October 2016 in Pennsylvania. The Florida rallies drew the attention of the Trump Campaign, which posted about the Miami rally on candidate Trump's Facebook account."[87]

Beginning in June 2016, "the IRA contacted different U.S. persons affiliated with the Trump Campaign in an effort to coordinate pro-Trump IRA-organized rallies inside the United States." In every case involving contacts with the Trump campaign, IRA agents claimed "to be U.S. political activists working on behalf of a conservative grassroots organization." IRA agents asked for "signs and other materials to use at rallies, as well as requests to promote the rallies and help coordinate logistics." In some cases, "campaign volunteers agreed to provide the requested support." However, there is no proof that "any Trump Campaign official understood the requests were coming from foreign nationals."[88]

THE LIKELY IMPACT OF RUSSIAN INFORMATION WARFARE

Empirical analysis suggests that activity on social media by Russian cyber troops influenced public opinion in the United States in the months preceding the 2016 presidential election. One experiment tested the hypothesis that Russian tweets affected public opinion by "comparing time series of election opinion polling during 2016 versus numbers of re-tweets or 'likes' of IRA tweets."[89] The study used "a database of 3315 national polls from 54 pollsters asking whether the participant intended to vote for Donald Trump or Hillary Clinton. . . . Time series were built by averaging all national polls in a given week across all pollsters." The analysis demonstrated that "changes in opinion poll numbers for Trump were consistently preceded by corresponding changes in IRA re-tweet volume, at an optimum interval of one week before." Statistical tests demonstrate "that IRA Twitter success (measured as both retweets and likes per tweet) predicted future increases for Trump in the [public opinion] polls, but did not predict Clinton's polls." Here, "predicted" means that "information in one time series contains information about the future activity in other time series." Interestingly, "the raw number of original IRA tweets [did not] predict the polls. Instead, it is the re-tweets, not total volume of original IRA tweets, that predicts the opinion polls." The authors of the study conclude: "Overall, the effect is quantified such that a gain of 25,000 re-tweets per week over all IRA tweets . . . predicted [an] approximately one percent increase in Donald Trump's poll numbers."[90]

Did Russian information warfare contribute to Trump's electoral victory? In attempting to answer that question, it is helpful to utilize the legal vocabulary of burdens of persuasion. In a criminal trial, the prosecution must prove its case beyond a reasonable doubt. In partisan debates about whether the Russians helped elect Trump, it is not possible for either side to prove its case beyond a reasonable doubt. There are too many "what ifs" to satisfy that burden of proof in either direction. In the usual civil trial, though, the plaintiff must prove his or her case by a preponderance of the evidence. This is a "more likely than not" standard. My central claim here is this: An impartial observer who weighed all of the evidence could reasonably conclude that it is more likely than not that, absent Russian information warfare, Hillary Clinton would have won the 2016 election. Kathleen Hall Jamieson conducted a comprehensive analysis of the available evidence. She argues that Russian interference probably tipped the balance in Trump's favor in key battleground states in the final weeks before Election Day 2016.[91] It is impossible to do justice to her analysis in a few pages, but here is a brief summary of the argument.

First, the Russians shaped the information environment through agenda setting and framing. Agenda setting is "a media effect that shapes what audiences think about." Framing is "a message effect that influences the ways that they think about a topic or issue."[92] On October 7, 2016, two days before the second presidential debate, the *Washington Post* published a recording (the *Access Hollywood* tape) in which "Donald Trump could be heard bragging . . . not only that he kissed women without their consent but that, because of his status as a star, he could do whatever else he wanted, including grabbing them 'by the pussy'." Less than one hour later, "Wikileaks released a first cache of emails stolen by Russian operatives from the account of Clinton campaign director John Podesta."[93] The WikiLeaks release of Russian hacked material "redirected the media agenda" and altered the framing "from one focused on Trump's proclivities . . . to one concentrating on the vulnerabilities of both candidates."[94] Two days later, in a televised presidential debate seen by 66 million viewers, the moderator read an excerpt from a document stolen by the Russians in which Clinton appeared to suggest that there was a difference between her public and private positions on some issues. The moderator then posed the following question: "Is it okay for a politician to be two-faced?"[95] A subsequent analysis of survey data showed that "those who viewed the second or third [presidential] debate were more likely than those who did not view those debates to consider Clinton someone who says one thing in public and something else in private."[96] That negative perception likely affected decision-making by undecided voters in the final weeks before the election.

Second, "the amount and relative weight of messaging matter" because increased exposure to messages supporting one candidate over the other "support the candidate with the messaging advantage."[97] In a typical election, members of the public are "exposed to messages from both sides . . . but the effects tend to be mutually canceling."[98] In 2016, Russia's social media operation "reweighted the communication environment . . . by increasing the visibility of existing anti-Clinton messages" through liking and sharing. Moreover, Russian social media activity "increased the likelihood that nontrolls would post stories . . . that were hostile to the Democrat."[99] In fact, "91 percent of first retweeters of IRA tweets were non-IRA bots, which suggests that [Russian] propaganda spread into networks of real U.S. citizens."[100]

Third, persistent attacks on Clinton by Russian cyber troops in the final weeks before the election amplified negative public perceptions of Clinton. Social science analysis of prior elections shows that campaign-related messaging "is likely to elicit small, short-term effects" and that "reinforced priming of negative attributes has produced shifts in" voter behavior in prior elections.[101] The volume of weekly posts by Russian cyber troops on Facebook and Instagram increased substantially in the last two months before the November 2016 election.[102] All of the IRA's Clinton-related posts focused on her alleged negative attributes. Survey data from fall 2016 show a sharp decline in the percentage of U.S. adults who thought Clinton was qualified to be president. Specifically "the results of the surveys show that those who saw Hillary Clinton as qualified to be president declined significantly . . . from 59 percent to 48 percent between the first sample, interviewed in early October, and the final sample" collected from October 20–25.[103] Russia's social media campaign was one of several factors that contributed to changing perceptions of Clinton's qualifications. Voters' increasingly negative assessment of Hillary Clinton undoubtedly affected decision-making by undecided voters in the final weeks before the election.

Fourth, voters in the 2016 election were unusually susceptible to Russian influence operations because there was "(1) an unusually high level of voter disaffection with both parties; (2) a higher than average percentage of self-identified independents . . . and (3) a larger than ordinary proportion of the population . . . making a decision in the last week before the election."[104] Moreover, "in key swing states, the results were driven by late deciders."[105] Wisconsin voters who "selected a candidate in the last week broke for Trump over Clinton, 59 percent to 30 percent. In Pennsylvania, the Republican carried those who made up their minds in the final days by seventeen points and in Michigan by eleven."[106] Of course, many factors contributed to the pro-Trump swing among late deciders in battleground states, but Russian information warfare was clearly one of those factors.

Finally, the Russians helped mobilize Trump voters and demobilize potential Clinton voters. "Negative emotion produces more powerful contagion effects than does the positive kind. . . . Facebook is a contagion machine built to order for many good ends but also for fake pages and posts bent on inciting and then harnessing economic anxieties and fears of cultural change." Russian cyber troops exploited social media to channel that fear and anxiety "against Clinton and for Trump."[107] The Russians (and the Trump campaign) sought to mobilize evangelicals to support Trump. He "actually outperformed prior Republican nominees with this group. Exit polls found that 81 percent of self-identified, white, born-again, evangelical Christians cast their ballots for Trump in 2016," compared to "78 percent for Romney in 2012, 74 percent for McCain in 2008, and 78 percent for Bush in 2004."[108] The Russians also made a concerted effort in the final months of the campaign to mobilize veterans to support Trump. "In mid-August, an NBC SurveyMonkey poll found Trump leading Clinton by only 10 points among military households . . . . By Election Day . . . exit polls suggest that he bested Clinton among that group by a substantial 60 percent to 34 percent."[109]

The Russians (and the Trump campaign) also sought to suppress the black vote. In 2016, "the black voter turnout rate declined for the first time in 20 years in a presidential election, falling to 59.6% in 2016 after reaching a record-high 66.6% in 2012. The 7-percentage point decline from the previous presidential election is the largest on record for blacks."[110] The Russians "also attempted to peel votes away from Clinton by urging balloting for Green Party candidate Jill Stein."[111] The data on Stein voters in key battleground states is revealing because Stein was also on the ballot in 2012. Stein garnered almost 30,000 more votes in Michigan in 2016 than she did in 2012. Trump's margin of victory in Michigan was less than 11,000 votes. Stein garnered 23,407 more votes in Wisconsin in 2016 than she did in 2012. Trump's margin of victory in Wisconsin was 22,748 votes. Stein garnered 28,600 more votes in Pennsylvania in 2016 than she did in 2012. Trump's margin of victory in Pennsylvania was about 44,000 votes. "If one assumes . . . that the 2012 Green Party vote is that party's base level of support, and grants that the additional votes Stein drew in 2016 . . . [would have gone] to Clinton, the results would have changed the Trump-Clinton outcome in Wisconsin and Michigan but not Pennsylvania."[112] (If Trump won Pennsylvania, but lost Wisconsin and Michigan, he still would have won the election.)

Even assuming that Russian interference was not sufficiently impactful to swing the 2016 election in Donald Trump's favor, one should not conclude that Russian information warfare was or is inconsequential. As discussed earlier in this chapter, one key Russian objective was to increase political polarization in the United States. Russia has continued to exploit social media to pursue that objective since the 2016 election. Several studies show that partisan polarization has increased in the past few years. A 2019 survey by Pew Research Center found that "the level of division and animosity—including negative sentiments among partisans toward the members of the opposing party" had deepened since 2016.[113] Similarly, a 2019 Gallup poll showed an "average 79-percentage-point difference between Republicans' and Democrats' job approval ratings of President Donald Trump during his second year in office." That was "the largest [such difference] Gallup has measured in any presidential year to date."[114] Of course, numerous factors have contributed to increasing polarization in the United States—including Donald Trump himself—but Russian information warfare is undoubtedly one such factor.

Russia has also tried to undermine trust in government, but the evidence suggests that Russian information warfare has had negligible effects in this respect. Polling data show that Americans' trust in government declined steadily after 2001 and has remained consistently low for several years. In October 2001, shortly after the 9/11 attacks, 55–60 percent of survey respondents said that they "trust the government in Washington to do what is right." That figure had declined to 20 percent by

February 2013; it has generally hovered between 17 and 20 percent since that time.[115]

NEW DEVELOPMENTS SINCE 2016

Russian objectives remained the same in 2020 as they were in 2016. According to David Porter, an agent on the FBI's Foreign Influence Task Force: "To put it simply, in this space, Russia wants to watch us tear ourselves apart."[116] Alina Polyakova, a leading Russia expert, adds: "A more divided United States means a more inward-looking White House that will be less concerned with pushing back against Russia's activities in Syria, Ukraine, and elsewhere."[117] Another pessimistic commentator notes: "It is entirely possible that the current disinformation disorder will render the country ungovernable despite barely convincing any mass of voters to cast ballots that they would not otherwise have cast."[118]

Although Russia's goals remained unchanged, its tactics evolved—at least partly in response to enhanced detection methods adopted by U.S. companies. Nathaniel Gleicher, the head of cybersecurity policy at Facebook, says: "If you go viral very, very fast that's exactly the sort of thing that our automated systems will detect and flag."[119] The Russians know this, and they want to avoid detection, so they are "using an updated playbook that typically involves more targeted—but less viral—efforts to affect political debates and elections."[120] Gleicher says: "They've gotten better at hiding who they are, but their impact has gotten smaller and smaller."[121] Gleicher's conclusion makes sense only if you measure impact in terms of virality. However, the Russians have arguably devised strategies to achieve high impact in other ways.

Young Mie Kim, a scholar at University of Wisconsin, claims that Russian cyber troops "are getting even more brazen in tactics."[122] They are relying less on fictitious user accounts and making greater use of impostor accounts and stolen accounts, which are more difficult to detect. In Kim's words, they are using "the identity of legitimate, relatively popular nonprofits, political action committees (PACs), or grassroots organizations." For example, Russian agents "mimicked the official account of the Bernie Sanders campaign, 'bernie2020,' by using similar names like 'bernie.2020_.'" Kim says "it is unclear whether the IRA is simply stealing names, logos, and materials already used by legitimate organizations, or unwitting collaboration between those legitimate organizations and the IRA's shell groups occurred." Either way, it is difficult for social media companies to detect these types of accounts. Moreover, Kim notes: "This tactic works favorably overall for IRA election interference strategies that exploit existing sharp political divides in our society, as it boosts the credibility of messages and helps amplify them among members and supporters of the domestic groups."[123]

Russian agents have also paid unsuspecting American journalists to write stories for them. Russian cyber troops "created fictitious personas on Facebook to direct people to a new site called Peace Data, which billed itself as a global news organization."[124] "One of the journalists who wrote columns for Peace Data . . . said that an editor reached out to him through a direct message on Twitter . . . offering $200 per article. He said he pursued the opportunity in part because he had lost his job in the pandemic." The American journalist had no idea that Peace Data was part of a Russian operation that "recruited U.S. journalists to write articles critical of Democratic nominee Joe Biden and his running mate, Sen. Kamala D. Harris, in an apparent bid to undermine their support among liberal voters." By hiring "people who are fluent in the language and culture" to write stories, the Russians can more easily evade detection.[125]

Experts say that "the Russians are relying increasingly on English-language news sites to push out incendiary stories that can be picked up and spread by Americans."[126] For example, during a Black Lives Matter protest in Portland, Oregon, in August 2020, "a few protesters among the many thousands appear to have burned a single bible." Ruptly, a video news agency financed by the Kremlin, posted a video of the protesters burning a bible. RT, a government-sponsored Russian news agency, "wrote an entire story about the Bible burning." The RT story caught the attention of Ian Miles Cheong, a Malaysian man with a large Twitter following. He posted a message that misrepresented what the Ruptly video actually showed. He tweeted: "Left-wing activists bring a stack of Bibles to burn in front of the federal courthouse in Portland."[127]

Mr. Cheong's tweet "quickly became the basis for an entire day of outrage from right-wing news outlets." Donald Trump, Jr., tweeted about the bible burning story, as did Senator Ted Cruz. The story was "held up as evidence of the protesters' depravity by prominent alt-right conspiracy theorists like Jack Posobiec, a correspondent for the One America News Network." "Yet in the rush to paint all the protesters as Bible-burning zealots, few of the politicians or commentators who weighed in on the incident took the time to . . . figure out that it had originated with a Kremlin-backed video news agency." The *New York Times* reporters who covered the story concluded that "the Portland Bible burnings appear to be one of the first viral Russian disinformation hits of the 2020 presidential campaign."[128] But the Russians did not use bots or fake accounts to spread disinformation. They used accounts that are openly linked to the Kremlin to light a spark, and then watched while Americans spread the fire.

The bible burning story provides a good example of how Russian agents can plant a story for others to disseminate. Sometimes, though, the Russians help amplify a false story initiated by Americans. Robby Mook was Hillary Clinton's 2016 campaign manager. On the night of the Iowa caucuses in February 2020, "the hashtag #RobbyMookCaucusApp" was trending on Twitter.[129] The hashtag was used to spread a conspiracy theory that accused Mook "of developing a mobile app to rig the Democratic primary against Senator Bernie Sanders." In fact, the Democrats were using an app to tabulate caucus votes, but Mr. Mook "had never even heard of the app, which was developed by a company called Shadow Inc."[130]

An American woman named Chelsea Goodell initiated the conspiracy theory by tweeting that the app "was a Democratic ploy to steal a victory from Mr. Sanders" in the Iowa caucuses. She "added the hashtag #RobbyMookCaucusApp to her tweets." Then Ann Louise La Clair, a Sanders supporter with a Russian Twitter following, retweeted Goodell's claim. Shortly after La Clair tweeted about the conspiracy theory, an account named "@DanWals83975326 shared it." The DanWals account was controlled by a Russian cyber warrior. "By the time Mr. Mook could correct the record on Twitter . . . the false claim had been shared more than 20,000 times." Clint Watts, a former FBI agent, commented: "It was a textbook example of suspected Russian trolls exploiting unwitting Americans to sow discord." He added: "The Kremlin doesn't need to make fake news anymore. It's all American made."[131]

CHAPTER THREE

RUSSIAN INFLUENCE OPERATIONS IN EUROPE

ALINA POLYAKOVA, A LEADING Russia expert, says: "Since Putin's return to power in 2012, the Kremlin has accelerated its efforts to resurrect the arsenal of 'active measures'—tools of political warfare once used by the Soviet Union that aimed to influence world events through the manipulation of media, society, and politics."[1] Since 2014, Russia has conducted foreign influence operations in at least twenty-one countries that are members of NATO, the European Union (EU), or both. These include Austria, Bulgaria, Canada, Czech Republic, Denmark, Estonia, Finland, France, Germany, Italy, Latvia, Lithuania, Malta, Montenegro, the Netherlands, Norway, Poland, Spain, Sweden, the United Kingdom, and the United States.[2] Russia has also interfered in EU parliamentary elections.[3]

Russia clearly wants to weaken both NATO and the EU. Additionally, "the Kremlin wants to see Europe fractured from within . . . a Europe that is inward-looking and that will not frustrate Russia's strategic interests in the shared neighbourhood and farther abroad. Most importantly, the Kremlin wants a Europe that cannot or will not defend liberal-democratic values—nor inspire them elsewhere."[4] Polyakova adds that "the long-term goal is to upend the Western liberal order by turning Western virtues of openness and plurality into vulnerabilities to be exploited."[5] Finally, in the short term, Russia hopes to persuade EU member states to remove the sanctions that the EU initially imposed in response to Russia's illegal annexation of Crimea in 2014.[6]

Russia's foreign influence operations in Europe fall into four broad categories. First, Russia exploits social media platforms to conduct information warfare. Second, Russia uses RT and Sputnik—two large, global media organizations controlled by the Russian government—to disseminate propaganda to Western audiences. Third, Russia has steadily been cultivating ties to European political parties and politicians on the far-right and far-left who are sympathetic to Russian foreign policy interests. Finally, Russia has utilized a variety of covert financing schemes to channel funds to pro-Russian politicians and political parties. A report from the Alliance for Securing Democracy documents covert Russian financing operations designed to influence political developments in the Czech Republic, Estonia, France, Germany, Italy, Latvia, Lithuania, the Netherlands, Poland, Sweden, and the United Kingdom.[7]

This chapter presents case studies of three Russian influence operations. The first section examines Russia's efforts to influence the Brexit referendum in the United Kingdom in June 2016. The next section analyzes Russian interference with the French presidential election in spring 2017. The final section discusses Russian influence operations related to the national election in Sweden in 2018. My emphasis throughout is on social media. However, I also touch upon other aspects of Russian influence operations that complement Russia's information warfare activities.

THE UK REFERENDUM ON BREXIT IN 2016

In February 2016, Prime Minister David Cameron announced that the United Kingdom would hold a referendum to allow British citizens to decide whether the UK should remain in the European Union. The referendum was presented as a simple binary choice between "Leave" and "Remain." The British electorate was deeply divided on the issue. In the final vote, held on June 23, 2016, the Leave campaign won by a margin of 52 to 48 percent. The vote sent political shock waves through Europe and beyond. It was a resounding defeat for proponents of European economic integration, and more broadly for the liberal internationalist project of removing barriers to the free movement of goods and people across national borders. Vladimir Putin could not have been more pleased with the outcome. The decision to leave the EU "suited the Kremlin, because it weakened the EU overall and made exits by other states more likely."[8]

We know that Russia tried—through both overt and covert means—to persuade voters to vote Leave. However, it remains unclear whether Russia's influence efforts had a significant impact on the referendum. Several studies have concluded that the outcome of the referendum is attributable primarily to domestic factors and that Russia's influence operations had at most a marginal impact.[9] That conclusion may be correct, but we cannot be too confident. For several years, members of Parliament have urged the British government to conduct a thorough investigation to determine the scope and impact of Russian intervention. However, according to one MP, "the UK government have actively avoided looking for evidence that Russia interfered" in the Brexit referendum.[10] Despite the UK government's refusal to conduct a detailed, systematic investigation, there is evidence that Russia attempted to swing the vote in favor of leaving the EU. Based on available information, it appears that Russia's overt influence operation through RT and Sputnik was more consequential than its covert social media campaign.

RT and Sputnik

RT is a global media organization that operates as a "propaganda outlet for transmitting the values and objectives of the Russian government across the world."[11] RT operates a twenty-four-hour television service in multiple languages in more than 100 countries. As of 2018, RT's global television programming had more than 100 million weekly viewers, including 43 million weekly viewers in fifteen European countries.[12] In the United Kingdom, RT has "an average weekly reach of one per cent of UK adults."[13] Sputnik describes itself as "a modern news agency whose products include newsfeeds, websites, social networks, mobile apps, radio broadcasts and multimedia press centers."[14] Like RT, Sputnik is effectively a propaganda arm of the Russian government.

Shortly after Prime Minister Cameron announced the referendum, both RT and Sputnik began covering the issue. Ben Nimmo, an expert on digital disinformation, reported that "the Russian government's English-language TV station, RT, and news website, Sputnik, have conducted systematically one-sided coverage whose effect has been to magnify the 'Out' campaign and marginalize the 'In' campaign." "Coming from outlets paid for by the Russian government," he added, "it looks distinctly like an attempt to influence the UK debate."[15]

After the referendum, a communications agency called 89up analyzed the influence of RT and Sputnik on British voters.[16] 89up examined RT and Sputnik stories about the EU and the referendum published between January 1, 2016, and the close of polls on June 23, 2016. The analysis concluded that "there was a heavy Leave bias to the most shared RT and Sputnik articles." RT articles were 73 percent pro-Leave, 6 percent pro-Remain, and 21 percent neutral. Sputnik articles were somewhat less biased: 58 percent pro-Leave, 4 percent pro-Remain, and 38 percent neutral.[17] In contrast, PBS coverage was evenly balanced: 25 percent pro-Leave, 25 percent pro-Remain, and 50 percent neutral. Although RT and Sputnik had a legal duty to provide impartial coverage, they clearly violated that duty. In 2019, British regulators fined RT 200,000 pounds for breaching impartiality rules.[18] That fine was unrelated to RT's coverage of the Brexit referendum, but it is indicative of the type of news coverage provided by RT and Sputnik.

RT and Sputnik's pro-Leave bias provided the equivalent of free advertising for the Leave campaign. That free advertising was important because "the result was very close, and a close vote offers an opportunity to shift enough voters to influence the outcome of the election." Moreover, "a significant segment of the electorate . . . was undecided and could potentially be influenced."[19] Additionally, the UK imposed a campaign spending limit of $9.8 million for each side in the referendum.[20] 89up worked with Kantar, a media monitoring organization, to estimate the value to the Leave campaign of the free advertising provided by RT and Sputnik. They focused specifically on 98 pro-Leave articles published by RT and 163 pro-Leave articles by Sputnik. Based on Kantar's analysis, they assigned a media value of $8,237 for each RT article and $7,085 for each Sputnik article.[21] (In essence, this is what a commercial advertiser would pay RT and Sputnik, respectively, given the size of their audiences.) In total, 89up concluded that RT and Sputnik provided the equivalent of $1.95 million in free advertising for the Leave campaign: an extra 20 percent beyond the legal limit of $9.8 million.[22] It bears emphasis that this estimate is based on the advertising value of RT and Sputnik articles on television, radio, and print media. It does not account for the additional distribution of RT and Sputnik stories via social media (which is discussed below).

In July 2018, the UK Electoral Commission found that Vote Leave—the officially designated representative of the Leave campaign—violated electoral law by spending about $664,000 in excess of the $9.8 million limit.[23] Social media scholar Philip Howard analyzed how that extra spending might have influenced the ultimate vote on the referendum if Vote Leave had spent all of it on Facebook advertising in the final ten days of the campaign.[24] He notes that "the Brexit campaign won by just over 1.2 million votes. A swing of about 600,000 people would have been enough to secure victory for Remain."[25] After conducting a thorough analysis of Vote Leave's social media advertising strategy, Howard concluded that the extra $664,000 might well have altered the referendum outcome by enabling Vote Leave to purchase enough extra Facebook ads to influence the votes of a sufficient number of undecided voters in the final days of the campaign.[26]

If Howard is correct that an extra $664,000 for Facebook ads was sufficient to alter the outcome, it seems plausible that an extra $1.95 million in free advertising provided by RT and Sputnik could also have been a critical factor in persuading undecided voters to vote Leave. Of course, by paying for ads on Facebook, Vote Leave was able to engage in sophisticated microtargeting, tailoring particular messages to particular demographic groups. Indeed, Howard's analysis relies on the fact that Vote Leave had state-of-the-art data analysis tools to help them identify and target undecided voters via social media. In contrast, disseminating pro-Leave articles on RT and Sputnik is a much blunter tool. We do not know whether British voters who watched RT television news and listened to Sputnik radio broadcasts were undecided voters, or whether they were firmly committed to the pro-Leave camp. If the vast majority of them were already firmly committed, then 89up's estimate of $1.95 million significantly overstates the value of RT and Sputnik articles to the Leave campaign.

Regardless, RT also reached a significant number of UK voters through its presence on social media. According to data compiled by 89up, RT has 292,000 likes on Facebook, 66,000 Twitter followers, and 54,000 YouTube subscribers in the UK. Ruptly, a subsidiary of RT that specializes in video, has 230,000 likes on Facebook, 52,000 Twitter followers, and 304,000 YouTube subscribers in the UK.[27] (The comparable figures for Sputnik are much smaller.) RT claims that, on a worldwide basis, it is the most watched news channel on YouTube. A report by Stanford University's Cyber Policy Center, which focuses on the U.S. audience, notes that "RT's YouTube viewership at times has rivaled and surpassed CNN's."[28]

89up analyzed the engagement of UK citizens with RT and Sputnik posts on social media. As noted above, their analysis focused specifically on 98 pro-Leave articles published by RT and 163 pro-Leave articles by Sputnik. Between January 1 and June 23, 2016, the RT articles achieved 215,337 engagements on Facebook and a total of more than 270,000 engagements across Facebook, Twitter, LinkedIn and Pinterest. The Sputnik articles achieved 40,465 engagements on Facebook and a total of almost 48,000 engagements across the four platforms.[29] (It is unclear why 89up did not include YouTube in this analysis. Given what we know about RT's presence on YouTube, engagement numbers for YouTube were probably much larger.) 89up provides two different comparisons to put these figures in context. First, the official Vote Leave website (not including paid advertising) achieved a total of 287,000 engagements on Facebook, compared to a total of 256,000 engagements on Facebook for RT and Sputnik.[30] Second, they compare RT and Sputnik to government-funded media outlets from France and the United States. Stories related to the Brexit referendum achieved only about 7,300 engagements on France24 and about 3,900 engagements on PBS. Thus, "compared to other major foreign state-funded media outlets, the Russian media outlets led to significantly larger social media exposure."[31]

These figures suggest that the pro-Leave articles on RT and Sputnik achieved a fairly high level of social media engagement. However, engagement with Russian-operated covert social media accounts in the United States during the 2016 presidential election campaign was an order of magnitude greater. A report prepared for the Senate Intelligence Committee shows that, during the 2016 U.S. campaign, four Facebook pages controlled by Russian cyber troops achieved more than 10 million engagements each, and ten other covert Russian Facebook pages achieved more than one million engagements each.[32] Comparable data for the UK referendum is not available because, as noted previously, the British government has not done the type of investigation that would be necessary to obtain such data. Given the limited available data, though, there are reasons to believe that pro-Leave articles on RT and Sputnik may have given a significant boost to the Leave campaign.

Covert Social Media Activity

As I write this chapter, more than four years after the referendum, we still know surprisingly little about Russian information warfare activity related to the Brexit vote. In October 2017, more than one year after the referendum, researchers from the City University of London identified "a network of more than 13,000 suspected bots that tweeted predominantly pro-Brexit messages before being deleted or removed from Twitter in the weeks following the vote." Their research "suggests that suspected bot accounts were eight times more likely to tweet pro-leave than pro-remain content."[33] However, that study did not produce any information definitively linking the bot accounts to Russia.

In January 2019, "Facebook removed 289 Pages and 75 accounts from its site, accounts that had about 790,000 followers. . . . The sites had been run by employees at the Russian state-owned news agency Sputnik, who represented themselves as independent news or general interest Pages."[34] The choice by Sputnik employees to operate Facebook accounts without identifying themselves as Russian agents has the trappings of a covert influence operation rather than an overt media campaign. However, there is no publicly available information linking these accounts to the Brexit referendum.

Revelations that Russia engaged in covert social media operations related to the Brexit vote first emerged in November 2017, more than sixteen months after the referendum. At that time, the U.S. Congress was investigating Russian interference in the U.S. election. In response to a congressional request, Twitter publicly released information about 2,752 accounts linked to Russia's Internet Research Agency. Several researchers analyzed those accounts and found evidence of Russian interference in the Brexit vote. CNN reported that "a network of Twitter accounts with ties to the Russian government . . . posted dozens of pro-Brexit messages on the day of the referendum."[35] *Wired* magazine said that "a coordinated network of Russian-based Twitter accounts . . . posted pro and anti-Brexit, anti-immigration and racist tweets around the EU referendum vote."[36] A study conducted "by researchers at the University of Edinburgh analyzed the 2752 accounts that Twitter handed over to the U.S. Congress." They "found that more than 400 of those accounts posted divisive messages about the Brexit referendum, the majority after the polls closed."[37] A different study found that "150,000 Twitter accounts with ties to Russia tweeted about Brexit in the days before the Brexit vote."[38]

Analysis of the Russian Twitter accounts, however, does not reveal anything remotely like what Robert Mueller called Russia's "sweeping and systematic" attempt to interfere in the 2016 U.S. election. Scholars at Oxford University analyzed the set of 2,752 accounts released by Twitter, as well as about 150 other Russia-linked Twitter accounts that they identified independently. They also examined the influence of bots.[39] They concluded that "bots have a small but strategic role in the referendum conversations." A different study prepared by the same group at Oxford said that, during Brexit, bots "were active for both the leave and remain campaign, generating large amounts of traffic."[40] However, the Oxford study found that Russian influence was marginal, at best: "Altogether, only 105 of these [Russian] accounts produced any tweets or retweets about Brexit, and they generated only 15,964 tweets in our sample, which represents less than 0.3% of the total traffic. We also found that overall, only 3% of the Russian accounts initially 'outed' by Twitter generated any traffic during the Brexit debate."[41]

The UK Parliament's Intelligence and Security Committee released an unclassified report on Russia in July 2020.[42] The committee sharply criticized the government for its failure to investigate allegations of Russian interference. The report stated: "The written evidence provided to us appeared to suggest that [Her Majesty's Government] had not . . . sought evidence of successful interference in UK democratic processes."[43] The committee noted: "This situation is in stark contrast to the US handling of allegations of Russian interference in the 2016 presidential election, where an intelligence community assessment was produced within two months of the vote."[44] The committee politely urged the UK intelligence community to prepare an analogous report. Stewart Hosie, a member of the parliamentary committee, was less diplomatic in his public comments. He said: "The report reveals that no one in government knew if Russia interfered or sought to influence the referendum because they did not want to know."[45] Given the failure of the British government to conduct a systematic investigation, it is possible that Russia operated hundreds or thousands of covert social media accounts related to the Brexit referendum that have not yet been discovered. However, based solely on Russian accounts that have been identified as such, it appears that covert social media accounts operated by Russian cyber troops had very little influence on the final vote in the UK referendum.

The Scent of Russian Money

One of the most intriguing stories to emerge from reporting by investigative journalists about Russia and Brexit involves a British businessman named Arron Banks. Banks donated 8 million pounds (about $11.6 million) to the Leave.EU campaign and an associated entity. His donation was "by far the largest political donation in U.K. history."[46] Leave.EU operated independently from Vote Leave, which had been designated by the Electoral Commission as the official Leave campaign. Hence, Leave.EU was not bound by the $9.8 million campaign spending limit that applied to Vote Leave. Some commentators have suggested "that the rambunctious Leave.EU campaign—which stoked fears of uncontrolled immigration— had roused voters who had been unmoved by the more technocratic messages of Vote Leave."[47] Public opinion polling data indicates that anti-immigration sentiment was a key factor supporting the final vote in favor of Brexit.[48]

ABC News noted in April 2019 that "doubts persist around the source of [Banks's] money, with allegations speculating that the money could have Russian roots."[49] Banks claimed that he had a net worth of $130 million, but an independent investigation found that "Banks' gross earnings since 2001 stood at only $32 million."[50] If the lower figure is correct, it is questionable whether he could afford to give a donation of more than $10 million without outside assistance. A report from a parliamentary committee stated that "Arron Banks discussed business ventures within Russia and beyond, in a series of meetings with Russian Embassy staff." Moreover, the report added, Banks "misled the Committee on the number of meetings that took place with the Russian Embassy."[51] According to a different source: "In the months before the 2016 Brexit referendum, a Russian spy under diplomatic cover at the Russian embassy in London connected Banks to the Russian ambassador to the U.K., who introduced Banks to a Russian oligarch, who in turn offered Banks" an opportunity "to make highly profitable investments in Russian gold and diamond firms."[52]

In November 2018, the Electoral Commission referred the matter of Banks's donation to the National Crime Agency (NCA) for investigation. The Electoral Commission said, among other things, it had reasonable grounds to suspect that "Mr. Banks was not the true source of the £8m reported as loans," that "Leave.EU . . . Mr. Banks, and possibly others, concealed the true details of these financial transactions," and that "various criminal offenses may have been committed."[53] Approximately eleven months later, the NCA said that it "found no evidence that any criminal offences have been committed under PPERA or company law by any of the individuals or organizations referred to it by the Electoral Commission."[54] However, outside commentators note that "the NCA defined its investigation narrowly" and that the NCA "hinted in a postscript that it was still delving into the allegations at the center of its investigation, which involve South Africa and Banks's assets there."[55] The South African connection is significant. "If Banks has used his South African mines to illegally launder the origin of gems secretly sourced from Zimbabwe (which has been alleged but not proven) . . . such a scheme would require support from Moscow, because . . . the Russian intelligence services have indirectly controlled the underground diamond trade in Harare for over a decade."[56]

In sum, there is some evidence to suggest that Russia may have provided covert financing for the Leave.EU campaign—indirectly through Arron Banks—and that Russian government agents may be supporting Banks's investment in a questionable African mining venture in exchange for his help in financing the Leave campaign.

Assessment

A British polling organization has been tracking public opinion about Britain's relationship with the EU since 1992. Each year, pollsters give people five options for summarizing their views: (1) leave the EU; (2) stay in the EU but reduce its powers; (3) leave things as they are; (4) stay in the EU and increase its powers; (5) or work for a single European government.[57] To simplify, let us say that the first two options reflect anti-EU sentiment. In 2008, only 55 percent of British citizens manifested anti-EU sentiment. By 2016, that number had increased to 76 percent, with a jump from 65 to 76 percent between 2015 and 2016. The authors of the study conclude that "the referendum campaign had profound consequences. First, it seems to have moved public opinion as a whole in a more skeptical direction. . . . Second, the campaign seems to have exacerbated the social and cultural division about the merits of EU membership that already existed in British society" before the referendum.[58]

Given the British governments' refusal to conduct a thorough investigation, it is difficult to say with confidence that Russia's influence operations did, or did not, have a significant impact on the outcome of the referendum. Based on available information, it seems likely that pro-Leave articles by RT and Sputnik were probably more influential than Russia's covert social media operation. Regardless, there is no question that Vladimir Putin is very pleased with the result.

THE 2017 FRENCH PRESIDENTIAL ELECTION

Russia's key goals in France are similar to its goals in other western European nations: to weaken support for both NATO and the EU. Russia has pursued these goals in France by "building political alliances with ideologically friendly political groups" and by "establishing pro-Russian organizations in civil society."[59] There is a sizeable Russian diaspora community in France. Additionally, "there is a powerful and well-structured net of civil society organizations and think tanks that promote Russian interests."[60]

France held its most recent presidential election in spring 2017. Eleven candidates competed in the first round of the election, held on April 23. The two candidates with the most votes in the first round competed in a runoff election on May 7: Emmanuel Macron, leader of the centrist party La République en Marche, and Marine Le Pen, leader of the far-right National Front (later renamed the National Rally). Macron defeated Le Pen in the runoff election by a decisive margin of 66 to 34 percent. Macron's victory was a significant loss for Russia because he was the only one of the leading first-round candidates who did not adopt a pro-Russian foreign policy position.

Three major political parties in France have espoused pro-Russian foreign policy views. The center-right Republican party (Les Républicains) was traditionally one of the two main political parties in France. François Fillon, a former prime minister, was the Republican presidential candidate in 2017. The Republicans are "divided on their relationship to Russia. However, there is a distinct pro-Russian group around" Fillon.[61] The Republican's "pro-Russian stance is partly based on the party's deep connections with elements of French big business, which have operations in Russia." Some of Fillon's allies in the Republican party "have been publicly supportive of the Russian position on the Ukrainian crisis" and others have "called for discontinuing European sanctions against Russia."[62]

Marine Le Pen is one of the most pro-Russian politicians in Europe. She publicly supported Russia's annexation of Crimea in 2014. Russia reciprocated her support by arranging a loan of 9.4 million euros from the First Czech Russian Bank.[63] Le Pen's party "completely subscribes to the Russian interpretation of events [in Ukraine] and has given very vocal support to Moscow's position."[64] Jean-Luc Mélenchon, leader of the far-left party La France Insoumise, also favors a close relationship with Russia.[65] Le Pen, Fillon, and Mélenchon collectively won more than 60 percent of the votes in the first round of the 2017 election.[66] Although Macron's ultimate victory in the runoff was a disappointment for Russia, the fact that three of the top four candidates in the first round were generally pro-Russian augurs well for Putin's longer-term effort to nudge French policy in a more Russia-friendly direction.

The Campaign against Macron

François Fillon was the front-runner for several months at the beginning of the presidential election campaign. However, a scandal erupted in January 2017 when the "newspaper *Le Canard Enchaîné* reported that Fillon had paid his wife a total of €800,000 from public funds to work as his parliamentary assistant."[67] The problem, allegedly, was that she did not actually do any work to earn the money. After the scandal broke, Macron began to rise in the polls as support for Fillon dropped sharply. When Macron became the front-runner, two different groups began to spread disinformation about him: official Russian news media and the American alt-right (who are ideologically aligned with Marine Le Pen).[68] The American alt-right "were active on Reddit, 4chan's political board, and other similar forums. Using fake French identities and sock-puppet social media accounts . . . [they] portray[ed] Macron as a stooge of Jewish financiers who will sell out the working class and capitulate to Muslim terrorists."[69]

Whereas the American alt-right operated covertly, Russian news media acted more overtly. RT operates a French-language television station that "is progressively growing a network of like-minded, French-speaking, pro-Russian individuals from across the political spectrum."[70] Before the 2017 election, RT and Sputnik disseminated anti-Macron propaganda. Specifically, they reported that he was "a puppet of U.S. political and business leaders, alleged he held an offshore account in the Bahamas to evade taxes, and fueled rumors of an extra-marital gay relationship."[71] "The French polling commission . . . issued a warning against polls deemed illegitimate under French law, after Kremlin-controlled news outlet Sputnik pushed out polls that showed François Fillon, a Russia-friendly candidate, to be in the lead."[72] During the campaign, Macron's team barred RT and Sputnik journalists from his campaign headquarters, a move that the Russian Foreign Ministry denounced as "outrageous . . . bare-faced discrimination."[73] After Macron won the election, he invited Putin to a meeting at Versailles. When they appeared together publicly for a press conference, "a Russian journalist [asked] why it had been so difficult for certain reporters to get access to [Macron's] campaign headquarters during the election." Macron's reply is illuminating: "I have always had an exemplary relationship with foreign journalists, but they have to be journalists. RT and Sputnik were organs of influence that spread counterfeit truths about me."[74]

In addition to spreading disinformation about Macron through RT and Sputnik, Russia also carried out covert operations. According to one source, "Russian intelligence agents attempted to spy on President Emmanuel Macron's election campaign . . . by creating phony Facebook personas."[75] In April 2017, "a Macron campaign spokesman said that 2000 to 3000 attempts have been made to hack the campaign, including denial-of-service attacks that briefly shut down Macron's website."[76] The French government never formally attributed those attacks to Russia. However, the head of the U.S. Cyber Command told the Senate Armed Services Committee that the United States "had become aware of Russian activity to hack French election-related infrastructure in the months prior to the French election." Additionally, "a private cybersecurity firm indicated that the Macron campaign was a target of APT 28," the Russian government intelligence unit responsible for hacking the Democratic National Committee in the 2016 U.S. election. [77]

The runoff election between Macron and Le Pen was scheduled for Sunday, May 7, 2017. French law imposes a pre-election media blackout, which took effect at midnight Friday night and lasted until the polls closed at 8:00 p.m. Sunday. On the evening of Friday, May 5, Macron's campaign announced that "it had been the target of a massive computer hack that dumped its campaign emails online." Reuters reported that "as much as 9 gigabytes of data were posted on a profile called EMLEAKS to Pastebin, a site that allows anonymous document sharing."[78] The leaked data consisted mostly of emails stolen from "the professional and personal email accounts of at least five of Macron's close colleagues."[79] Subsequent commentary noted that, given the official media blackout, "the leak was so timed to leave Macron and his party powerless to defend themselves, to block the mainstream media from analyzing the documents and their release, and to make social media, especially Twitter, the primary space where the content could be discussed."[80]

Conversation about the leaked documents quickly exploded on Twitter. An analysis published on Saturday, May 6, "found that the hashtag #MacronLeaks reached 47,000 tweets in three and a half hours after it was first used by Jack Posobiec," a far-right activist in the United States who has more than 100,000 Twitter followers.[81] The initial conversation was primarily in English. "This makes it clear that the hashtag #MacronLeaks was launched and spread in the United States, by the American alt-right."[82] Soon, though, WikiLeaks helped spread the hashtag #MacronLeaks to a French audience with a link to the files on Pastebin. "Only then came the first French amplifiers, who happened to be Le Pen supporters." The early Twitter conversation "was dominated by the anti-Macron voices but a shift happened overnight, which coincided with a shift in language: at the same time the conversation became more French . . . it also became more critical of the leak."[83]

We know that the American alt-right helped spread the #MacronLeaks hashtag, but it is not entirely clear who initially hacked the email accounts or who posted the files on Pastebin. The person who posted the files on Pastebin used a Latvian IP address. However, he/she probably used a proxy server to hide his/her true location.[84] The French government never officially blamed Russia for the hack, but several other sources suggest that Russia was probably responsible. An information security analyst known as "The Grugq" predicted the leaks against Macron in February. "In his expert opinion, it was a Russian operation."[85] Similarly, the Japanese cybersecurity firm Trend Micro attributed the hack "to APT 28 (also known as Fancy Bear or Pawn Storm), a cyberespionage group linked to the Russian military intelligence agency GRU."[86] Another cybersecurity group, ThreatConnect, identified "consistencies with Fancy Bear registration and hosting tactics," but said that they could not "definitely confirm Trend Micro's assessment that Fancy Bear aka Pawn Storm is behind this activity."[87] The head of the French National Cybersecurity Agency said: "The modus operandi is very similar [to APT 28], but we cannot exclude that a very competent group can try to imitate them."[88] In October 2020, a federal grand jury in the United States issued an indictment charging six Russian intelligence agents with various crimes; the indictment alleged, among other things, that in spring 2017 they conducted "spearphishing campaigns and related hack-and-leak efforts targeting French President Macron's . . . political party, French politicians, and local French governments prior to the 2017 French elections."[89]

Most analysts concluded that the so-called Macron Leaks operation was a failure because Macron won the election. Several factors help explain why the operation failed. First, most of the social media conversation about #MacronLeaks took place on Twitter. Twitter is not a very good vehicle for influencing French elections because there are only about 7.1 million French Twitter users in a population of 65 million—roughly 11 percent of the population. Moreover, French citizens "do not trust social networks as news sources: a survey showed that while 75 percent of the population trusts news from 'traditional' media, only 25 percent trusts news found on social networks."[90] Second, social media manipulation is likely to be most effective in a close election. The first-round voting was close: the top four candidates each won between 19 and 25 percent of the vote. However, the runoff election was not close. The French legal requirement for a runoff election after the first round, combined with Le Pen's second-place finish in round one, virtually guaranteed that round two would be a landslide because Le Pen was perceived as being too far right to garner anything close to majority support in the French political environment in 2017. (In contrast, recent polling data gives her a fair chance of winning a runoff election against Macron in 2022.[91])

Third, "the media environment of the election is also more regulated in France than in the United States."[92] After the hacked emails were released on social media, "the French electoral commission issued an instruction to news media in France not to publish the contents of the leaked information . . . [and] the media effectively complied with the government ban."[93] Finally, after the 2016 U.S. presidential election, social media companies were more alert to the danger of foreign electoral interference. "Facebook stated publicly in April 2017 that it had suspended 30,000 accounts for promoting propaganda or election-related spam before the French poll," and subsequent reports indicate that "the number of accounts ultimately suspended could have been as many as 70,000."[94]

Social Media in France and the 2017 Presidential Election
This section summarizes three empirical studies of French social media use in the period surrounding the 2017 French presidential election. Readers should bear in mind two key dates: the first-round election was on April 23, 2017, and the runoff between Macron and Le Pen was on May 7. Emilio Ferrara, a scholar at the University of Southern California, analyzed a "Twitter dataset of nearly 17 million posts . . . between April 27 and May 7, 2017."[95] A group of scholars from Oxford University analyzed two different Twitter datasets. The first included about 842,000 tweets posted from March 13–19 (before the first round),[96] and the second included about 960,000 tweets posted from April 27–29 (after the first round and before the runoff).[97] In contrast to the Ferrara and Oxford studies, which focused exclusively on Twitter, Bakamo, a private media consultancy firm, collected data from a wider variety of sources over a longer time period. Bakamo used the TalkWalker platform, which "collects data not just from social media platforms like Twitter, Facebook, Instagram, and YouTube, but also from forums, blogs, newspaper comments, and the like."[98] Bakamo captured more than 20 million conversations from November 1, 2016, to May 22, 2017.

Ferrara's analysis focused primarily on bots. He identified "the presence of bots that existed during the 2016 U.S. Presidential election campaign to support alt-right narratives, went dark after November 8, 2016, and came back into use" shortly before the French presidential election. Those bots were used to disseminate anti-Macron propaganda during the French election campaign. Ferrara's most striking conclusion is that "a black market of reusable political disinformation bots may exist."[99] It is unclear how many of those bots are controlled by Russian agents and how many are controlled by alt-right activists in the United States.

The Oxford studies found that bots accounted for a fairly small portion of the election-related Twitter conversation in France. The first study, completed before the first-round election, concluded: "On average, 7.2 percent of the traffic about French politics is generated by the bots we are able to track."[100] That percentage increased significantly before the runoff. The second study, which focused on the runoff election, concluded that "16.4 percent of the traffic about the election is generated by the bots we are able to track."[101]

Both Bakamo and the Oxford team analyzed the links in social media posts to determine the sources of information that French netizens are sharing. The authors of the Bakamo report analyzed 20 million social media posts and 8 million shared links in public social media conversations from November 1, 2016, to May 22, 2017.[102] They measured the influence of different media sources by counting the number of times that social media users shared links to articles, videos, and images from different sources. They divided the "media map" into five categories:

- "Traditional" sources are media sources "that belong to the established commercial and conventional media landscape." This category accounted for 50 percent of shared links.
- "Campaign" sources include "the official web presences of the candidates and parties." This category accounted for 7 percent of shared links.
- "Extend" sources include "media sources that act to extend the journalistic scope of the traditional media." They generally "contribute to the public's discourse in a constructive manner." This category accounted for 20 percent of shared links.

- "Reframe" sources are media sources that "share the motivation to counter the Traditional Media narrative." They "see themselves as part of a struggle to 'reinform' readers of the real contexts and meanings hidden from them when they are informed by Traditional Media sources." This category accounted for 19 percent of shared links.
- "Alternative" sources constitute "an incoherent, confusing space [that] fuses radical left and right views which are unified in their opposition to globalization." This category accounted for 4 percent of shared links.[103]

The Oxford studies also divided linked sources into different categories, but they used a very different typology. The first two categories in the Oxford studies—professional news content and professional political content—correspond fairly closely to the first two categories in the Bakamo scheme: traditional sources and campaign sources. Table 2 displays the data from the Bakamo report and the two Oxford studies. The Bakamo and Oxford results for these two categories are fairly consistent, suggesting that about 40–50 percent of shared links refer to traditional

TABLE 2. Shared links in French social media posts. Sources: Bakamo, "French Election Social Media Landscape: Final Report"; Howard et al., "Junk News and Bots during the French Presidential Election"; Desigaud et al., "Junk News and Bots during the French Presidential Election."

	Percentage of shared links	
	Professional news content (traditional sources)	Professional political content (campaign sources)
First Oxford report (March 13–19, 2017)	46.7	15.7
Second Oxford report (April 27–29, 2017)	40.2	11.8
Bakamo final report (November 1, 2016— May 22, 2017)	50	7

media sources, and another 7–16 percent refer to campaign sources. The differences between Bakamo and Oxford are primarily attributable to the fact that Bakamo collected data over a longer time period from a broader range of sources.[104]

Beyond these two categories, the Bakamo report and the Oxford studies use very different classification schemes to categorize the other types of sources that appear in shared links. The Oxford studies group together "junk news," "Russian content," and "religious content" under the heading of "other political news and information." The combination of the three categories accounted for 7 percent of shared links in the first-round election and 10 percent of shared links in the runoff election.[105] If we group the three categories together under the heading of "junk news," the Oxford studies suggest that the ratio of professional news to junk news was almost 7:1 in the first-round election and about 4:1 in the runoff. The authors conclude that French voters "share political news and information of better quality than US voters."[106] In a separate study of Michigan voters in the 2016 U.S. presidential election,[107] the Oxford team found that Michigan voters shared "professional news and junk news" at a roughly 1:1 ratio.

The Oxford team's rather upbeat assessment of the French social media environment contrasts fairly sharply with two key conclusions from the Bakamo report. First, the Bakamo report found that about 23 percent of shared citations refer to sources that challenge traditional media narratives. These are the sources in the Reframe and Alternative categories. There is "clear evidence that these sources are exposed to Russian influence. Nearly one in five sources in the Reframe section and almost half of Alternative sources refer to Russian media sources."[108]

Second, according to Bakamo, "there is virtually no common ground to connect people who receive political news from Alternative/Reframe sources and those who receive political news from Traditional sources. Sharing across the divide separating Traditional from Reframe/Alternative sources is almost non-existent. . . . With no agreement on 'facts' (much less interpretation), these sources talk past each other."[109] Thus, the report provides compelling evidence of an echo chamber effect that tends to polarize French politics. However, the primary axis of polarization is not along traditional left/right lines. Rather, it is the divide between mainstream media sources and the Reframe/Alternative sources dominated by nationalist, anti-globalization, and anti-Islam narratives. The authors conclude: "With little common ground between users who accept traditional media narratives and those who contest them, techniques of disinformation will continue to be effective."[110]

In sum, there is an evident tension between the Oxford studies' conclusion that French netizens tend to share fairly high-quality political news and information, and the Bakamo report's conclusion that almost one-quarter of French netizens are stuck in an echo chamber that is heavily influenced by Russian propaganda and that professional news sources are largely unable to penetrate. Bakamo's main conclusions are reminiscent of a study of the U.S. media environment conducted by a group of scholars at Harvard University, although the Harvard study focused on traditional media, not social media.[111] Regardless, the Harvard scholars concluded that the U.S. media environment is sharply divided between "the right-wing media ecosystem" and everyone else. Roughly 30 percent of American citizens rely on the right-wing media ecosystem—including Fox News, Breitbart, and (previously) Rush Limbaugh—as their primary source of news and information. Like the French netizens who rely on Reframe/Alternative sources, Americans who rely on the right-wing media ecosystem are easily swayed by misinformation because they do not trust mainstream media and are therefore impervious to fact-checking by mainstream sources.[112]

Assessment

Russia actively sought to undermine Macron's candidacy through a combination of hacking and disinformation. The American alt-right supported Russia's effort in this respect. In contrast to the 2016 U.S. election, though, there is scant evidence to suggest that Russian agents relied heavily on fictitious user accounts. Bots clearly played some role in the

2017 French election, but they were probably not very influential, and it is unclear what percentage of bots were actually controlled by Russian cyber troops.

Several commentators have characterized the 2017 French election as a victory for liberal democracy over Russian interference and the potentially pernicious effects of social media. That assessment is clearly correct insofar as Macron scored a decisive victory over Le Pen in the second round. Nevertheless, those who are committed to liberal democracy should not be overly complacent. The fact that Marine Le Pen advanced to the runoff is itself grounds for concern. Like the strong showing of the Sweden Democrats in the 2018 Swedish elections (discussed in the next section), Le Pen's performance is indicative of the rise of the far-right in Europe, which is a boon for Putin and a threat to the future of liberal democracy. Additionally, the fact that Le Pen, Fillon, and Mélenchon collectively won more than 60 percent of the votes in the first round was good news for Putin because all three, to varying degrees, favor a pro-Russian foreign policy stance.

Bakamo's detailed analysis of the French social media landscape also sounds a cautionary note. Liberal democracy cannot function effectively if partisans on opposite ends of the political spectrum lack a common set of facts that provide a basis for reasoned discussion of policy issues. The Bakamo report suggests that almost one-quarter of the French electorate inhabits its own informational echo chamber that is filled with disinformation, including Russian disinformation. The French government clearly needs to do more to break down the barriers that inhibit effective communication between citizens who get their news and information from mainstream sources and those who occupy a separate, insulated media ecosystem.

2018 ELECTIONS IN SWEDEN

Sweden is a multiparty democracy with a unicameral legislature, the Riksdag. Eight parties currently hold seats in the 349-person Riksdag. The two largest parties are the center-left Social Democratic Party (100 seats) and the center-right Moderate Party (70 seats). The far-right Sweden

Democrats have gained a progressively larger share of the vote in the last three national elections, held in 2010, 2014, and 2018. After the 2010 elections, the Social Democrats and the Moderate Party held a combined 219 seats in the Riksdag, compared to a mere 20 seats for the Sweden Democrats. After the 2018 election, though, Social Democrats and Moderates between them held 170 seats—a combined loss of 49 seats in two election cycles—and the Social Democrats held 62 seats, a gain of 42 seats in the same two election cycles. Overall, the center-right coalition that governed Sweden from 2010 to 2014 (which included the Moderates, Centre Party, Liberals, and Christian Democrats) lost 30 seats between 2010 and 2018, while the far-right Sweden Democrats gained 42 seats.[113] Vladimir Putin is surely pleased to see the rise of the Sweden Democrats and the weakening of traditional, centrist parties. Russian information warfare is one of several factors that has contributed to these trends.

Sweden joined the European Union (EU) in 1995. Although Sweden has traditionally maintained a policy of neutrality, it began to cooperate with NATO on defense matters under the Partnership for Peace program in 1994. Swedish cooperation with NATO remained quite limited for the next two decades, but Russia's forcible annexation of Crimea in 2014 was a wake-up call for non-NATO countries in close geographic proximity to Russia. "Since Russia annexed Crimea in 2014, Sweden's public opinion has shifted in favor of Sweden joining NATO."[114] "In 2017, a Pew poll found that 47 percent of the population favored joining NATO, while only 39 percent were opposed."[115] Both Sweden and Finland strengthened their defense cooperation with NATO by joining the "partnership interoperability initiative" in 2014.[116]

Russia perceives NATO's closer cooperation with Sweden and Finland as a significant threat. "The encirclement hypothesis, which argues that the United States and its allies are threatening Russian security with the installment of military bases near Russian borders," provides a key analytic framework for Russian security doctrine.[117] The Russian defense minister has said "that the greater inclusion of Finland and Sweden into the Alliance's exercises and command-and-control systems lead[s] to the destruction of the existing system of global security and generate[s] ever greater mistrust, forcing us to take response measures."[118] Since 2014, Russia has stepped up its foreign influence operations in both Sweden and Finland, at least partly in response to their decisions to strengthen defense cooperation with NATO.

One key goal of Russia's foreign influence operations in Sweden is to weaken support for both NATO and the EU. Sputnik International launched a Swedish language news site in 2015. Two scholars affiliated with the Swedish Institute of International Affairs conducted a comprehensive content analysis of 3,963 news items published on Sputnik's Swedish language website between April 2015 and spring 2016. They concluded that about 60 percent of all articles involved "criticism of the EU and NATO" and that this messaging was probably "the dominant narrative which Russia wants to communicate . . . to the Swedish target audience."[119]

Another key Russian goal is to increase polarization on divisive issues. Accordingly, Russian agents have spread disinformation to Swedish audiences on the topic of immigrants. Sweden admitted 165,000 asylum seekers in 2015. With a population of 10 million people, "this gave Sweden the highest per capita immigration rate of any OECD country."[120] Since that time, Sweden has struggled with a "rising public backlash against [the] influx of refugees." Indeed, migration was "the dominant political issue" in the 2018 election cycle,[121] and the anti-immigrant policies of the far-right Sweden Democrats help explain their strong electoral gains in 2018. The political salience of the immigration issue made it a prime target for Russian disinformation. "Russian information operations have polarized the debate by criticizing both sides of the immigration argument."[122] For example, one false claim alleged that the Swedish government ordered police not to investigate rapes committed by immigrants. According to an EU database on Russian disinformation, "There is no evidence to support the claim that the Swedish government has forbidden the police authority to investigate sexual violence, performed by immigrants. . . . However, the narrative against immigrants . . . [is] in line with a recurrent pro-Kremlin narrative on migration."[123]

In February 2016, "the Supreme Commander of the Swedish Armed Forces reported that Russian cyber attacks against the country occur daily."[124] In August 2017, the Swedish defense minister confirmed "that Russia was carrying out hybrid warfare against Sweden, including military action, cyber attacks, disinformation, and false news."[125] Also in 2017, the defense ministers of Sweden and Denmark "condemned Russian fake news as a danger to their countries and pledged to increase their work in combatting Moscow's hybrid warfare."[126] The Authoritarian Interference Tracker—a database maintained by the Alliance for Securing Democracy— identifies eight discrete examples of Russian information manipulation and cyber operations targeting Sweden between February 2015 and the 2018 elections.[127]

Russian covert measures targeting Sweden since 2014 include the dissemination of "disinformation, forged telegrams and fake news items," the use of "troll armies" on social media to target journalists and academics, the "hijacking of Twitter accounts," "falsified interviews with Swedish citizens," and harassment of Swedish journalists and diplomats working in Russia.[128] Shortly before the 2018 elections, a foreign actor launched a "Distributed Denial of Service (DDoS) attack [that] twice brought down the website of Sweden's largest political party, the Social Democrats."[129] Although the Swedish government did not formally accuse Russia of launching the attack, the "Social Democrats' IP provider stated that the IP addresses behind the attack were linked to Russia and North Korea."[130] Moreover, Russia has launched similar DDoS attacks against other targets in the past, and Russia had a clear motive to attack the Social Democrats, because they led the government that decided to increase defense cooperation with NATO.

Russian operatives have a long history of using forgeries in their foreign influence operations. Two Swedish scholars documented "26 forgeries and fake articles appearing in the Swedish information climate" between December 2014 and July 2016.[131] In one case, for example, a letter ostensibly signed by the Swedish minister of defense "appeared on social media through a Twitter identity of a well-known Swedish military affairs journalist." The letter indicated that Sweden was planning to export advanced military equipment to Ukraine. The claim was false and the letter was a forgery. Nevertheless, the story "surfaced on a German news website and has since reappeared on pro-Kremlin websites and social media."[132] Although it is difficult to identify with certainty the person or government responsible for specific forgeries, it is likely that Russian agents are responsible for most of them. One piece of evidence pointing to Russia is that "the most active social media account used for disseminating Swedish language forgeries is 'George Kobzaru' (a fake name), who is also present on pro-Kremlin Facebook groups."[133]

Russian agents probably helped spread disinformation related to Sweden's relationship with NATO in 2015 and 2016. "In May 2016, Swedish lawmakers ratified an agreement that allows NATO to more easily operate on Swedish territory during training or in the event of a conflict or other crisis."[134] Three false claims about that agreement spread on both traditional and social media in 2015 and 2016. Stories alleged that NATO "will be allowed to place nuclear weapons on Swedish military bases, use Swedish territory to launch a first-strike attack on Russia and enjoy legal immunity for crimes committed by NATO troops on Swedish territory. All three claims are false but have nevertheless reappeared frequently in Swedish media and public debate."[135] There is no definitive proof that Russian agents fabricated these stories, but the stories clearly advance Russia's goal of undermining support for Swedish defense cooperation with NATO.

The Swedish Defense Research Agency conducted a study on the role of bots on Twitter during the 2018 election campaign. They "found a substantial presence of bots engaging in the Swedish political debate."[136] In the period under review, "bots generated nearly 17 percent of all election-related content." The far-right "Sweden Democrats received significantly more support from the bots than they received from human-operated accounts. . . . Moreover, the material shared by these bots often came from immigration-critical alternative media."[137] It is unclear whether Russian agents were responsible for creating some or all of these bot accounts.

A group of scholars at Oxford University studied activity on Swedish Twitter over a ten-day period approximately one month before the 2018 Swedish elections.[138] They applied a coding system that divided Twitter messages into several categories, including (1) professional news content,

(2) professional political content, (3) junk news and information, and (4) other political news and information. Junk news includes "misleading, deceptive or incorrect information purporting to be real news" and "ideologically extreme, hyper-partisan or conspiratorial news and information." Two conclusions from that study are especially noteworthy. First, "the ratio of professional news to junk news shared over social media was roughly 2:1." This ratio is similar to the United States, but "significantly lower than in the UK, Germany, and France." Comparable studies in those countries showed that "Germany had the ratio of 4:1 and UK and France had 5:1 and 7:1 respectively."[139] Thus, junk news constituted a substantially higher proportion of content on Swedish Twitter in the weeks before the 2018 Swedish election than the proportion of junk news in France, Germany, or the UK in the weeks before their elections.

Second, "analysis of the junk news sources revealed that out of the top-ten most shared junk news sources eight were Swedish."[140] In other words, domestic sources of junk news were shared much more widely than foreign sources. Even so, as other scholars have noted, "a disinformation operation is most likely to succeed when it enters a target group's independent media climate."[141] Based on available information, one cannot exclude the possibility that Russian cyber troops initiated much of the junk news content and successfully induced domestic Swedish actors to disseminate that content on Twitter.

Sweden recognized the threat of Russian interference well in advance of the 2018 elections. Accordingly, Sweden adopted a whole-of-society approach to protect its democracy from the threat of information warfare. Key elements of that approach include a comprehensive national cybersecurity strategy; measures to strengthen election infrastructure and protect election security; improved coordination between the government and traditional media organizations; a collaborative approach to fact-checking by five of Sweden's largest media outlets to combat disinformation; joint public and private sector efforts to improve media literacy; and a nationwide curricular reform to increase elementary and high school students' ability to recognize disinformation.[142] Several commentators have lauded Sweden's approach as a model for other democratic countries.[143]

I agree that Sweden's effort to shield its democratic system from the threat of Russian information warfare before the 2018 national elections was commendable. Even so, there are several reasons to be concerned. First, Putin is undoubtedly pleased to witness the increased strength of the far-right Sweden Democrats—who went from twenty seats in the Riksdag in 2010 to sixty-two seats in 2018—because their opposition to NATO and the EU promotes Moscow's foreign policy interests. Second, it was not until eighteen weeks after the election that Stefan Löfven, the Social Democrat party leader, "finally won enough support in the Swedish Parliament . . . to secure a second term as prime minister."[144] The protracted negotiation necessary to build a coalition is evidence of a deeply fractured Swedish polity. Under Swedish rules, a prime minister can be elected without majority support "so long as there is not a majority against his or her candidacy." Löfven secured the prime minister's job with only 115 votes in favor, 153 votes against, and 77 abstentions.[145] (After the 2014 election, the center-left governing coalition held 159 legislative seats.) With a governing coalition that holds fewer than one-third of the seats in the 349-seat Riksdag, Löfven's government is likely to confront paralysis—a situation that clearly serves Moscow's interests.

Additionally, the proportion of junk news on Swedish Twitter is disturbingly high. The job of Russian cyber troops becomes quite easy if domestic actors in Sweden are already polluting the information environment with large amounts of disinformation. Finally, "there currently is no law that makes it illegal for foreign powers to influence Swedish elections."[146] Russian agents can lawfully make unlimited campaign donations to Swedish political parties, and they can purchase political advertisements, without any disclosure requirements. "This legislative omission is less of a loophole than it is a direct invitation for foreign meddling."[147]

Russia clearly has a substantial interest in weakening NATO, weakening the EU, and undermining liberal democracy in Europe. Russian agents will continue to engage in information warfare and other foreign influence operations to pursue these goals. European governments have taken some steps to protect their democracies from the threat posed by

Russian information warfare. However, more can and should be done. Members of the EU and NATO, including the United States, should share "lessons learned" to develop a set of best practices for defending liberal democracy. Additionally, as discussed in Part Two, some degree of regulatory harmonization would be helpful. Before discussing solutions, though, we need to consider the threat from China. That is the subject of the next chapter.

CHAPTER FOUR

CHINA'S GLOBAL INFORMATION OPERATIONS

WE SAW IN THE LAST TWO CHAPTERS that Russia is actively using social media to interfere with democratic elections in the United States and
western Europe. China's approach to information operations differs from
Russia's in several respects. First, China's ambitions are global: it aims to
reshape the global information environment to align with its authoritarian values. Second, social media is a fairly small element of China's global
information strategy: China is utilizing a broad range of communication
tools to achieve its goals. Third, whereas Russia's agenda is primarily negative—to undermine Western democracies—China has a much more positive agenda. Ultimately, China seeks to transform the liberal international
order created by the United States and its allies after World War II so that
international norms and institutions align more closely with China's authoritarian governance model.

The Chinese term *huayuquan* is translated as "discourse power." Discourse power is the "national capability to influence global values, governance, and even day-to-day discussions on the world stage."[1] One commentator notes: "The Chinese Communist Party's quest to dominate
thought and narrative has always been central to its pursuit of power. To
this end, every supreme party leader since Mao has reaffirmed the strategic
and national security importance of the party's control of media, culture,
and narrative."[2]

Recent events illustrate the Chinese Communist Party's (CCP's) use of discourse power to influence the global narrative on Hong Kong. China introduced new national security legislation that took effect in Hong Kong on June 30, 2020. The legislation—which China simply imposed on Hong Kong without giving its residents a vote—establishes draconian restrictions on individual liberties long enjoyed by Hong Kong residents. In practical effect, the legislation signals the end of the "one country, two systems" policy that China had respected for more than two decades since Great Britain officially returned Hong Kong to China in 1997. Henceforth, protection for fundamental human rights in Hong Kong will be greatly diminished.

The new national security law for Hong Kong sparked a flurry of diplomatic activity in the UN Human Rights Council, the chief UN organ responsible for promotion and protection of international human rights. On June 30, the United Kingdom's ambassador to the UN delivered a joint statement on behalf of twenty-seven democratic countries. The statement expressed "deep and growing concerns at the imposition of the legislation . . . on Hong Kong," and criticized the "erosion of the rights and freedoms that the people of Hong Kong have enjoyed for many years."[3]

On the same day, Cuba delivered a joint statement to the Human Rights Council on behalf of fifty-three mostly authoritarian states. Cuba's statement emphasized that "non-interference in internal affairs of sovereign states is an essential principle enshrined in the Charter of the United Nations and a basic norm of international relations."[4] The statement asserted that China's national security legislation for Hong Kong is "not a human rights issue and therefore not subject to discussion at the Human Rights Council" because "Hong Kong affairs are China's internal affairs that brook no interference by foreign forces."[5] The Cuba statement was almost certainly written by, or in close consultation with, the Chinese delegation. The fact that the statement attracted almost twice as many signatories as the UK statement represents a significant victory for China in its ongoing effort to shape global narratives in a manner that is consistent with authoritarian ideas about sovereignty and noninterference, but inconsistent with liberal democratic ideals related to universal human rights.

Both sides in the debate could cite language from the UN Charter to support their positions. Under Articles 55 and 56 of the charter, states are obligated "to take joint and separate action" to promote "universal respect for, and observance of, human rights and fundamental freedoms for all."[6] Article 2(7) states: "Nothing in the present Charter shall authorize the United Nations to intervene in matters which are essentially within the domestic jurisdiction of any state."[7] For most of the period since World War II, liberal democracies, led by the United States, shaped the discourse within the Human Rights Council and other UN bodies to be consistent with the liberal view that Article 2(7) does not provide a valid excuse for states to violate internationally recognized human rights. The claim in the Cuba statement that the new Hong Kong legislation is "not a human rights issue" because it concerns only "internal affairs"—and the fact that fifty-three states endorsed that statement—demonstrates that China has achieved notable success in changing the global narrative to be consistent with Chinese concepts of sovereignty and noninterference. Moreover, the fact that the Cuba statement was delivered to the Human Rights Council is highly significant because the Council and its predecessor, the Human Rights Commission, have historically been champions of liberal human rights values.

Two caveats are important here. First, in one of the Trump administration's most self-defeating moves, the United States withdrew from the Human Rights Council in June 2018. In light of the U.S. withdrawal, the two-to-one ratio supporting China's Hong Kong legislation could plausibly be explained as a failure of U.S. diplomacy rather than a victory for Chinese discourse power. If the United States had maintained its membership in the council and had lobbied hard for a strong statement criticizing the Hong Kong legislation, the split between pro- and anti-China statements might have been more even. Regardless, the fact that fifty-three states endorsed a statement suggesting that legislation imposing draconian restrictions on individual liberties is a purely internal matter that does not implicate human rights is a clear sign of China's growing discourse power.

Second, it is impossible to know how many states joined the Cuba statement because government leaders actually agree with the illiberal principles it endorses, and how many joined simply because they fear China's economic and political power. Clearly, one goal of China's global information operations is to persuade other national leaders to agree with its vision of international relations, which emphasizes authoritarian control over internal affairs at the expense of universal human rights. However, in the final analysis, China may not care very much whether states endorse documents like the Cuba statement because they agree with the principles it espouses, or because they fear provoking China's wrath. Insofar as states remain silent when other countries commit serious human rights violations, China has succeeded in shaping the global narrative, regardless of whether it secured their silence by means of persuasion or coercion.

For present purposes, the key takeaway from the story about dueling Hong Kong statements is that China's use of social media to conduct foreign influence operations is merely one element of a multifaceted global information strategy. A report from the Stanford Internet Observatory states: "China entered the internet age with a sophisticated propaganda model already in place and decades of experience refining the institutional, psychological, and tactical aspects of its application. The CCP has successfully integrated into that model every new wave of technology since the dawn of radio."[8]

China's global information operations can be explained in five parts. We look first at China's overall strategic goals in international affairs. Next we examine Chinese information operations broadly, focusing on traditional media. The third part zeroes in on social media as a tool for Chinese information warfare, followed by an analysis of Chinese interference in established democracies. The final part addresses China's use of information technology to support the diffusion of an authoritarian governance model throughout the global South.

CHINA'S STRATEGIC GOALS

When Deng Xiaoping was the de facto leader of China in the 1980s, he famously said that China should "hide its brilliance and bide its time." In practice, this meant that the CCP took a fairly cautious approach to international affairs. Since Xi Jinping became the general secretary of the CCP in 2012, China has adopted a more assertive foreign policy. In an essay in *Foreign Affairs*, two leading China experts summarized developments since early 2020 as follows: China "has tightened its grip over Hong Kong, ratcheted up tensions in the South China Sea, unleashed a diplomatic pressure campaign against Australia, used fatal force in a border dispute with India, and grown more vocal in its criticism of Western liberal democracies."[9] In the past, they note, China "generally sought to maintain a relatively stable security environment . . . without provoking undue international backlash." Now, by contrast, "the world may be getting a first sense of what a truly assertive Chinese foreign policy looks like."[10] The Chinese refer to this new approach as "wolf warrior diplomacy."[11]

Despite China's increased assertiveness, it is important not to exaggerate the magnitude of the threat that China poses to Western values and interests. In a speech delivered in June 2020, U.S. National Security Advisor Robert O'Brien compared Xi Jinping to Stalin. Describing the Chinese Communist Party as a Marxist-Leninist organization, O'Brien said that "[t]he Party General Secretary Xi Jinping sees himself as Josef Stalin's successor."[12] However, as Ambassador Michael McFaul notes, China's foreign policy under Xi is not nearly as aggressive as the Soviet Union's foreign policy under Stalin. "In the early years of the Cold War, [Stalin's] Red Army soldiers, intelligence officers, and Communist Party agents aggressively imposed communism across Eastern Europe. . . . [Stalin provided] covert assistance to communists in Greece, encouraged proxy military forces in the Korean War, and supported coups around the world."[13] In contrast, Xi "has not orchestrated the overthrow of a single regime."[14]

In a speech delivered at the Nixon Presidential Library in July 2020, Secretary of State Michael Pompeo claimed that Xi seeks nothing less than the "global hegemony of Chinese communism."[15] That is a gross exaggeration. To borrow the Cold War metaphor of falling dominoes, if Hong Kong is a single domino that has fallen from democracy to authoritarianism, it does not mean that China wants to extend that pattern to the rest of the world. China is perfectly content for the United States, Canada, and numerous other states to continue to function as liberal democracies. However, as Jessica Chen Weiss contends, China does want "to make the world safe for its authoritarian form of government."[16] At a minimum, making the world safe for autocracy means that China would strongly resist aggressive U.S. efforts to spread democracy to every corner of the globe. Additionally, the CCP wants "to preserve its monopoly on political power [domestically, and] . . . restore China to its rightful place as the dominant power in Asia."[17]

Beyond that, I suggest, China's goal of making the world safe for autocracy entails three distinct sets of policies and practices. First, with respect to information operations, China is actively disseminating narratives on a global scale that convey a positive image of China to national leaders and citizens in other countries. At the same time, China is trying to silence or marginalize voices that are critical of China and the CCP. Second, China is trying to reshape international norms and institutions to minimize the importance of universal human rights values (or, more generally, liberal values) and to emphasize the importance of national sovereignty and non-intervention in domestic affairs.[18] Chinese leaders have stated repeatedly "that the Party believes it is in an ideological war with liberalism generally and the U.S. specifically."[19] Thus, China's policies are "helping to sustain authoritarianism and corrode liberalism."[20] Third, China seeks to preserve friendly relations with numerous countries to maintain a positive environment for Chinese companies to engage in international trade and investment. China is eager to maintain international economic relations with both democratic and autocratic countries. It remains to be seen whether, and to what extent, China's increasingly assertive foreign policy will harm its economic relationships with democratic countries, and to what extent China may be willing to moderate its more aggressive behavior to help preserve those relationships.

AN OVERVIEW OF CHINA'S GLOBAL
INFORMATION OPERATIONS

China's information operations strategy is distinctly different from Russia's. One commentator, using exceptionally colorful language, described Russia as a "hurricane. It comes in fast and hard. China, on the other hand, is climate change: long, slow, pervasive."[21] Russia's agenda is almost entirely negative: like a hurricane, it leaves destruction in its wake. China has a more positive agenda: it wants to reshape the international order to align with its authoritarian governance model. China recognizes that its attempt to transform the liberal international order will necessarily be a slow, gradual process, like climate change.

China has developed an impressive range of capabilities to influence the global information environment. Its global information operations include: disseminating propaganda designed to convey a positive image of China; engaging in various activities to silence and/or intimidate China's critics; expanding its control over content delivery systems in many parts of the world; and exporting surveillance technology to support digital authoritarianism in the global South. The range of actors involved in these global information operations include: state-owned media outlets; Chinese social media platforms; a group of large technology companies that are nominally private but are ultimately accountable to the CCP;[22] and the United Front system, which is "a network of party and state agencies responsible for influencing groups outside the party."[23] This section summarizes the activities of key actors involved in China's effort to reshape the global information environment. The next section focuses specifically on social media.

State-Run Media Organizations

China has by far the largest network of state-run media organizations of any country in the world. In 2009, Hu Jintao made a commitment to spend 45 billion yuan ($9.3 billion) on a major media expansion campaign.[24] Since that time, the Chinese government and the CCP have expanded several global media organizations that they control, including the

China Global Television Network (CGTN), *China Daily, People's Daily,* China Radio International (CRI), Xinhua News Agency, and China News Service.

CGTN operates TV channels in English, Spanish, French, Arabic, and Russian that are available in more than 170 countries. CGTN also operates several digital platforms with more than 150 million followers outside of China.[25] CGTN "claims to be broadcasting to 1.2 billion people . . . including 30 million households in the U.S.—which would make it the world's largest television network."[26] *China Daily* is an English language newspaper owned by the CCP. The China Daily Group publishes a total of sixteen newspapers in China, Hong Kong, North America, Europe, Asia, Africa, and Latin America, with a total circulation of 900,000 daily newspapers.[27] *People's Daily* describes itself as "the most influential and authoritative newspaper in China."[28] Others describe it as the official "mouthpiece" of the CCP.[29] *People's Daily* publishes a total of ten newspapers, several of which are targeted to foreign audiences. One of the leading newspapers published by *People's Daily* is the *Global Times,* an English-language newspaper founded in 2009 that "has rapidly become the major English newspaper" in China.[30]

CRI "has nearly 70 overseas, dedicated affiliate radio stations and 18 global internet radio services . . . [It] has six overseas main regional bureaus and 32 overseas correspondent bureaus." CRI "uses 44 languages in its overseas reporting work and broadcasts a daily total of 2,700-plus programming hours."[31] "China Plus is CRI's overseas all-in-one English-language media brand, combining such entities as the China Plus app and website, China Plus Radio and China Plus News."[32] The Xinhua News Agency is "the official press agency of the People's Republic of China . . . . Xinhua employs more than 10,000 people. . . . [It] owns more than 20 newspapers and a dozen magazines, and it prints in eight languages: Chinese, English, Spanish, French, Russian, Portuguese, Arabic and Japanese."[33] Xinhua "launched 40 new foreign bureaus between 2009 and 2011 alone." The number of foreign bureaus "jumped to 162 in 2017."[34] China News Service is a news agency owned by the United Front Work Department. It has more than a thousand employees with offices in "Tokyo,

Bangkok, Kuala Lumpur, New York, Washington, Los Angeles, San Francisco, Vancouver, London, Paris, Sydney and Moscow."[35]

All these global media organizations ultimately answer to the CCP. CCP control is evidenced by the fact that, on some occasions, several Chinese newspapers have printed virtually identical front pages on the same day.[36] Since the CCP is hostile to liberal, democratic values, the overall messaging of China's state-run media organizations is also hostile to liberal, democratic values. All the aforementioned news organizations are charged with spreading propaganda that casts China in a favorable light and countering narratives disseminated by China's critics. Sometimes, they are also charged with disseminating propaganda that presents a negative image of other countries, including the United States. For example, during the protests that erupted after the police killing of George Floyd, Chinese state media published numerous stories "to tout the strength of [China's] authoritarian system and to portray the turmoil as yet another sign of American hypocrisy and decline."[37]

China's Large Tech Companies

China's large internet, telecommunications, and technology companies are major players in the global information technology landscape. Although most of the major companies are nominally private, "the CCP's influence and reach into private companies has increased sharply over the past decade. In 2006, 178,000 party committees had been established in private firms. By 2016, that number had increased sevenfold to approximately 1.3 million."[38] Article 33 of the CCP's constitution states that party committees are expected to "ensure the implementation of party policies and principles, and discuss and decide on major issues of their enterprise."[39] "Internet and technology companies are believed to have the highest proportion of CCP party committees in the private sector." An independent study conducted in 2017 "identified 288 companies listed in China that changed their articles of association to ensure management policy that reflects the party's will."[40] In short, China's large technology companies, although nominally private, operate to a large extent as agents of the CCP.

Chinese officials have stated publicly that they seek "to develop controls so that the party's ideas always become the strongest voice in cyberspace. This includes enhancing the global influence of internet companies like Alibaba, Tencent, Baidu and Huawei and striving to push China's proposition of internet governance toward becoming an international consensus."[41] In keeping with this strategy, Chinese "companies have supplied telecommunications hardware, advanced facial-recognition technology, and data analytics tools to a variety of governments with poor human rights records. . . . Digital authoritarianism is being promoted as a way for governments to control their citizens through technology, inverting the concept of the internet as an engine of human liberation."[42] Aided by Chinese tech companies, authoritarian states around the world are increasingly using Chinese technology "for repression, censorship, internet shutdowns and the targeting of bloggers, journalists and human rights activists."[43]

Consider two examples. Huawei has become a world leader in the development of so-called "smart city" technologies. Smart city projects "include the provision of surveillance cameras, command and control centers, facial and license plate recognition technologies, data labs, intelligence fusion capabilities and portable rapid deployment systems for use in emergencies."[44] "In 2017, Huawei listed 40 countries where its smart-city technologies had been introduced; in 2018, that reach had reportedly more than doubled to 90 countries (including 230 cities)."[45] Smart city technologies can provide significant benefits for citizens if government use of the technology is regulated by laws designed to protect individual privacy. However, China imposes no such legal requirements when Huawei exports its technology to authoritarian governments. Moreover, that technology provides powerful surveillance tools that help authoritarian governments tighten state control over citizens who present actual or potential challenges to autocratic rulers.[46]

The government of Zimbabwe is one of the most corrupt authoritarian regimes in the world.[47] China is "Zimbabwe's largest source of foreign investment, partly as a result of sanctions imposed by Western countries over human rights violations."[48] Both Huawei and ZTE (another large Chinese company) are key players in Zimbabwe's telecommunications sector. The Zimbabwean government "has openly been looking to China as a model for controlling social media, including by creating a cybersecurity ministry, which a spokesperson described as like a trap used to catch rats."[49] In March 2018, "Zimbabwe signed a strategic partnership with a Chinese startup, CloudWalk Technology, to implement facial recognition screening across the country, with cameras expected to be installed at airports, transit facilities, and potentially city streets by the Chinese firm Hikvision."[50] The deal with CloudWalk potentially "compromises the personal data of [Zimbabwe's] citizens . . . because CloudWalk has insisted that Zimbabwe share all facial recognition data with China so that CloudWalk can refine its algorithms."[51]

Chinese Social Media Platforms

WeChat is a Chinese social media platform owned by TenCent. *The Economist* describes WeChat as "the digital bedrock of Chinese society."[52] "It is used not only for messaging, but for reading news, shopping, ordering taxis, booking flights, paying bills, making appointments with a doctor and donating to charity."[53] WeChat is reportedly the third-largest social media platform in the world. As of March 31, 2020, WeChat had about 1.2 billion monthly active users,[54] including about 240 million monthly active users outside of China.[55] Many of the users outside China are members of the Chinese diaspora in Australia, Canada, the United States, and other Western democracies. Since TenCent monitors all communications on WeChat (see pp. 84–86), and since the CCP exercises substantial control over TenCent, WeChat provides a valuable tool for the CCP to monitor and influence members of the Chinese diaspora around the world.

TikTok is an app that reportedly has about 800 million monthly active users, including about 344 million outside of China.[56] As of this writing, there are roughly 100 million monthly active users in the United States. TikTok enables users to make their own short videos and post those videos on the internet. ByteDance, a large Chinese company, purchased the platform in 2017. Journalists often refer to TikTok as a "social media platform," but that label is somewhat misleading. For Facebook and most other social media platforms, the user-generated content that you see depends on "who your friends are."[57] Not so for TikTok: TikTok's algorithm decides which videos its users see. "TikTok's algorithm, unmoored from the constraints of your social network or professional content creators, is free to promote whatever videos it likes."[58] Since ByteDance is ultimately accountable to the CCP, TikTok's algorithmic design makes it an ideal tool for disseminating CCP propaganda. Hence, TikTok "censored Tiananmen Square, Tibetan independence, and the Falun Gong," as well as "Hong Kong protests."[59]

President Trump issued two executive orders on August 6, 2020, that effectively banned both WeChat and TikTok from the United States, unless the U.S. operations were segregated from Chinese operations on the platforms.[60] Plaintiffs have filed lawsuits to challenge both executive orders. Several district courts have granted preliminary injunctions to block enforcement of those executive orders, at least temporarily.[61] As of April 2021, the Biden administration was reportedly still deciding whether to support the WeChat and TikTok bans.[62]

The United Front System

The United Front system is best described as a sprawling octopus with thousands of tentacles reaching across the globe. United Front work, carried out on behalf of the CCP, "encompasses a broad spectrum of activity from espionage to foreign interference, influence and engagement."[63] The system includes "hundreds of thousands of united front figures and thousands of groups, most of which are inside China." Its overseas functions "include increasing the CCP's political influence, interfering in the Chinese diaspora, suppressing dissident movements, building a permissive international environment for a takeover of Taiwan, intelligence gathering, encouraging investment in China, and facilitating technology transfer."[64] United Front groups carry out these activities through both overt and covert means. The leader of the United Front system is Wang Yang, "the fourth-ranked member of the seven-man Politburo Standing Committee,"[65] which is the highest leadership body in the CCP.

United Front work "involves four lines of operations" that are conducted internationally.[66] "First, united front work seeks to assert control over ethnic Chinese communities abroad, using them as agents of CCP influence . . . . Second, it coopts foreigners, enticing them to defend and advance the Chinese Communist Party's positions abroad and to furnish valuable intelligence and know-how."[67] "Third, it wages a sophisticated and complex global strategic communications campaign via a vast network of print and online media to promote the CCP's foreign policies . . . . Finally, it mobilizes global support to China's ambitious Belt and Road Initiative."[68]

The British Chinese Project illustrates the type of covert foreign influence activities conducted by the United Front system. The BC Project "is a group that says it seeks to foster the political participation of ethnic Chinese and build their influence on [British] policy. . . . However, the BC Project's close links to the united front system call into question its independence and ability to genuinely represent ethnic Chinese."[69] Christine Lee is the chair and founder of the BC Project. She "is an executive member of the China Overseas Friendship Association and a committee member of the CPPCC [Chinese People's Political Consultative Conference]," both of which are run by the United Front Work Department (UFWD).[70]

"Since 2009, Lee has donated hundreds of thousands of pounds" to Barry Gardiner, who is the "Labour Party shadow secretary of state for international trade." Lee's son has worked for Gardiner since 2015.[71] In his previous position as shadow secretary for energy, "Gardiner was an outspoken advocate of a controversial proposal for Chinese Government involvement" in a nuclear reactor project in the United Kingdom. The proposed Chinese partner on that nuclear project "is a state-owned nuclear company that's been involved in espionage and is subject to a US Government export ban because of its history of diverting nuclear technology to the Chinese military."[72] In sum, it appears that Christine Lee, a UK resident of Chinese descent—acting covertly through the United Front system as an agent of the CCP—persuaded a British member of Parliament to use his influence to try to secure a role for a state-owned Chinese company in a British nuclear project that could have given China's military access to sensitive nuclear technology.

Representatives of the United Front system also engage in various overt foreign influence activities. For example, as noted previously, the UFWD operates China News Service, one of China's largest media organizations. China News Service owns or controls numerous "overseas Chinese-language media outlets . . . including Qiaobao in the US and Australia's Pacific Media Group. At least 26 WeChat accounts run by nine Chinese media outlets are in fact registered to a subsidiary of China News Service."[73] Those social media accounts on WeChat operate in Australia, Brazil, Canada, the European Union, Japan, New Zealand, Russia, the United Kingdom, and the United States. "Many of the accounts appear to have tens of thousands if not hundreds of thousands of followers."[74] Although publicly available information links those accounts to the United Front, and ultimately to the CCP, it seems likely that most of the people who are engaging with the WeChat accounts do not realize that the accounts are operated by CCP agents.

To summarize, China employs a full spectrum of communication tools—including traditional diplomacy, traditional media, social media, and United Front work—in its effort to shape global narratives about China and about issues that are important to the CCP. The CCP's global information strategy is supported by a large number of Chinese information and communications technology companies that are indirectly controlled by the CCP. As discussed later in this chapter, many of those technology companies are actively disseminating China's model of authoritarian information control to countries in the global South.

CHINESE AGENTS ON U.S. SOCIAL MEDIA PLATFORMS

China's approach to foreign influence operations on social media is still evolving, but the CCP is clearly integrating social media into its broader strategy for global information operations. In doing so, the CCP can draw on nearly two decades of experience with domestic internet controls. The Chinese government built the so-called "Great Firewall of China" in 2002 with help from Western information technology companies. The Great Firewall "is a massive, sophisticated, national censorship system that uses a number of techniques . . . to automatically control and restrict the stream of internet communication entering or leaving China."[75] China has used its domestic control over the internet to block Chinese residents' access to Facebook, Twitter, and YouTube since 2009. The government closely monitors communications on domestic social media platforms. "The censorship apparatus allows a great deal of criticism of the regime . . . but stops discussions that can generate collective action on the ground."[76]

To help manage the conversation on domestic social media platforms, the government employs as many as two million people in its so-called "50 cent party." Members of the 50 cent party "surreptitiously post large numbers of fabricated social media comments, as if they were the genuine opinions of ordinary Chinese people."[77] Scholars estimate that party members post about 448 million messages per year. However, "almost none of the Chinese government's 50c party posts engage in debate or argument of any kind. . . . Instead, most 50c posts are about cheerleading and positive discussions of valence issues." The observed behavior is consistent with the theory that "the strategic objective of the regime is to distract and redirect public attention."[78]

China utilizes both overt and covert strategies in its global social media operations. As shown in table 3, major Chinese media organizations have cultivated a large number of followers on Facebook, Twitter, and other U.S. social media platforms. "As of December 2019 . . . three of the 10 media accounts on Facebook with the largest number of followers were Chinese state media."[79] The fact that Facebook and Twitter are both banned in China means that the data for Chinese state media organizations displayed in table 3 is based almost entirely on people who reside outside of China.[80]

Table 3 includes comparable figures for a few major U.S. media organizations. The data show that large Chinese state media organizations attract more likes on Facebook than their U.S. counterparts, but large U.S. media companies attract more Twitter followers than their Chinese counterparts. Facebook pages associated with Chinese state media outlets

TABLE 3. Media organizations on Facebook and Twitter. Sources: Data about the number of likes on Facebook is taken from each organization's Facebook page. Data about the number of Twitter followers is taken from each organization's Twitter profile. All data was current as of June 22, 2020.

	Facebook (likes)	Twitter (followers)
Chinese state media companies		
CGTN	105 million	13.9 million
China Daily	94 million	4.3 million
People's Daily	84 million	7.1 million
Xinhua News	80 million	12.6 million
Global Times	57 million	1.7 million
China Plus News (CRI)	21 million	772 thousand
Selected U.S. media companies		
CNN	33.5 million	49.5 million
Fox News	18.6 million	19.5 million
New York Times	17.4 million	47.1 million
Wall Street Journal	6.5 million	17.9 million

generate fairly low audience interaction rates, whereas the Facebook pages for major U.S. news organizations generate "significantly higher audience interaction rates" than their Chinese counterparts.[81]

Apart from state-run media organizations, the CCP also enlists Chinese diplomats to engage in public diplomacy on social media. As of May 2020, "the number of diplomatic Twitter accounts has tripled, to 135, up from just 40 accounts this time last year."[82] A few Chinese diplomats have developed a substantial following on Twitter. Zhao Lijian, a spokesperson for the Ministry of Foreign Affairs, had more than 750,000 Twitter followers as of July 2020. Hua Chunying, the director of the Foreign Ministry's Information Department, had roughly 575,000 Twitter followers.[83]

Whereas China's state-run media organizations have operated overt social media accounts for years, Chinese use of U.S. social media platforms to conduct covert foreign influence operations is a relatively recent development. In 2018, China's People's Liberation Army (PLA) reportedly operated social media accounts covertly "to manipulate Taiwan public opinion . . . [and] to spread fake news."[84] In fall 2018, Chinese cyber troops allegedly exploited fake accounts on Facebook to help a pro-Beijing candidate win an election for mayor in the Taiwanese city of Kaohsiung.[85] Wang Liqiang, a self-declared Chinese spy who defected to Australia, claimed that he created 200,000 fake social media accounts to meddle in that mayoral election.[86] A 2019 report from the Oxford Internet Institute states: "Until recently, we found that China rarely used social media to manipulate public opinion in other countries. . . . However, in 2019 the Chinese government began to employ global social media platforms to paint Hong Kong's democracy advocates as violent radicals with no popular appeal."[87]

We turn now to two cases where China made extensive use of covert operations on social media to support foreign influence operations. The first relates to pro-democracy protests in Hong Kong in 2019. The second relates to the Covid-19 pandemic in 2020. In both cases, the CCP deployed the full spectrum of information operation tools—including domestic censorship, television, newspapers, radio, diplomacy, and both overt and covert social media operations—in an effort to control the narrative in China and around the world. The Hong Kong and Covid-19 campaigns support the conclusion that China's "ongoing efforts to manipulate social media audiences . . . [are] unlikely to relent. The Chinese party-state is invested in information management as a fundamental pillar of its global engagement."[88]

Hong Kong Protests in 2019

For many years, Hong Kong residents have enjoyed a much broader range of individual freedoms than the residents of mainland China. In June 2019, "more than a million people in Hong Kong took to the streets to protest a Chinese extradition bill." Critics feared that the bill would put Hong Kong residents "at risk of arbitrary detention, unfair trials, and torture."[89] Many of the protesters sought greater local autonomy for Hong Kong; the

Chinese government viewed calls for local democracy as a threat to CCP control. China responded by launching a sustained propaganda campaign that involved tight coordination among traditional diplomacy, overt messaging on state-run media, and covert operations on U.S. social media platforms. "The Hong Kong campaign provided the first concrete evidence that the CCP is willing to execute online covert influence operations targeting Western audiences using inauthentic social media personas."[90]

In August 2019, Facebook, Twitter, and YouTube all announced that they were blocking or removing numerous accounts linked to the Chinese government. The nearly simultaneous actions by U.S. social media companies were highly significant because "this takedown was the first information operation publically attributed to China on Western social media platforms."[91] Twitter disclosed "a significant state-backed information operation focused on the situation in Hong Kong, specifically the protest movement and their calls for political change." Twitter suspended approximately 200,000 accounts for violating its platform manipulation policies. It said that the suspended accounts "were deliberately and specifically attempting to sow political discord in Hong Kong, including undermining the legitimacy and political positions of the protest movement on the ground."[92] Facebook announced that it had "removed seven Pages, three Groups and five Facebook accounts involved in coordinated inauthentic behavior as part of a small network that originated in China and focused on Hong Kong." According to Facebook, "about 15,500 accounts followed one or more of these Pages and about 2200 accounts joined at least one of these Groups."[93] Similarly, Google announced that it had disabled 210 YouTube channels that "behaved in a coordinated manner while uploading videos related to the ongoing protests in Hong Kong."[94]

China's response to the Hong Kong protests illustrates several points about its covert use of social media manipulation. First, China's covert use of social media was closely integrated with its formal diplomatic activity, its overt use of state-run newspapers, television channels, and radio stations, and the overt use of social media by various actors who are directly or indirectly controlled by the CCP. In both overt and covert channels, China described the protesters as "thugs" who threatened the rule of law in Hong Kong. The messages were designed to counter "unfavorable narratives that had reached both domestic and international audiences . . . to shape the global perception of the protesters and refute any sense that the CCP's control over Hong Kong was in jeopardy."[95] The CCP's long tradition of imposing discipline on a broad range of actors enabled the party to conduct a propaganda campaign like a professional orchestra, with numerous instruments playing in harmony.

Second, many of the Chinese accounts were old accounts that had been repurposed. For example, one of the Twitter accounts was created in 2013. "It originally posted primarily in Malay . . . about Islam and the Arsenal football team." Then it went dormant for four years "and suddenly became active again in July 2019, with tweets, now in Chinese, that defended the Hong Kong police and derided the protesters."[96] On Facebook, "campaign operators appear to have purchased a number of accounts and pages formerly belonging to users in Bangladesh. In most cases, the campaign operators changed the account profile pictures but otherwise left the original account owner's content, including their name and personal photographs."[97] This pattern of behavior suggests that many of the accounts were either "purchased, hacked or stolen."[98]

Third, most of the Chinese accounts "had underdeveloped personas."[99] Whereas Russian cyber troops have developed a sophisticated ability to create fake identities that appear to be real Americans, or real Germans, Chinese cyber warriors made little effort to establish convincing identities. Their failure to develop convincing identities reduced the effectiveness of China's covert social media operations and made it easier for companies to identify them as fake accounts. However, as one study notes, "the CCP's propaganda apparatus has been watching the tactics and impact of Russian disinformation." If the Chinese learn from the Russians, "the party-state's online experiments will allow its propaganda apparatus to influence audiences on Western platforms with growing precision."[100]

Finally, most of the Chinese accounts got very little engagement. They "were highly prolific" in that they produced a large number of posts, but "about 78% of accounts had no followers."[101] Even so, it would be a mistake to evaluate the success or failure of China's foreign influence operation for Hong Kong simply by counting followers for covert social media accounts. To reiterate, covert use of social media was part of a broader operation involving diplomacy, traditional media, and overt use of social media. Although China's covert social media accounts were not very influential, the larger information operation was arguably quite successful. As noted earlier in this chapter, fifty-three countries co-signed a statement supporting the new national security law that China imposed on Hong Kong in June 2020. Broad support for that statement provides one indicator that China's foreign influence operation achieved notable success in shaping the global narrative to align with China's ideology. On the other hand, the fact that China was forced to enact such draconian legislation to control the situation on the ground in Hong Kong indicates that China's effort to control the domestic narrative within Hong Kong failed miserably.

The Covid-19 Pandemic in 2020

Doctors first detected Covid-19 in Wuhan, China, in December 2019. The CCP initially responded by engaging in the familiar tactic of censorship, trying to suppress information about the virus that might portray China unfavorably. However, when suppression was no longer possible, China modified its communication strategy. "To manage the public relations crisis, the CCP . . . leveraged all of the traditional and digital media capabilities at its disposal in its attempt to control the narrative and deflect blame, both within China and abroad, using both overt and covert tactics."[102]

Perhaps because initial reporting on the pandemic blamed China as the source of the virus, the CCP responded by significantly increasing its output on social media in both overt and covert channels. One report published early in the pandemic analyzed "social media posts from accounts run by Chinese state-run media organizations and associated foreign influence accounts on Western social media platforms."[103] As of March 9, 2020, the report concluded, "Chinese overt influence accounts had published over 32,000 posts related to COVID-19 on several Western social media platforms."[104] As of May 20, a different study concluded that China had more than doubled "its number of official government tweets since January" and had "pushed out 90,000 tweets since the start of April from 200 diplomatic and state-run media accounts as part of an offensive in the COVID-19 information war."[105]

China also significantly increased the number of paid advertisements on Western social media platforms in response to the coronavirus pandemic. One research report examined paid "advertisements run by the English-language Chinese state media Pages . . . from January 1, 2019 to March 29, 2020."[106] The number of ads increased after the pandemic arose: about half of the advertisements in the data set were created after January 1, 2020. Moreover, 77 percent of the advertisements in 2020 related to the coronavirus. "The coronavirus-related subset of ads" amassed at least 36 million impressions.[107] "Facebook ads provide accounts with a way to push posts to people who do not already follow them, and can be targeted to viewers by country, interest, or other demographic criteria."[108] The ads targeted audiences in Russia, Pakistan, Turkey, Saudi Arabia, Mexico, and numerous African countries. The authors of the study conclude "that paid promotions are helping to cultivate a global audience for Chinese state media outlets."[109]

In June 2020, Twitter suspended 173,000 covert accounts linked to China "for various violations of our platform manipulation policies." These covert accounts included "23,750 accounts that comprise the core of the network" and about "150,000 accounts that were designed to boost this content."[110] An independent analysis of the 23,750 core accounts found that "most accounts were created around late 2019 to January 2020," when news about the coronavirus first began to emerge.[111] That report identified more than 32,000 tweets related to Covid-19. "From mid-March, as the outbreak evolved into a global pandemic, the number of coronavirus-related tweets significantly increased."[112] The covert accounts linked to the Chinese government were supported by "a loosely coordinated pro-China trolling campaign on Twitter."[113] Unlike the covert accounts that Twitter attributed to the Chinese government, analysis of the troll accounts showed "no clear evidence of state direction." Thus, analysts concluded, the troll accounts "may simply reflect nationalistic pro-China trolls responding on their own initiative to events as they unfold."[114]

Both overt and covert social media accounts pushed three main narratives. First, China put a positive spin on its response to the pandemic, emphasizing that "the CCP's model of social governance is one that can successfully manage crises, that the PRC's economy is rapidly recovering from the period of lockdown, and that the PRC is a generous global citizen that can rapidly mobilize medical support and guide the world through the pandemic."[115] China also attempted "to counter the view that Taiwan's Covid-19 response was successful while the PRC's was not."[116] Second, China criticized other governments—especially the United States—for their failure to contain the virus. Over time, as Black Lives Matter protests developed, China's messaging combined criticism of the U.S. government's handling of the pandemic with a critique of systemic racism in the United States.[117] Third, China attempted to shift the blame for Covid-19 by challenging the claim that the virus had originated in Wuhan, China.[118] Both overt and covert accounts aggressively spread the theory that the virus actually originated in the U.S. Army Research Institute for Infectious Diseases at Fort Detrick, Maryland.[119] (There is no evidence to support that theory.)

Analysis of Chinese activity on social media reveals some significant differences between the overt and covert accounts. First, the overt and covert accounts targeted different audiences. Seventy-nine percent of the tweets in the suspended Twitter accounts were in Chinese, suggesting that the covert accounts were targeted toward social media users in Hong Kong and Taiwan and the broader Chinese diaspora.[120] In contrast, overt accounts associated with Chinese state-run media organizations targeted English speakers worldwide,[121] and accounts associated with Chinese embassies targeted local audiences, using "the language of an embassy's host country."[122] The overt accounts reached a much broader audience than the covert accounts. "Most of the [covert] accounts had very small followings: over 92% of accounts had less than 10 followers." Engagement with the covert accounts "was generally low."[123] In contrast, as discussed previously, overt social media accounts associated with state-run media organizations have attracted very large followings. Their messaging related to Covid-19 also achieved much greater audience engagement. For example, on April 30, Xinhua posted a video on Twitter titled "Once upon a Virus" that criticized the U.S. response to Covid-19 and praised China's response. Less than three weeks later, that message had "been retweeted almost 26,000 times and liked 50,000 times."[124]

China's information offensive related to Covid-19 is significant for at least two reasons. First, the Covid-19 campaign provides the first substantial evidence of China's willingness and ability to utilize covert social media accounts to carry out a Russian-style disinformation campaign. In the words of one leading commentator: "Beijing has taken a more aggressive approach than usual, even experimenting with tactics drawn from Russia's more nihilistic information operations playbook. That strategy aims not so much to promote a particular idea as to sow doubt, dissension, and disarray . . . in order to undermine public confidence in information and prevent any common understanding of facts from taking hold."[125] China's covert social media operations are not yet as sophisticated as Russia's, but China's covert operations are likely to become increasingly sophisticated over the next few years.

Second, China's Covid-19 campaign implicates one of the central themes of this book: the ongoing battle of ideas between democratic and authoritarian modes of governance. One of the fundamental responsibilities of all governments is to protect the health and safety of their people. After the Chinese government contained the spread of the coronavirus pandemic within China, the CCP used the opportunity to tell a simple story to the world: our authoritarian system of government is superior to Western, liberal democracy because we protected our people, whereas liberal democracies failed to do so. The CCP disseminated that message through all available channels, including diplomatic channels, television, radio, newspapers, overt state-run social media accounts, and covert social media operations.

Officially reported data provide some support for China's story. Table 4 presents data about the global spread of Covid-19, as of November 11, 2020. Assuming that the official Chinese numbers are accurate, China really has done a better job protecting the health and safety of its people than many (but not all) democracies. Granted, there are reasons to be

TABLE 4. Covid-19 cases and deaths (as of November 11, 2020). Source: *Washington Post* Staff, "Mapping the Worldwide Spread of the Virus."

	Deaths per 100,000 population	Cases per 100,000 population
Taiwan	0	2.5
China	.3	6.6
South Korea	.9	53.8
Japan	1.5	88.7
Germany	14.3	870.0
France	61.2	2769.6
United States	73.2	3133.8
United Kingdom	74.6	1851.2

skeptical about China's published data. To some extent, the published data may simply indicate that China's dictatorship is better able to suppress truthful information than Western democracies. However, even if the actual numbers from China are ten times higher than the reported numbers, it would still be true that China has done a better job protecting its people from Covid-19 than many Western democracies. Thus, the data about Covid-19 illustrates a basic point about information competition. If the United States and like-minded countries want to win the battle of ideas between democracy and authoritarianism, liberal democratic governments need to do a better job promoting the welfare of their citizens, not just in terms of individual liberty but also in terms of health, safety, and economic security.[126]

MEDDLING IN ESTABLISHED DEMOCRACIES

The Australian Strategic Policy Institute reports that China has engaged in "cyber-enabled foreign interference" in 2016 elections in Hong Kong; 2018 elections in Cambodia, Hong Kong, Malaysia, and Taiwan; 2019 elections in Australia and Indonesia; and 2020 elections in Taiwan and the United States.[127] The CCP takes advantage of the openness of Western democracies by employing tactics designed to shape the information environment in democratic countries and nudge public opinion and government policies in a more China-friendly direction. This section examines three different types of foreign influence operations targeted at Western democracies: electoral interference in Taiwan; exploiting WeChat to influence the Chinese diaspora; and spending money to influence foreign media.

Electoral Interference in Taiwan

In its 2019 report on threats to democracy, the Varieties of Democracy (V-Dem) Institute rated countries on the degree to which they are targets of disinformation spread by foreign governments. Taiwan and Latvia were "the two countries with the absolute worst scores" on this indicator, meaning that foreign states interfere frequently in their democratic processes.[128] Not surprisingly, China is the country primarily responsible for spreading disinformation in and about Taiwan. Taiwan is a vulnerable target for social media manipulation because Taiwanese citizens are active on social media. "As of January 2020, the social media penetration rate was 88%."[129] Facebook and YouTube are the two most popular platforms in Taiwan, followed by LINE, a messaging app that has 21 million monthly active users in a country of 24 million people.[130]

Although Taiwan functions as an independent country, the CCP maintains that Taiwan is an integral part of China. Now that China has effectively abolished Hong Kong's independence, many observers fear that Taiwan is next in line.[131] The Chinese military arguably has the capacity to terminate Taiwan's independence through brute force. However, the Chinese government would strongly prefer to accomplish its goal of unification through information warfare and other influence operations, if possible, because that approach is far less costly.

The citizens of Taiwan voted for president on January 11, 2020. The election pitted the incumbent, President Tsai Ing-wen of the Democratic Progressive Party (DPP), against Han Kuo-yu of the Kuomintang (KMT).[132] China had a clear preference for Han because the DPP has historically favored greater independence from China, whereas the KMT supports unification. China conducted an "aggressive disinformation campaign . . . designed to sow confusion on the island and tilt the race against incumbent Tsai Ing-wen."[133] "The campaign amounts to more than spreading 'fake news.' It is best understood as an information influence operation—a comprehensive attempt to control every step of the information supply chain."[134] Ultimately, China's information warfare campaign failed: President Tsai won 57 percent of the vote, compared to 39 percent for Han.

One factor that helped Tsai and hurt Han was a major news story that broke in the midst of Taiwan's presidential election campaign. In November 2019, Australian media reported that a self-declared Chinese spy named Wang Liqiang had sought asylum in Australia. Wang provided the Australian Security and Intelligence Organization (ASIO) a trove of information about Chinese covert operations in Hong Kong and Taiwan.[135] Most importantly, for present purposes, "Wang claimed that he had participated in meddling in the 2018 Taiwanese local elections by creating 200,000 fake social media accounts" and that "a Hong Kong front company created twenty other 'internet companies' to attack the DPP."[136] Wang's allegations triggered a flood of commentary on both traditional media and social media in Taiwan. Sources sympathetic to China and the KMT attempted to discredit Wang's allegations. Sources sympathetic to the DPP cited Wang to sound the alarm about the threat of Chinese interference in Taiwan's domestic political affairs. Wang's allegations—combined with the fact that the Chinese-backed government in Hong Kong had recently conducted a major crackdown against protesters in Hong Kong—probably strengthened support for the DPP by stoking fears of a potential Chinese takeover of Taiwan.

Although China's intervention in the 2020 election was ultimately unsuccessful, it presents an interesting case study because it represents the most aggressive Chinese effort to date to interfere in a foreign election. In the months preceding the January 2020 election, China utilized a combination of traditional media channels, covert social media accounts, content farms, and overt social media accounts to disseminate its preferred narratives.

Any effort to analyze the impact of Chinese interference on Taiwan's information environment is complicated by the fact that "key media outlets in Taiwan are owned by individuals and companies with extensive business interests in China."[137] For example, in 2008, "the pro-Beijing chairman of Want Want China Holdings, a Taiwanese food and beverage company that makes 90 percent of its revenue in mainland China, purchased one of Taiwan's largest media groups, the China Times Media Group."[138] Owners of Taiwanese media companies who have strong business ties to China "exercise self-censorship . . . or, more problematically, follow editorial lines suggested to them by their Chinese interlocutors" because the continued profitability of their Chinese businesses requires them "to remain in the good graces of Chinese government or Party officials."[139] Thus, when Taiwanese newspapers and television stations report the news with a pro-China spin, should the story be viewed as Chinese propaganda, or as the authentic expression of the views of Taiwan's citizens? The line between the two is so fuzzy that it is virtually nonexistent.

For example, when the Wang Liqiang story broke, "media outlets considered friendly toward Beijing (e.g., *China Times*) and KMT-supportive press (e.g., *United Daily News*) aligned their narratives with those from the mainland." Like news outlets based in mainland China, "these Taiwanese publications uniformly aimed to discredit Wang."[140] However, articles published by Taiwanese newspapers gained much more traction on Taiwanese social media than did similar articles published by Chinese newspapers. For example, one article about Wang Liqiang published by the *Global Times,* a Chinese newspaper, "was only posted to two Facebook Pages and shared 17 times on Facebook." In contrast, a similar article published by "the Taiwan-based *China Times* . . . was posted to over 100 [Facebook] Pages and Groups and shared 1,100 times."[141] Thus, the CCP was able to shape narratives on Facebook in Taiwan by influencing the stories disseminated on Taiwanese media outlets, many of which are owned by Taiwanese businessmen with substantial economic ties to China.

In addition to influencing traditional Taiwanese media, Chinese agents— or people who appear to be Chinese agents—operated "content farms [that] helped spread false information through networks of Facebook

Pages and the messaging app LINE."[142] Two content farms, in particular, whose names translate as "Mission" and "Roar," "amplified rumors and criticized the DPP and Tsai Ing-wen. . . . Roar published content that promoted misinformation and deepened party divisions."[143] During the presidential election campaign, a fact-checking organization "was asked to verify 39 articles from Mission; of those, only four of the contested claims turned out to be true." In fall 2019, "Facebook blocked hundreds of content farms' URLs from being shared, including Mission."[144] A report from the Stanford Internet Observatory concludes: "Though the extent of China's influence on Taiwan's content farms is difficult to quantify," several factors indicate "that these media properties are a useful tool with which to plant false information and influence conversations about Taiwanese politics, including during the presidential campaign."[145]

China also tried to influence the 2020 election by operating fictitious user accounts on YouTube and Twitter. One YouTube channel "was run by a YouTuber who appeared to be a concerned Chinese citizen. . . . The channel creator was subsequently revealed to be a Chinese state media reporter."[146] As noted previously, in June 2020 Twitter suspended 173,000 covert accounts linked to China that were posting content related to Covid-19. Twitter is not widely used in Taiwan, but several of the suspended Twitter accounts had posted links to YouTube content that targeted Taiwan, including videos that tried to discredit Wang Liqiang.[147] The Wang story first broke on November 22, 2019. According to the Stanford Internet Observatory, "a notable finding from the Twitter dataset was that about half of all Taiwan-related tweets were from November 25 to 27, when the story of the defecting spy was unfolding." "The fake Twitter accounts claimed that President Tsai Ing-wen had fabricated the Wang Liqiang case in order to slander Han Kuo-yu . . . a popular narrative that was additionally circulating in the pro-Han Facebook community."[148]

WeChat and the Chinese Diaspora

As noted previously, WeChat has about 240 million monthly active users outside of China, many of whom are members of the Chinese diaspora in Australia, Canada, the United States, and other Western democracies.

WeChat accounts can be divided between China-registered accounts, "which were originally registered to mainland China phone numbers," and non-China-registered accounts, which were originally registered to a phone number outside mainland China.[149] It is well known that WeChat strictly censors content posted on China-registered accounts. Notably, a report from the University of Toronto demonstrates "that WeChat communications conducted entirely among non-China-registered accounts are subject to pervasive content surveillance that was previously thought to be exclusively reserved for China-registered accounts."[150] Moreover, "files deemed politically sensitive are used to invisibly train and build up WeChat's Chinese political censorship system."[151]

A Dutch researcher, Victor Gevers, "found a database storing more than 1 billion WeChat conversations, including more than 3.7 billion messages . . . . Each message had been tagged with a GPS location, and many included users' national identification numbers. Most of the messages were sent inside China, but more than 19 million of them had been sent from people outside the country."[152] Gevers "says the system resembles the global surveillance methods used by the U.S. National Security Agency."[153] For example, "on March 18 alone, 3.6 billion messages in Chinese, 59 million in English, and 26 million in other languages were captured and routed to operators."[154] Those operators work directly for WeChat, and indirectly for the CCP. Thus, the CCP effectively uses WeChat to monitor the communications of tens or hundreds of millions of ethnic Chinese people who live in Western, democratic countries.

Consider the case of "David," a Chinese American doctor who lives in the United States. Like many other members of the Chinese diaspora, David uses WeChat to communicate with family in China. At some point, David noticed that his WeChat posts "were not going through" to his relatives in China.[155] "Undeterred, he kept sharing politically charged articles. Within days, he couldn't send messages to any group chat . . . David then dialed back his sharing of news articles, limiting his conversations to trivial chitchat and music-sharing. His group chat function was quickly restored. Emboldened, he began sharing his political posts in group chats, only to find himself blocked again."[156] In this way, the CCP uses its control over WeChat to extend its system of censorship to the Chinese diaspora community.

A report from the Australian Strategic Policy Institute notes that "WeChat is increasingly used by politicians in liberal democracies to communicate with their ethnic Chinese voters."[157] In Australia, for example, "Prime Minister Scott Morrison and Opposition Leader Bill Shorten both use WeChat to communicate with Chinese-Australian voters."[158] Since all such communications are subject to CCP surveillance and censorship, "there are concerns politicians using WeChat may have to self-censor their comments, avoiding criticism of China and dodging other topics Beijing finds sensitive."[159] For example, "in September 2017 Canadian parliamentarian Jenny Kwan posted a WeChat message of support for Hong Kong's [pro-democracy movement] . . . only to have it censored by WeChat."[160] Thus, China uses its control over WeChat to censor communications between politicians in liberal democracies and their ethnic Chinese constituents.

Chinese Money and Foreign Media

We saw previously that China has developed the most extensive global network of state-run media organizations of any country in the world. However, the CCP is not content to rely exclusively on state-run media organizations to disseminate its preferred narratives. Chinese officials have also developed a set of "opaque methods to exploit foreign media outlets." They use the phrase "borrowing the boat to reach the sea" to describe those methods.[161]

Media organizations linked to the CCP have made content-sharing arrangements with local news media in "Spain, the United Kingdom, Australia, Argentina, Peru, Senegal, and India."[162] "These content sharing agreements are commercial arrangements that allow China to publish its own coverage in newspapers around the world in the form of handouts or inserts. Newspapers adorned with full-page spreads and glowing assessments of China's President can now be found from Europe, to Africa, to Latin America."[163] Unfortunately, "the surreptitious nature in which these inserts are included means many readers are unlikely to be aware that they're consuming content sponsored by the Chinese government."[164]

China Daily, "an English-language newspaper controlled by the Chinese Communist Party," has deployed this strategy to influence news coverage in the United States.[165] Information filed with the Justice Department in June 2020 revealed that *China Daily* had "paid more than $4.6 million to the *Washington Post* and nearly $6 million to the *Wall Street Journal* since November 2016." That money pays for supplements, or inserts, that "are designed to look like real news articles, though they often contain a pro-Beijing spin on contemporary news events."[166]

China has also used its money to gain effective control over Chinese-language media around the world. China Radio International (CRI) has bought media companies throughout Australia. "A 2016 report in the *Sydney Morning Herald* quoted Australian Chinese media sources saying that the majority of the Chinese language media in the country was owned or controlled by the Chinese state or its affiliates."[167] Similarly, "a November 2018 investigation by the *Financial Times* found that party-affiliated outlets were reprinting or broadcasting their content in at least 200 nominally independent Chinese-language publications around the world . . . . In most cases, the content appears to have been provided for free and published under the masthead of the overseas news organizations, making it appear native to the independent publication."[168] Thus, people outside of China who read newspapers in Chinese, or listen to television or radio programs in Chinese, are likely to be receiving content approved by the CCP, even when they are getting their news from nominally independent sources.

CHINA AND THE GLOBAL SOUTH

China's activities in the global South related to information and communications technology raise two distinct concerns that are relevant to the central themes of this book. First, Chinese companies are exporting surveillance technology to authoritarian governments around the world. Such exports facilitate the rise of authoritarianism in the global South. Second, Chinese companies and government entities are increasingly exerting control over the channels of communication in countries throughout the global South. By controlling the channels of communication, China can shape the overall information environment in a way that supports its broader effort to make the world safe for autocracy.

Exporting Surveillance Technologies

Digital authoritarianism can be defined as "the use of digital information technology by authoritarian regimes to surveil, repress, and manipulate domestic and foreign populations."[169] The technology includes "high-resolution cameras, facial recognition, spying malware, automated text analysis, and big-data processing,"[170] all supported by sophisticated artificial intelligence (AI) to facilitate mass surveillance of ordinary citizens. "The Chinese Communist Party is forging a future of mass surveillance . . . and rapidly exporting those tools to other parts of the world."[171]

As discussed previously (see pp. 84–86), private Chinese companies are exporting the technology of digital authoritarianism, but they are not alone. "Firms based in the United States, France, the United Kingdom, Germany, Spain, and Israel are also key suppliers."[172] The technologies that support digital authoritarianism are not inherently evil. With appropriate laws and regulations in place, democratic countries can ensure that governments employ the technology to enhance public welfare in a manner that is consistent with liberal, democratic ideals. Unfortunately, when Chinese companies export the technology to authoritarian countries, neither the exporting nor the importing country is likely to insist on regulations to promote liberal, democratic ideals. Absent such regulations, the tools of digital authoritarianism enable autocratic rulers to conduct mass surveillance and identify political opponents. All too often, identification of opponents leads to arbitrary arrest, torture, and/or extrajudicial killing. A 2019 Freedom House report stated "that 47 of the 65 countries assessed featured arrests of [social media] users for political, social, or religious speech—a record high."[173]

The tools of digital authoritarianism strengthen autocratic rule. "Between 1946 and 2000—the year digital tools began to proliferate—the typical dictator ruled for around ten years. Since 2000, this number has more than doubled, to nearly 25 years."[174] Moreover, "those authoritarian regimes that rely more heavily on digital repression are among the most durable."[175] Hence, commentators legitimately fear "the emergence of an AI-powered authoritarian bloc led by China . . . [that] could prevent billions of people, across large swaths of the globe, from ever securing any measure of political freedom."[176] China doves contend that "material interests, not a universalist mission of promoting autocracy abroad, are the key drivers of China's global strategy."[177] Assuming the doves are correct, their analysis should not be construed as an argument for complacency. Chinese companies driven by the profit motive will likely help autocratic rulers entrench their control unless there is countervailing pressure to regulate surveillance technologies. Notably, the Chinese government is not applying any such pressure.

It bears emphasis that U.S. social media platforms, in the hands of autocratic rulers, function as surveillance technologies. That is no accident. Facebook and Google earn most of their revenue through advertising. Companies and political candidates pay substantial amounts of money for microtargeted advertising because Facebook and Google have amassed a tremendous amount of information about us, the targets of the ads. Thus, private companies routinely engage in surveillance of social media users by collecting huge amounts of information from billions of internet users to support the delivery of microtargeted advertising. The information that social media companies collect from their users is the raw material of "surveillance capitalism."[178]

In the United States and other liberal democracies, governments do not generally conduct surveillance on social media platforms because laws enacted by democratic legislatures restrict government surveillance. However, authoritarian governments are increasingly exploiting U.S. social media platforms for surveillance purposes. A 2019 Freedom House report stated: "At least 40 of the 65 countries covered by this report have instituted advanced social media monitoring programs."[179] Moreover, "of the 15 countries in Asia assessed by this report, 13 have social media surveillance programs under development or in use."[180] The report notes that "China is a leader in developing, employing, and exporting social media surveillance tools."[181]

For example, a Chinese company called Semptian has developed the Aegis surveillance system. The Aegis system "is designed to be installed inside phone and internet networks, where it is used to secretly collect people's email records, phone calls, text messages, cellphone locations, and web browsing histories."[182] The company's equipment is helping the CCP "covertly monitor the internet and cellphone activity of up to 200 million people" in China. More recently, Semptian "has supplied the equipment to authoritarian governments in the Middle East and North Africa." Although a company spokesman refused to identify those countries, an investigative journalist suggests that Semptian may have sold Aegis to "Saudi Arabia, Bahrain, Morocco, the United Arab Emirates, Oman, Sudan, and Egypt."[183]

Knowlesys is a Chinese company described as "an award-winning surveillance industry veteran."[184] Knowlesys "sells social media and open source internet monitoring and analysis tools to . . . private sector giants from both the East and West." The Knowlesys Intelligence System "is available in almost a dozen languages including Arabic, English, Chinese and Uighur." Governments use it "to effectively monitor and analyze social media."[185] In August 2020, a group of hackers "obtained internal files from three Chinese social media monitoring companies," including Knowlesys.[186] The hackers offered journalists "a large dump of files" that allegedly exposed "social media monitoring and disinformation campaigns conducted by [Knowlesys and two other] companies at the behest of the Chinese government."[187]

Thus, Chinese companies are strengthening autocratic rule in the global South by exporting surveillance technology to authoritarian governments, including technology that helps those governments exploit U.S. social media platforms to conduct surveillance of their own citizens.

Controlling Channels of Communication

Marshall McLuhan famously declared that "the medium is the message." The CCP has built a global information strategy around this idea. According to Peter Mattis, a China expert at the Jamestown Foundation:

"Over the last ten years . . . the push has been less about messaging and more about the medium. This way they can crowd out other stories, they can have essentially a monopoly on the information environment—that makes it easier for their narratives to be received and accepted."[188] China's effort to augment its control over communication channels in the global South includes both hardware and communications media.

With respect to hardware, a report by the Australian Strategic Policy Institute shows that twelve key Chinese technology companies, in the aggregate, are involved in "52 5G initiatives, across 34 countries . . . 56 undersea cables, 31 leased cables and 17 terrestrial cables; 202 data centres and 305 telecommunications & ICT projects spread across the world."[189] A 2018 Freedom House report notes that Chinese companies have "installed internet and mobile network equipment in at least 38 countries."[190] China can potentially use its control over information pipelines to engage in both surveillance and censorship. "As more of the world's critical telecommunications infrastructure is built by China, global data may become more accessible to Chinese intelligence agencies."[191] Indeed, according to one source, "there is already evidence of Chinese companies using their control over dissemination channels . . . to suppress information deemed undesirable by Beijing. But even where this potential has not yet been activated, the foundations are being laid to facilitate future manipulation."[192]

With respect to communications media, as discussed previously, Chinese state-run media operate hundreds of television and radio stations and dozens of newspapers in countries throughout the world. In addition, China has been engaged in an "opaque campaign of buying up broadcast space on foreign airwaves and inside newspapers. . . . Beijing has been able to infiltrate local media across the world by using overseas airwaves to disseminate its message."[193] For example, a "Reuters investigation revealed there were at least 33 radio stations across 14 countries that are part of a global radio web structured in a way that obscures its majority shareholder: state-run China Radio International (CRI)."[194] Xinhua "has signed exchange agreements with local counterparts" in many countries, including Bangladesh, India, Nigeria, Egypt, Thailand, Vietnam, Belarus, and Laos.[195] Xinhua concluded an agreement with the Thai News Network allowing Xinhua to broadcast its "*China Report* program in Thailand on a daily basis." In South America, "TV Peru's Channel 7 broadcast 12 documentaries about China . . . in 2016, nearly all of which were produced by CGTN and aired during prime time."[196]

China's attempt to control the information environment in the global South appears to be gaining substantial traction in Africa. StarTimes is a privately owned Chinese television distribution company with close ties to the Chinese government. "StarTimes has been a key player in the transition from analog to digital transmission [in Africa], accruing over 10 million subscribers in 30 countries."[197] The company determines "which stations those viewers are able to access." It appears to prioritize channels operated by Chinese state media "at the expense of independent international news stations."[198] In early 2020, StarTimes launched a daily TV show with news about the coronavirus pandemic for an African audience.[199] StarTimes also entered into a joint venture with the state broadcaster in Zambia. The deal allegedly "paves the way for a Chinese company to control Zambia's national broadcasting service."[200]

One analysis suggests that "audiences in the West may prove a challenge to win over—but there is concern that Africa is more vulnerable to China's creeping media buy-ups. . . . With a less robust media environment and countless cash-strapped local networks, China has been more active in infiltrating and controlling African media."[201] Public opinion polling data from the Pew Research Center suggest that China's information operations in Africa are yielding positive results. Polling data "indicated an overall decrease in China's global favorability rating—but African nations were among the most likely to express favorable attitudes towards Beijing."[202]

The next chapter focuses on a single question: "If China and Russia are using information warfare to attack liberal democracies, why don't we do the same to them?" The short answer is that the situation is not symmetrical. Russia and China are closed societies. The United States and other liberal democracies are open societies. Social media offers Russia and China a powerful tool to exploit our openness to undermine democratic governance. However, we cannot use social media to undermine authoritarian control in China and Russia because, in both countries, authoritarian governments control social media. Chapter 5 shows that the playing field is not level because social media and other digital technologies systematically tilt the field in favor of authoritarian governance and against liberal democracy. The tilt in favor of authoritarianism is not an inherent feature of the technology. Rather, the uneven playing field results from the interaction between technology and regulatory strategies.

CHAPTER FIVE

AN UNEVEN PLAYING FIELD

FOR THE FORESEEABLE FUTURE, the world will be divided between democracies and autocracies. The United States is currently the most powerful democratic country in the world. China and Russia are the two most powerful authoritarian states. I assume that, other things being equal, the United States and other liberal democracies would prefer to nudge autocratic states in the direction of becoming more liberal and more democratic. Similarly, I assume that, other things being equal, China and Russia would prefer to nudge democratic states in a more authoritarian direction. Traditional military forces are not well suited for this type of ideological competition. Instead, the ideological battle will be fought, at least in part, with propaganda, public diplomacy, and other types of information operations, including operations on social media.

Many Americans believe that, in a battle of ideas, the best ideas inevitably prevail. Assuming that liberal democracy is a better form of government than authoritarianism, should we assume that liberal democracy will inevitably prevail in an ideological competition with authoritarianism? Not necessarily. The outcome of the competition depends partly on whether the contestants are competing on a level playing field. This chapter demonstrates that the playing field is not level because social media and other digital technologies systematically tilt the field in favor of authoritarian governance and against liberal democracy.[1]

The tilt in favor of authoritarianism is not an inherent feature of the technology. Rather, the uneven playing field results from the interaction between technology and regulatory strategies.

Many authoritarian states practice "digital authoritarianism"—they have developed a set of laws, policies, and technical practices that empower governments to exploit social media and other digital technologies for surveillance, censorship, and online content manipulation. Empirical analysis shows "that those authoritarian regimes that rely more heavily on digital repression are among the most durable."[2] In short, the exploitation of social media by states that practice digital authoritarianism strengthens autocratic control.

In contrast, organized social media manipulation (OSM)—when applied domestically within democracies—erodes the quality of democratic governance in democratic states. (See the glossary for a definition of "organized social media manipulation.") As of this writing, no democratic state has enacted comprehensive regulations to protect the integrity of democratic self-government from the threat posed by OSM. In effect, liberal democracies have made a policy choice to delegate to large technology companies the task of protecting democracy from both domestic OSM and information warfare conducted by foreign cyber troops. That laissez-faire approach is not working. The preceding three chapters showed that Facebook, Twitter, and Google have failed to protect Western democracies from information warfare conducted by foreign cyber troops. This chapter shows that social media companies have failed to protect Western democracies from domestic OSM. Granted, Twitter banned Donald Trump after the January 6 insurrection, and Facebook "indefinitely suspended" him from both Facebook and Instagram, but those responses merely scratch the surface of a much deeper problem. As explained in more detail below, without the necessary government regulation, domestic OSM erodes the quality of democratic governance in liberal democracies by heightening political polarization and accelerating the spread of lies and misinformation.

The combination of digital authoritarianism in autocratic states and the laissez-faire approach to regulating social media in democratic states creates an uneven playing field in the ideological competition between liberal democracy and authoritarianism. This chapter explains the uneven playing field in four parts. The first part presents some basic data about the current state of play in the global, ideological competition between autocracy and democracy. The next part explains how social media generally, and OSM particularly, undermines democracy in countries that are, or previously were, liberal democracies. The third part explains how China and Russia utilize digital authoritarianism to strengthen autocratic control domestically. The final part explains how authoritarian rulers in other countries are copying the Chinese and Russian models of techno-social control to bolster autocratic rule in their own countries.

To reiterate, I am not suggesting that social media is inherently antidemocratic. If liberal democracies join together to enact sensible laws and regulations to protect the integrity of democratic governance, then social media could potentially promote democratic ideals—or at the very least, not undermine those ideals.

DEMOCRACY VS. AUTHORITARIANISM: A SNAPSHOT

Table 5 presents a snapshot of the distribution of regime types across geographic regions as of 2019. The data in table 5 is based on the v2x_regime variable in the V-Dem database.[3] Per the V-Dem database, the United

TABLE 5. Democracies and autocracies, as of 2019. Source: V-Dem database.

	Liberal democracies	*Electoral democracies*	*Electoral autocracies*	*Closed autocracies*	*Total*
Europe	20	13	5	0	38
Americas	7	14	5	1	27
Asia-Pacific	7	8	12	5	32
Africa	2	13	28	3	46
Former Soviet Union	0	2	9	1	12
Arab League	1	0	7	14	22
Total	37	50	66	24	177

States is classified as a liberal democracy, Russia is classified as an electoral autocracy, and China is classified as a closed autocracy.

As of 2020, the United Nations has 193 member states. However, the V-Dem data for 2019 covers only 179 "states." The V-Dem database presents data for several entities that are not UN member states, including Kosovo, Taiwan, Hong Kong, Palestine (Gaza), and Palestine (West Bank). I chose to exclude Hong Kong because China has effectively abolished Hong Kong's independence. I chose to count Palestine as one state, not two, because the Arab League treats Palestine as one state. Thus, table 5 displays data for 177 "states."

The V-Dem data excludes numerous small states that are UN member states. Those exclusions may skew the data to some extent. For example, the V-Dem database excludes eight states in the Caribbean region that are UN member states: Antigua and Barbuda, Bahamas, Belize, Dominica, Grenada, Saint Kitts and Nevis, Saint Lucia, and Saint Vincent and the Grenadines. Freedom House classifies all eight states as "free."[4] If we added them to table 5 as either liberal or electoral democracies, the Americas region would appear to be more democratic. However, to ensure an apples-to-apples comparison, I chose to include in table 5 only those countries that are included in the V-Dem database.

I include all twelve states that are members of the Commonwealth of Independent States (CIS) as part of the "Former Soviet Union" group. Latvia, Lithuania, and Estonia were also once part of the Soviet Union. However, they are not CIS members and they are all members of the European Union. Accordingly, I include those three states in the European group. All states that are members of the Arab League (including Palestine) are included in the Arab group. All other states are classified strictly on the basis of geography.

It bears emphasis that the geographic distribution of democratic and authoritarian states is not uniform across regions. Former Soviet states and Arab states are predominantly authoritarian. European states and states in the Western Hemisphere are predominantly democratic. Both Africa and the Asia-Pacific region have large numbers of states in the two middle categories, but Africa is more autocratic than Asia.

Regional groupings matter because social scientists have demonstrated that states often imitate other states. Imitation facilitates policy diffusion across states. In the words of two leading scholars, "states imitate legitimated models in areas such as education, market liberalization and privatization, the environment, arms control, warfare, science policy, and human rights."[5] In other words, contrary to rationalist models of state behavior, states often behave as "copycats." Copycat behavior is especially pronounced in regional groupings where states in a given region share a common legal and/or cultural heritage.[6] As discussed later in this chapter, autocratic states in the former Soviet Union manifest substantial regional similarities in their approaches to digital authoritarianism.

ORGANIZED SOCIAL MEDIA MANIPULATION AND DEMOCRATIC DECAY

Over the past decade, several scholars have argued that social media is undermining democracy. Broadly speaking, the scholarly commentary falls into two groups. One group focuses on polarization, arguing that social media has a polarizing effect on society and that polarization erodes the quality of democratic self-government.[7] A different group focuses on misinformation, arguing that social media accelerates the spread of lies and half-truths, thereby undermining the agreement on basic facts that is an essential foundation for effective democratic governance.[8] I believe that both groups present compelling arguments. In short, social media generally, and OSM specifically, tends to weaken democratic governance in established democracies by heightening political polarization and accelerating the spread of lies and misinformation.

The argument proceeds as follows. First, I present quantitative data showing that there is a positive correlation between heightened OSM activity and greater democratic decay. The quantitative analysis does not prove causation, but it does show that—within the group of liberal democracies—countries with higher levels of OSM activity were more likely to experience significant democratic decay. The next section presents a case study of Poland, showing how OSM has contributed to significant democratic backsliding in Poland. The final two sections, respectively, analyze the effects of misinformation and polarization on democratic governance. It bears emphasis that the polarizing effects of social media are not primarily attributable to OSM: social media would have polarizing effects even if governments and political parties did not practice OSM. In contrast, OSM is the primary mechanism, although not the exclusive mechanism, for spreading misinformation via social media.

OSM and Democratic Decay

I referred earlier to the v2x_regime variable in the V-Dem database, which is helpful for classifying countries in groups. In this section, rather than assigning states to different categories, we want to measure democratic decay by examining changes over time in a country's "liberal democracy" score. For this purpose, the "libdem" variable is more useful because that variable scores countries on a thousandths-point scale from 0 to 1, with 1 being the highest score. Here, we want to measure democratic decay in states that could plausibly be called "liberal democracies." There are 53 countries that scored .650 or better on the libdem index for at least one year in the past twenty years. For present purposes, I classify those 53 countries as liberal democracies. Note that this figure is considerably higher than the 37 states classified as liberal democracies in table 5.

I measured democratic decay for those 53 countries by identifying each country's highest score on the libdem index between 2000 and 2019. For each country, I calculated the difference between its highest score and its score in 2019: that difference provides a quantitative measurement of democratic decay. For ease of expression, I multiplied all scores by 100 so that democratic decay is measured on a scale from 0 to 100. Nine countries registered a decline of more than ten points. Presenting them in order by the magnitude of democratic decay, they are: Hungary (37.0), Poland (36.8), Brazil (28.2), Croatia (17.4), the United States (15.6), Suriname (15.2), Czech Republic (14.6), Israel (12.0), and South Africa (10.8). Notably, only two of these states—Israel and the United States—qualify as liberal democracies under the criteria used in table 5. The quality of democracy in the other seven countries has eroded sufficiently that they are all classified as electoral democracies in table 5—except for Hungary, which is an electoral autocracy.[9]

I did two different tests to determine whether there is a positive correlation between OSM and democratic decay. A report from the Oxford Internet Institute (the "Oxford disinformation report") identifies 70 countries that practice OSM,[10] including 21 of the 53 states that are classified as liberal democracies for the purpose of this analysis. The Oxford disinformation report purports to be comprehensive, so it is fair to assume that states omitted from the Oxford report did not practice OSM, or there is no substantial evidence that they did. Therefore, we can divide the 53 liberal democracies into two groups: 21 states that practiced OSM and 32 states that did not. I calculated the average democratic decay for those two groups of states. States that practiced OSM, on average, registered a decline of 11.3 points. States that did not practice OSM registered an average decline of 5.1 points. Thus, the decline in liberal democracy scores was more than twice as great for states that practiced OSM compared to states that did not practice OSM.

Based on data in the Oxford disinformation report, I developed an (admittedly crude) measure of the level of OSM activity in states that do practice OSM. Under that measure, which is explained in the endnotes,[11] the maximum possible score for any state was 23. Brazil and the United States registered the two highest OSM levels; each had a score of 18. The Czech Republic, with a score of 5, registered the lowest OSM score among the states included in the Oxford report. I assigned a score of zero for all states excluded from the Oxford report. Figure 4 displays a scatter plot with OSM scores on the horizontal axis and democratic decay scores on the vertical axis.[12] Each dot represents one of the 53 states in the data set (although dots for states with very similar scores are hard to distinguish). The line depicts the best linear fit for the data. The upward slope of the line shows a positive correlation: higher OSM scores are associated with greater democratic decay. Applying a Pearson's test, that correlation is statistically significant at the .05 level. If we exclude Hungary and Poland from the analysis—the two states that registered the highest levels

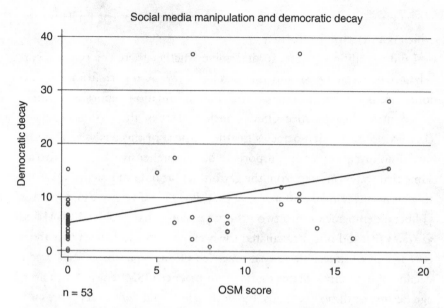

FIGURE 4. OSM activity and democratic decay in fifty-three liberal democracies. Sources: V-Dem database; Bradshaw and Howard, *The Global Disinformation Order.*

of democratic decay—the correlation is still significant at the .05 level, but the line in the graph would have a flatter slope, indicating a weaker correlation.

Thus, there is a positive correlation between increased OSM activity and greater democratic decay. Of course, correlation does not prove causation. However, the analysis supports the claims of scholars who argue that OSM activity is contributing to democratic decay in liberal democracies. The next section presents a brief case study of OSM in Poland to show how governments and political parties utilize OSM to erode the quality of democratic governance.

OSM and Democratic Decay in Poland

Poland was a model liberal democracy from 1991 (after the fall of the Berlin Wall) until about 2015. In 2015, the right-wing Law and Justice Party

(PiS) won federal elections and secured a majority in the Polish legislature. Since gaining power, the PiS has enacted a series of legislative reforms that pose a substantial threat to judicial independence.[13] Moreover, "the public media and their governing bodies have been purged of independent or dissenting voices since PiS came to power."[14] Since 2015, Poland's score on the libdem index has declined dramatically. Indeed, Poland registered the second-highest level of democratic decay among all fifty-three countries included in the preceding analysis. There is no doubt that democratic decay in Poland is attributable to the rise of PiS. The question is: Did a successful OSM campaign help PiS win the federal elections in 2015?

Robert Gorwa, a doctoral student at Oxford University, conducted a detailed study of OSM in Poland. He notes: "The Internet has become very important for political life in the country. In particular, Facebook has emerged as a central source of political information and news."[15] As of 2017, there were reportedly 22.6 million Facebook users in a country with about 37 million people. Since the 2011 federal election, political campaigns in Poland "have been using an increasingly professionalized set of tools to manage their online self-presentation and mobilize supporters."[16]

Gorwa interviewed several people for his project, including an anonymous source "who is a political consultant and marketer, and works for a communications firm that has experience in using fake identities on Polish social media platforms."[17] The firm works for both commercial and political clients. Over the past decade, the firm has "created more than 40 thousand unique identities, each with multiple accounts on various social media platforms . . . forming a universe of several hundred thousand specific fake accounts that have been used in Polish politics and multiple elections."[18] Philip Howard refers to these unique identities as "legends." "In social media terms, a legend is the biographical background, supported by a stream of photos, comments, and online activity, that makes an account appear to represent a genuinely social, real person."[19]

Each employee of the Polish communications firm manages up to fifteen legends at a time. Based on his interviews with anonymous sources, Gorwa describes the work as follows:

[The firm's] trolls/bots/influencers cannot, and do not attempt to influence public opinion directly. Rather, the firm's strategy is to target opinion leaders, including journalists, politicians, bloggers, and key activists. By infiltrating influential Facebook groups, mining comment sections, and directly striking up conversations with these opinion leaders, the goal is . . . to provide long-term nudges towards certain strategically devised positions. The amount of work which goes into these efforts is staggering, and the most involved campaigns will include multiple employees bringing their networks of accounts together to stage threads on discussion boards and steer conversations on forums. An entire thread on such a platform can feature dozens of fake accounts. . . . All this occurs invisibly and behind the scenes, and the ordinary person that logs onto these forums may believe that they are receiving a legitimate signal for public opinion on a topic when they are in effect being fed a narrative by a secret marketing campaign.[20]

For obvious reasons, Gorwa's anonymous source could not say whether the firm in question worked for PiS in the 2015 election. Even so, there are reasons to believe that PiS's electoral success is at least partially attributable to an OSM campaign of the type described by that source. First, "Pawel Szefemaker, a Secretary of State in the Chancellery of the Polish Prime Minister . . . has been referred to as PiS's 'internet genius' and is widely believed to be the mastermind behind its successful online efforts."[21] Gorwa reports that "several interviewees suggested that Polish right-wing and nationalist groups were mobilizing online in a highly effective way that seems to combine new and traditional modes of organization."[22] Some commentators claim that PiS "won the Internet" in the 2015 election. Gorwa says: "The broad consensus seems to be that PiS managed to mobilize their supporters and control media narratives far more effectively than its opponents."[23]

Gorwa also performed an independent analysis of Twitter activity in Poland in spring 2017. Based on that analysis, he concluded "that right-wing pro-government and nationalist accounts form the majority of suspect bot accounts [on Twitter], and indeed are far more prolific on the collected political hashtags than their left-wing counterparts." In his view, the Twitter data "provides another element of evidence to corroborate the commonly held assumption that the Polish right has been more effective online, having implemented a variety of new tools and practices more effectively than their rivals."[24]

In sum, we know that PiS won the 2015 election and that legislative reforms adopted by the PiS government triggered dramatic democratic decay in Poland. We also know that there is at least one major political communications firm in Poland that has developed a very sophisticated capability to utilize online social media manipulation to influence public opinion. Moreover, many knowledgeable people in Poland agree that right-wing groups associated with PiS have utilized social media to advance their political agenda much more effectively than their opponents, and Twitter data provides some support for that conclusion. However, it is impossible to determine conclusively the degree to which a successful OSM campaign contributed to PiS's electoral success in 2015.

Social Media, Misinformation, and Democratic Governance

Governments were practicing disinformation long before the advent of social media. However, social media accelerates the spread of false information by enabling people to reach a large audience at low cost. Social media accelerates the spread of both misinformation and disinformation. "Misinformation" includes any false or misleading information. "Disinformation" is false or misleading information that is purposefully crafted or strategically placed to achieve a political goal.[25] (See glossary.)

The political objectives of a disinformation campaign could be either foreign or domestic. Prior chapters focused on foreign affairs. Here, let us consider domestic disinformation campaigns. The "Pizzagate" story is a good example. In fall 2016, a Twitter post alleged that Hillary Clinton was "the kingpin of an international child enslavement and sex ring."[26] The story quickly spread on social media, leading to the creation of a discussion board on Reddit with the title "Pizzagate." As various contributors embellished the story, they identified a specific pizza parlor in Washington, DC, Comet Ping Pong, as the base of operations for the child sex operation. "These bizarre and evidence-free allegations soon spread beyond the dark underbelly of the internet to relatively mainstream right-wing media such as the Drudge Report and Infowars." Alex Jones, the creator of Infowars, "has more than 2 million follows on YouTube and 730,000 followers on Twitter; by spreading the rumors, Jones vastly increased their reach."[27] (Jones has since been banned from most major social media platforms.) Ultimately, a young man who believed the story arrived at Comet Ping Pong with "an AR-15 semiautomatic rifle . . . and opened fire, unloading multiple rounds."[28] Although the story was debunked, "pollsters found that more than a quarter of adults surveyed were either certain that Clinton was connected to the child sex ring or that some part of the story must have been true."[29]

Several features of the current information environment accelerate the spread of misinformation. Before the rise of the internet, major media companies like CBS and the *New York Times* had the capacity to distribute stories to millions of people. However, they were generally bound by professional standards of journalistic ethics so that they would not deliberately spread false stories. They were far from perfect, but they did help prevent widespread dissemination of false information. The internet effectively removed the filtering function of large media organizations, enabling anyone with a social media account—and a basic working knowledge of how messages go viral on social media—to spread misinformation to a very large audience very quickly.[30]

The digital age has given rise to automated accounts known as "bots." A bot is "a software tool that performs specific actions on computers connected in a network without the intervention of human users."[31] Political operatives with a moderate degree of technical sophistication can utilize bots to accelerate the spread of messages on social media.[32] Moreover, social media platforms facilitate the use of microtargeting: "the process of preparing and delivering customized messages to voters or consumers."[33] In summer 2017, political activists in the United Kingdom built a bot to disseminate messages on Tinder, a dating app, that were designed to attract new supporters for the Labour Party. "The bot accounts sent between thirty thousand and forty thousand messages in all, targeting eighteen- to twenty-five-year-olds in constituencies where the Labour candidates needed help." In the ensuing election, "the Labour Party either won or successfully defended some of these targeted districts by just a few votes. In celebrating their victory over Twitter, campaign managers thanked . . . their team of bots."[34] There is no evidence in this case that the bots were spreading false information, but unethical political operatives can also use bots and microtargeting to spread false messages quickly via social media.

In the past two decades, we have seen the growth of an entire industry of paid political consultants who have developed expertise in utilizing social media to influence political outcomes.[35] The Polish firm discussed earlier in this chapter is one example. Philip Howard, a leading expert on misinformation, claims: "It is safe to say that every country in the world has some homegrown political consulting firm that specializes in marketing political misinformation."[36] Political consultants work with data mining companies that have accumulated huge amounts of information about individuals by collecting data from a variety of sources, including social media platforms, and aggregating that information in proprietary databases. The data mining industry "supplies the information that campaign managers need to make strategic decisions about whom to target, where, when, with what message, and over which device and platform."[37]

Political consulting firms use both bots and human-operated "fake accounts" to disseminate messages via social media. (A "fake account" is a social media account operated by someone who adopts a false identity for the purpose of misleading other social media users about the identity of the person operating the account.) They take advantage of data from the data mining industry and the technical features of social media platforms to engage in very sophisticated microtargeting, sending customized messages to select groups of voters to shape public opinion and/or influence political outcomes. "Social media algorithms allow for the constant testing and refinement of campaign messages, so that the most advanced techniques of behavioral science can sharpen the message in time for those strategically crucial final days" before an important vote.[38] Many such messages are undoubtedly truthful, but there are several well-documented cases where paid political consultants have deliberately spread false information in service of some political objective. For example, Howard has documented the strategic use of disinformation by the Vote Leave campaign in the final weeks before the UK referendum on Brexit.[39]

It bears emphasis that disinformation does not have to be believed to erode the foundations of our democratic institutions. Disinformation "does not necessarily succeed by changing minds but by sowing confusion, undermining trust in information and institutions, and eroding shared reference points."[40] For democracy to function effectively, we need shared reference points. An authoritarian government can require citizens to wear masks and practice social distancing during a pandemic by instilling fear that leads to obedience. In a democratic society, by contrast, governments must persuade a large majority of citizens that scientific evidence demonstrates that wearing masks and practicing social distancing saves lives. Unfortunately, misinformation spread on social media undermines trust in both government and scientific authority. Without that trust, it becomes increasingly difficult for government leaders to build the consensus needed to formulate and implement effective policies to address pressing social problems, such as slowing the spread of a pandemic.

Social Media, Polarization, and Democratic Governance

The United States has become much more polarized since the 1970s.[41] Social scientists disagree about the underlying causes of polarization. One important book, co-authored by a group of Harvard scholars, contends that the root cause of polarization in the United States is "the right-wing media ecosystem," led by Fox News, Breitbart, and the late Rush Limbaugh.[42] Another important book, written by a journalist, contends that political polarization in the United States has its roots in the civil rights debates of the 1960s.[43] Both books marshal impressive bodies of evidence to support their claims. However, both suffer from an exclusive focus on the United States. As legal scholar Amy Chua contends, growing political polarization in the United States is closely related to "the wider, global populist surge that led to Brexit in the United Kingdom, France's yellow vest protests, and the rise of the nationalist politician Matteo Salvini in

Italy."[44] The rise of social media provides a plausible explanation for global trends because increasing reliance on social media as a source of news and information is a phenomenon common to almost all modern democracies.

To be clear, I am not claiming that social media is the sole cause, or even the primary cause, of political polarization in the United States. Such a claim is not tenable because the trend of growing polarization started several decades before the advent of social media. However, I am claiming that growing reliance on social media for political communication has exacerbated the preexisting trend of polarization in the United States, and that the use of social media for political communication is also contributing to polarization in other Western democracies.

Political communication on social media contributes to both cognitive and affective polarization. In one of the earliest books warning about the anti-democratic effects of social media, Eli Pariser argued that social media creates "filter bubbles" and that social media users are "more and more enclosed in our own bubbles." Democracy, he argued, "requires a reliance on shared facts; instead we're being offered parallel but separate universes."[45] Cognitive polarization means that Democrats and Republicans in the United States—and people who occupy opposite sides of key political fault lines in other countries—increasingly inhabit separate factual universes. Filter bubbles exacerbate the problem of cognitive polarization. OSM contributes to the problem, but OSM is only partly to blame. Social media algorithms and the business models of social media companies create filter bubbles. Companies make money by selling advertising. They sell more advertising if more people spend more time on their platforms. So, they create algorithms that are designed to induce people to spend more time on their platforms. Those algorithms push people into filter bubbles that drive social media users into separate factual universes.[46]

Cognitive polarization undermines democracy in much the same way that misinformation undermines democracy: by eroding shared reference points. For example, a recent Pew survey found that 71 percent of Democrats believe that "policies aimed at reducing climate change generally provide net benefits for the environment." In contrast, "43% of Republicans said such policies make no difference" and 22 percent of Republicans "said they do more harm than good for the environment."[47] It is difficult for Republican and Democratic politicians to strike bipartisan deals on legislation if they cannot agree on scientific evidence about the likely effects of proposed legislation.

Empirical evidence shows that social media also exacerbates the problem of affective polarization. "A large and likely growing proportion of Americans have very negative attitudes toward people and candidates who identify with the opposing political party."[48] Jaime Settle refers to these negative attitudes as "affective polarization." Settle conducted a series of experiments—focusing specifically on the Facebook News Feed—to test the impact of the News Feed on affective polarization. One of her most interesting findings is that engagement with the News Feed induces affective polarization in people who are not politically active. She summarizes those findings in a vignette about a hypothetical person named Janet Lewis.

> Janet Lewis now knows more about the political opinions of her family, friends, and acquaintances than she ever has before, but not because she has sought out that information. When she scrolls through her Facebook News Feed—which she does every day in order to share pictures of her grandkids and keep tabs on what people from her past are doing—she inevitably encounters political content. . . . It seems in the months leading up to an election, she simply can't escape the onslaught. . . . Janet has always avoided political conversations. But for the first time, she has a window into the conversations of groups of people with whom she strongly disagrees. . . . As a consequence of seeing this, Janet has become more judgmental about those people with whom she disagrees, and she assumes the worst about the people who appear to have such extreme opinions.[49]

In short, the overall design of the Facebook platform means that people who spend time on Facebook—which currently has about 2.7 billion monthly active users—are exposed to political content even if they would otherwise prefer to avoid political conversations. Moreover, that exposure tends to induce affective polarization. Settle cites evidence that "large proportions of Americans would be displeased if their child married someone from another political party. Fewer than 15 percent of people view the out-party . . . as possessing core moral traits. . . . Majorities of people agree that voters of the out-party are ignorant, narrow minded, and ideologically driven."[50]

For democracy to function effectively, politicians must be willing and able to reach across the aisle to compromise with members of the opposing party. In the current political environment, though, many voters view bipartisan compromise as a betrayal of core moral principles—why should I compromise with someone who is ignorant and lacks core moral traits? Consequently, voters punish politicians who strike bipartisan deals and elect representatives who share their attitude that it is morally abhorrent to compromise with members of the opposing party. Facebook did not create this problem, but Facebook exacerbates the problem.

Social media tends to induce both cognitive and affective polarization in social media users. Cognitive polarization weakens democracy by driving people into separate factual universes. Affective polarization weakens democracy by eroding the bonds that lead people to feel that what unites us is more important than what divides us. Social media would magnify polarization even if governments and political parties did not practice OSM. OSM exacerbates the problem because politically motivated actors, including domestic actors, spread disinformation that undermines trust and erodes shared reference points. The remainder of this chapter explains how authoritarian states use social media domestically, in conjunction with other digital technologies, to bolster autocratic control at home.

DIGITAL AUTHORITARIANISM IN CHINA AND RUSSIA
China and Russia both practice digital authoritarianism. Under this approach, "the single ruling party remains in control while a wide range of conversations about the country's problems nonetheless occurs on websites and social networking services. . . . As a result, the average person with Internet or mobile access has a much greater sense of freedom."[51]

However, people "whom the rulers see as threats are jailed . . . and the courts and the legal system are tools of the ruling party."[52] In short, citizens enjoy a modicum of free speech on social media, provided that they do not cross a vague line—defined in practice by substantial administrative discretion—that separates permissible political expression from subversive activity.

The Chinese and Russian systems for internet regulation share many common features. In both countries, much of the telecommunications infrastructure is privately owned but ultimately subject to government control. In Russia, "Article 64 of the Law on Communication obliges service providers" to shut down networks whenever government authorities so request. Accordingly, in 2018, three mobile service providers shut down mobile internet networks in response to protests in the Republic of Ingushetia.[53] Similarly, in China, a cybersecurity law that took effect in 2017 "provides legal grounds for officials to instruct network operators to stop transmission of certain content." In extreme cases, the Chinese government has shut down access to entire communications systems. "The most dramatic example occurred in 2009, when authorities imposed a 10-month internet blackout in Xinjiang . . . after ethnic violence [erupted] in the regional capital, Urumqi."[54]

Both China and Russia have sophisticated systems for monitoring and surveillance of speech on social media. Russia's surveillance system, known as SORM, "is grounded in a legal framework allowing for the lawful interception of communications by a number of KGB-successor security organs." By law, the government has access "to all user metadata and communications."[55] In China, the government has "unfettered access to user communications and data" on social media platforms. The scope of surveillance is chilling. In April 2018, police investigated "an individual who had criticized Xi Jinping in a WeChat group with only eight members. Though the individual had used a pseudonym, the [police] identified him with his real name, address, and phone number."[56]

In both Russia and China, surveillance can lead to the arrest and detention of individuals who are deemed to be a threat to the regime.

"Detention, arrest, or imprisonment of selected individuals serves as an effective warning to others that they are being watched."[57] Thus, surveillance backed by the threat of imprisonment encourages many people to engage in self-censorship. In Russia, "the vague wording of laws that touch on online expression, the arbitrary manner in which they are enforced, and the general ineffectiveness of judicial remedies make ordinary users reticent to express themselves online."[58] In China, "self-censorship is pervasive among persecuted minorities, especially Uighurs. . . . Many block their own family members living abroad to avoid being detained for their foreign contacts."[59]

In both Russia and China, private companies actively support the system of surveillance and censorship on social media. In Russia, a 2016 anti-encryption law requires companies that use encryption to provide the government "with encryption keys or other means of decoding transmitted data."[60] In contrast to the United States, where social media companies are immune from liability for content posted on their platforms, both China and Russia impose liability on internet intermediaries, including social media companies. "All Internet companies operating within Chinese jurisdiction . . . are held liable for everything appearing on their search engines, blogging platforms, and social-networking services."[61] The same is generally true in Russia.[62] The threat of liability gives private companies a powerful incentive to censor content on their platforms. A company that fails to perform its delegated censorship responsibilities to the satisfaction of government overseers could have its license revoked, or worse.

Both the Chinese and Russian governments are actively involved in manipulating content on social media platforms. As discussed previously, the Chinese government employs as many as two million people in its so-called "50 cent party" (see p. 90). Scholars estimate that party members post about 448 million messages per year.[63] The Russian government uses "bots, trolls, leaks of compromising or manipulated content" and other techniques to create "an overall online environment that still appears relatively unrestricted . . . but in which the government exerts [substantial] control over the overall development of content and narratives." In this way, the government uses content production and narrative manipulation "to undermine and marginalize the voices of opposition movements and leaders."[64]

Despite these similarities, there are significant differences between China and Russia with respect to internet regulation. Overall, China's online environment is more restrictive than Russia's, as manifested by the countries' scores on Freedom House's Freedom on the Net report. Russia received a score of 31 out of 100. China received a score of 10 out of 100: worse than any other country covered in the report.[65]

Two features of the Chinese system are distinctive. First, the Chinese government built the so-called "Great Firewall of China" in 2002 with help from Western information technology companies. The Great Firewall "is a massive, sophisticated, national censorship system that uses a number of techniques . . . to automatically control and restrict the stream of Internet communication entering or leaving China."[66] China has used the Great Firewall to block Chinese residents' access to Facebook, Twitter, and YouTube since 2009. In contrast, Russian citizens have access to U.S. social media platforms, including Facebook, Twitter, and YouTube. Thus, it is generally easier for Russian residents than it is for Chinese residents to receive uncensored information from outside the country via social media.

Second, China's "social credit system" extends the scope of government (and Communist Party) surveillance and social control far beyond anything that exists in Russia. Every Chinese citizen is identified by an eighteen-digit "social credit unified code" associated with his/her identity card.[67] The term "credit," *xinyong* in Chinese, "is associated with the moral virtues of trustworthiness and integrity."[68] The primary goal of the system "is to single out people and organizations whose acts are considered to be 'breaking trust'." Those who are deemed "trust-breaking" are placed on blacklists. Those who are "trust-keeping" are placed on "Redlists." Addition of a person's name to blacklists gives rise to a range of sanctions. Unfortunately, the standard that determines whether particular activity is trust-breaking "is vaguely defined and hence triggers a great deal of legal uncertainties. For instance, spreading rumors on the Internet is . . . deemed trust-breaking."[69]

The Chinese government collects voluminous records from social media and other sources that "integrate a broad spectrum of information concerning 'trust-breaking' behavior."[70] Technology used to collect and process information includes "high-resolution cameras, facial recognition, spying malware, automated text analysis, and big-data processing,"[71] all supported by sophisticated artificial intelligence (AI) to facilitate mass surveillance of ordinary citizens. The technological features of the system are still being developed, but "recent trends indicate that the Chinese government will likely leverage big data to upgrade the [social credit system] to a near-omnipotent version. Given the power stemming from its technological advances, it is capable of doing so."[72]

Although China's version of digital authoritarianism is reminiscent of George Orwell's dystopian vision, the government and Chinese Communist Party (CCP) appear to enjoy a high degree of support and legitimacy among the people. Two social scientists conducted an online survey of 500 people in China. Their central conclusion is worth quoting at length.

> The CCP has gradually embraced more public participation in the political deliberation process to bolster regime stability and legitimacy. . . . [The] emerging online sphere should be understood as a part of CCP's broader strategic moves to manage and co-opt the Internet in a way to strengthen its hegemony . . . Partial public participation in the political deliberation process online serves the government in multiple ways: It operates as a "safety valve" to defuse any probable collective dissent against the party-state system, helps the government to monitor local governments and officials, [and] gauges and directs online public opinion in a way that reinforces CCP positions and policies.[73]

It is unclear whether, or to what extent, online political debate serves a similar legitimation function in Russia. Regardless, in both China and Russia, extensive government control over the online environment means that it is simply not feasible for the United States to engage in effective social media manipulation to support pro-democracy activism in either country. Instead, the "closed media environment of a nondemocracy provides efficient ways for these governments to censor, cut, or counter social media in ways that promote regime survival."[74]

DIGITAL AUTHORITARIANISM OUTSIDE RUSSIA AND CHINA

For a period of about fifteen years after the fall of the Berlin Wall, it appeared that liberal democracy was spreading around the world through a process of policy diffusion.[75] Countries that lacked strong, historical democratic traditions were embracing liberal norms and internalizing those norms in domestic laws, policies, and institutions. A set of transnational networks "served as the foot soldiers of U.S. hegemony by spreading broadly liberal norms and practices."[76] Now, however, the reverse is happening: a set of transnational networks is spreading illiberal norms and practices. Digital technology generally, and social media in particular, is facilitating the diffusion of illiberal norms and the incorporation of those norms into domestic laws, institutions, and practices in authoritarian states. Blogs and academic journals are filled with essays about "digital authoritarianism" and "authoritarian learning."

Many autocratic states are copying elements of the Chinese and/or Russian models of digital authoritarianism. The three central features of that model—surveillance, censorship, and content manipulation—have diffused widely to numerous authoritarian states. The Oxford disinformation report, referenced above, identifies 70 countries where governments and/or political parties are engaged in at least some OSM activity.[77] Combining the data from the Oxford report with data from table 5, governments and/or political parties in at least 38 of the 90 autocratic states included in table 5 are practicing some form of OSM. Chapter 4 explained how China exports digital authoritarianism to the global South. This section examines digital authoritarianism in the former Soviet Union and Arab states: the two most autocratic regions in the world.

Digital Authoritarianism in the Former Soviet Union (FSU)
In 2009, two Azerbaijani citizens posted a satirical YouTube video in which a group of "journalists interview a donkey . . . and note that this donkey would be afforded more civil liberties than Azerbaijani citizens."[78] Two

weeks later, "they were arrested for 'hooliganism' and sentenced to 30 and 24 months imprisonment, respectively." The so-called "donkey blogger" case "was widely reported on Web sites frequented by young Azerbaijanis. Over the months that followed, support for activism dropped precipitously among this population."[79] "The government would not have been able to instill" the requisite fear in the broader population merely by preventing the donkey bloggers from speaking.[80] Instead, the government achieved its objectives—encouraging self-censorship and discouraging online political activism—by permitting online political speech, monitoring that speech, arresting online activists for violating vague laws that give the government broad discretion to punish government critics, and publicizing the arrests. This approach to networked authoritarianism is common among autocratic states in the former Soviet Union (FSU).

The FSU region includes ten autocratic states and two electoral democracies (see table 5). The ten autocratic states are Armenia, Azerbaijan, Belarus, Kazakhstan, Kyrgyzstan, Russia, Tajikistan, Turkmenistan, Ukraine, and Uzbekistan. The two electoral democracies are Georgia and Moldova. Jaclyn Kerr, a research fellow at Lawrence Livermore National Laboratory, conducted a recent study of internet policy diffusion across former Soviet states. She concludes that "many of the region's [authoritarian] regimes have adopted similar approaches to control Internet content and use within their territories."[81] Although there are variations among states, the general model is characterized by three main elements: limited censorship combined with active content manipulation, communications interception and surveillance, and broadly similar "information security doctrines."[82]

The authoritarian FSU states combine "a relatively low level of static censorship . . . with significant degrees of pro-regime content production and manipulation."[83] They do occasionally "block access to critical sites and resources at politically sensitive moments." More commonly, though, "hackers, youth groups, trolls, bloggers, and other actors mount hard-to-attribute informational or cyberattack campaigns on behalf . . . of the regime, while seeking to maintain plausible deniability as to the government's actual involvement." In some cases, they pay trolls "to intervene in online discussions on topics and disrupt critical discourse." Such tactics are used "to target activists and change narratives." By applying these strategies, authoritarian governments are capable of "disrupting or drowning out critical speech, leaking compromising content about opposition figures, and providing the appearance of authentic discourse."[84]

Recall that Russia has implemented a surveillance system, known as SORM, "in which communications service providers and telecommunications equipment manufacturers are required to ensure that their network and equipment are . . . accessible to a monitoring facility from which [government] analysts request, receive, store, and analyze intercepted data."[85] The SORM model has diffused widely throughout the region, with active assistance from Russia. "Ukraine, Belarus, Kazakhstan, and Uzbekistan each have implemented sophisticated SORM-based systems, with Kyrgyzstan, Tajikistan, Turkmenistan, and Azerbaijan having made varying degrees of progress toward developing similar technical surveillance systems." "In Russia, a whole industry has developed around the production of hardware and software products to meet the SORM standards. As the model has spread through surrounding states, Russian companies . . . have often served as suppliers to the region."[86]

One distinctive feature of the FSU approach is that Russia's "information security approach has spread broadly within the FSU region." Formal national security documents in many countries—including Belarus, Ukraine, Uzbekistan, Tajikistan, Kazakhstan, Kyrgyzstan, and Moldova—have "integrated language similar to that of the Russian . . . Doctrine of Information Security." Under that doctrine, the concept of information security is not limited to "protection from data breaches, cyberattacks, and other threats to computer networks and data."[87] To the contrary, an express goal of information security measures is to protect those in power from popular uprisings that threaten the stability of autocratic rule. Authoritarian FSU states have incorporated this concept of information security into "summit agreements, cooperation pacts, [and] joint security operations." These multilateral "efforts emerge as part of a global normative contestation with Western democracies over the appropriate understandings of the relationship between state sovereignty, the Internet, and security."[88]

Digital authoritarianism strengthens autocratic control in authoritarian FSU states. The FSU governments "maintain a façade of democratic freedoms and processes" by permitting citizens to engage in a good deal of online political speech. Even so, Kerr concludes: "By limiting overt rights abuses to [a] handful of targets . . . while avoiding widespread and obvious abuses that would be evident to the majority of the population, these regimes are . . . able to maintain a low-intensity coercion approach to nondemocratic rule, which maintains regime stability partly through the maintenance of public support."[89]

Digital Authoritarianism in Arab States

During the Arab Spring uprisings in 2011, there were significant pro-democracy protests in several states in the region, including Bahrain, Egypt, Libya, Morocco, Syria, Tunisia, and Yemen. The pro-democracy activists made extensive use of social media to help organize their political activities.[90] Thus, for a brief period, many commentators were optimistic that social media would help fuel democratic reforms throughout the region. Unfortunately, the optimists were mostly wrong. Autocratic rulers in Bahrain, Egypt, and Syria have used the tools of digital authoritarianism to strengthen their dictatorial control. Libya and Yemen have descended into civil wars. The one bright spot is Tunisia, which has undergone significant pro-democracy reforms since 2011. Indeed, Tunisia is the only Arab state classified as a democracy in table 5. (Unfortunately, Tunisia may also be trending authoritarian since I compiled the data for table 5.[91])

In August 2019, Facebook reported that it had removed numerous Pages, Groups, and accounts linked to two separate operations in the Middle East, "one of which originated in United Arab Emirates and Egypt, and another in Saudi Arabia." According to Facebook, "both created networks of accounts to mislead others about who they were and what they were doing."[92] A few weeks later, Twitter announced that it had also removed a network of accounts linked to the UAE, Egypt, and Saudi Arabia.[93] At about the same time, the *New York Times* reported that social media influence operations in the Middle East "are being coordinated across borders in an effort to bolster authoritarian rule and douse the kind of popular protests that gave rise to the Arab Spring in 2011."[94]

The Arab League consists of twenty-two states, including Palestine. Most of the states are in North Africa or the Arabian Peninsula, but the league also includes Mauritania in West Africa, and Comoros, Djibouti, and Somalia in East Africa. According to the Oxford disinformation report, seven of the twenty-two Arab League states are actively engaged in OSM: Bahrain, Egypt, Qatar, Saudi Arabia, Sudan, Syria, and the United Arab Emirates (UAE).[95] The remainder of this section analyzes the practice of digital authoritarianism in those seven states.

Geopolitically, the seven states listed above are deeply divided. In June 2017, Bahrain, Egypt, Saudi Arabia, and the UAE severed diplomatic relations with Qatar. They also imposed an air, land, and sea blockade on Qatar.[96] Egypt, Saudi Arabia, and the UAE are supporting one side in the Libyan civil war; Qatar is supporting the other. Ironically, the dispute between Qatar and its neighbors may be partially attributable to Russian hackers. In May 2017, a story posted to the site of Qatar's state-run news agency (QNA) claimed that Qatar's hereditary ruler had affirmed good relations with Iran, Hezbollah, and Hamas. Saudi Arabia and the UAE then accused Qatar of supporting terrorism: that was the primary reason the other states cut diplomatic ties with Qatar. However, Qatar said that the story was false and that QNA's social media accounts had been hacked.[97] U.S. officials later backed Qatar's version of the story, claiming that "Russian hackers breached Qatar's state news agency and planted a fake news report that contributed to a crisis among the US' closest Gulf allies."[98]

The Oxford disinformation report documents the fact that the governments of Bahrain, Egypt, Qatar, Saudi Arabia, Sudan, Syria, and the United Arab Emirates all engage in OSM. All of the countries except Sudan have utilized bots for covert social media manipulation. All except Qatar have used human-operated fake accounts in which the human operator adopts a false identity to conceal the fact that he or she is acting as a government agent. Bahrain, Saudi Arabia, Syria, and the UAE all employ private contractors to support their social media influence operations.[99] According to the Oxford report, Egypt, Saudi Arabia, Syria, and the UAE all have "high" cyber troop capacity, whereas Bahrain, Qatar, and Sudan have "medium" capacity.

There is evidence that China is exerting influence over internet policy in six of the seven states—all except Qatar. China has been "cultivating media elites and government ministers around the world to create a network of countries that will follow its lead on internet policy."[100] Chinese companies have installed internet and mobile network equipment in Bahrain, Egypt, Saudi Arabia, and Sudan. Additionally, China hosted a three-week seminar for senior media staff from Arab countries. "Chinese officials have held trainings and seminars on new media or information management with representatives" from Egypt, Saudi Arabia, Syria, Sudan, and the UAE.[101] It is not entirely clear what transpires in those seminars, but China is likely teaching representatives from Arab states how to regulate the internet to strengthen authoritarian control.

All seven countries, to varying degrees, employ four different types of social media regulation strategies: overt censorship, surveillance, content manipulation, and other tactics that have the purpose or effect of encouraging people to practice self-censorship. Overt censorship can take the form of blocking or filtering content, or forcing platforms to delete content. Governments in Bahrain, Egypt, Saudi Arabia, Syria, and the UAE practice aggressive overt censorship of social media.[102] The government of Sudan also practices overt censorship, but Freedom House indicates that Sudan relies less heavily on overt censorship than the other states.[103] In Qatar, "the law requires internet service providers to block objectionable content upon request from judicial authorities. . . . The government-controlled internet service provider Ooredoo restricted the expression of views via the internet and censored the internet for political, religious, and pornographic content."[104]

Governments in Bahrain, Egypt, Saudi Arabia, Sudan, Syria, and the UAE exploit social media to engage in extensive surveillance of their domestic populations. In all six countries, in addition to direct state surveillance of online activities, governments require internet service providers and related technology companies to assist the government in monitoring private communications.[105] In Bahrain, for example, all telecommunications providers are "obliged to provide security forces access to subscriber data upon request." Any company that applies for an operating license "must develop a 'lawful access capability plan' that would allow security forces to access communications metadata."[106] Surveillance in Qatar appears to be less pervasive than in other countries. In Qatar, "residents enjoy some freedom of private discussion, [but] security forces reportedly monitor personal communications, and noncitizens often self-censor to avoid jeopardizing their work and residency status."[107]

Governments employ a variety of legal and extralegal measures that have the purpose and/or effect of encouraging individuals to practice self-censorship. All seven countries have laws that impose civil or criminal penalties for online activities. Individuals are frequently detained and prosecuted for violations of such laws, and penalties can be harsh. In all seven countries, with the possible exception of Qatar, individuals face the potential threat of extralegal harassment and violence in retaliation for their online activities.[108] In Sudan, for example, Freedom House reports that "arrests, prosecutions, and interrogations for online activities continued. . . . The arrests reflected government efforts to limit internet freedom by silencing critical voices and intimidating online journalists and users into self-censorship."[109]

Governments and supporting actors engage in online content manipulation for different purposes. Governments in Bahrain, Egypt, Qatar, Saudi Arabia, Syria, and the UAE (but not Sudan) employed cyber troops to spread pro-government propaganda and to amplify their preferred content on social media. Governments in Bahrain, Egypt, Saudi Arabia, Sudan, Syria, and the UAE (but not Qatar) employed cyber troops on social media to mount smear campaigns, attack political opponents or activists, and/or suppress political participation through personal attacks or harassment. Somewhat surprisingly, Arab governments were less likely than governments in other parts of the world to use social media to spread disinformation. Egypt, Saudi Arabia, Syria, and the UAE engaged in disinformation tactics, but there is no evidence that Bahrain, Qatar, or Sudan practiced disinformation.[110]

Available evidence suggests that the tools of digital authoritarianism strengthen autocratic rule. "Between 1946 and 2000—the year digital tools began to proliferate—the typical dictator ruled for around ten years. Since 2000, this number has more than doubled, to nearly 25 years."[111] Moreover, "those authoritarian regimes that rely more heavily on digital repression are among the most durable."[112] In contrast, whereas digital authoritarianism reinforces autocratic control in authoritarian states, the practice of OSM in liberal democracies tends to weaken or undermine democratic governance in those states. Therefore, absent effective regulation, social media will continue to create an uneven playing field by strengthening autocratic control in authoritarian states and weakening democratic governance in liberal democracies.

This concludes Part One. At this point, I have hopefully persuaded readers that Chinese and Russian information warfare presents a significant threat to liberal democracies. My goal in this book, though, is not merely to describe the threat but also to offer at least a partial solution. That is the subject of Part Two. The policy proposal developed in Part Two does not directly address either the problem of digital authoritarianism in autocratic states or the problem of domestic OSM in liberal democracies. Instead, my proposal for a new transnational regulatory system is designed to protect Western democracies from the threat presented by Chinese and Russian information warfare. Digital authoritarianism and domestic OSM are related, but distinct, problems that require different types of policy solutions.

PART TWO

PRESCRIPTION

CHAPTER SIX

A PROPOSAL FOR TRANSNATIONAL REGULATION

THIS CHAPTER SETS FORTH the contours of a detailed proposal for transnational regulation to protect liberal democracies from Chinese and Russian information warfare. The proposal assumes that the United States has an important foreign policy interest in preserving democracy in established liberal democracies. The proposed transnational regulatory system is designed to accomplish two primary objectives. The first goal is to prevent, to the maximum extent feasible, Russian and Chinese agents from using social media to exacerbate the problem of democratic decay in the United States. The second goal is to prevent, to the maximum extent feasible, Russian and Chinese agents from using social media to exacerbate the problem of democratic decay in other leading constitutional democracies, especially in states that are key U.S. allies.

The proposed transnational regulatory system includes seven central elements:

(1) A new alliance of democratic states that will cooperate with each other to protect themselves from Russian and Chinese information warfare (the "Alliance for Democracy").

(2) Rules guaranteeing robust protection for free speech on social media by citizens and nationals of Alliance member states.

(3) A rule prohibiting Chinese and Russian agents from creating or operating accounts on regulated social media platforms (the "ban"),

subject to an exemption for benign state agents. The ban would be implemented by appropriate legislation and/or regulations in all Alliance member states.

(4) A disclaimer regime that will provide warnings for domestic audiences in Alliance member states whenever foreigners from nondemocratic states transmit election-related messages via social media.

(5) A registration system that will require social media users to register their accounts and declare their nationalities, including a verification system enabling governments of Alliance member states to verify that social media users who claim to be nationals of member states are, in fact, nationals of those states.

(6) Rigorous safeguards to protect informational privacy and data security.

(7) An exemption from the registration system for social media users who choose to maintain private accounts rather than public accounts.

The first part of the chapter describes several circumvention strategies that Chinese and Russian agents might undertake in an effort to evade the ban and the disclaimer requirements. It is important for readers to understand these circumvention strategies because the proposed transnational regulatory system includes several elements that are specifically designed as anti-circumvention measures. After describing potential circumvention strategies, the remainder of the chapter presents a detailed explanation of the proposed transnational regulatory scheme. Chapter 7 evaluates the likely success of that scheme in accomplishing its intended objectives, and weighs the likely costs and benefits of the proposed regulatory system. Chapter 8 addresses potential First Amendment objections that would likely be raised in the United States. The appendix includes suggested language for certain key regulatory provisions that would be substantially similar in all Alliance member states.

LIKELY CIRCUMVENTION STRATEGIES

Russian and Chinese cyber troops have exploited U.S. social media platforms to pursue various foreign policy objectives. If Alliance member states enact statutes and regulations to prohibit Chinese and Russian agents from creating or operating accounts on regulated social media platforms, those foreign agents will undoubtedly attempt to evade that prohibition. This section describes seven distinct circumvention strategies that Chinese and Russian agents might pursue in an effort to evade the ban.

First, Chinese and Russian cyber troops might attempt to create *fictitious user accounts*. A *fictitious user account* is a social media account created in the name of a nonexistent person who pretends to be a citizen or national of an Alliance member state. Russian agents made extensive use of fictitious user accounts during the 2016 presidential election campaign in the United States.[1] Indeed, fictitious user accounts were one of the most potent weapons that Russia deployed in that information warfare operation. The registration system described later in this chapter is designed to prevent Chinese and Russian cyber troops from creating or operating fictitious user accounts. If that system is implemented effectively by Alliance member states, it would become practically impossible for foreign agents to operate fictitious user accounts.

Second, Chinese and Russian cyber troops might attempt to create *impostor accounts*. An *impostor account* is a social media account operated by a Chinese or Russian agent who misappropriates the identity of a real person without that person's knowledge or consent. There are three main ways to establish an impostor account. First, Chinese agents have hacked into existing accounts created by real people and taken control of those accounts ("hacked accounts").[2] Second, Chinese agents have purchased "stolen accounts" that are available for sale on the black market.[3] A stolen account is a hacked account that has been sold to a third party. Third, cyber troops could create an impostor account from scratch by obtaining the identifying information of a real person and using that information to create a new account. The registration system described later in this chapter, if implemented effectively, would make it much more difficult and costly (but not impossible) for Chinese and Russian cyber troops to create new impostor accounts from scratch. However, the proposed registration system would not address the problem of hacked or stolen accounts. The best way to prevent cyber troops from obtaining hacked or stolen accounts is to educate ordinary social media users and induce them to adopt better cyber security practices.

Third, Chinese and Russian cyber troops might attempt to create *rental accounts*. A *rental account* is a specific type of impostor account in which a foreign agent pays a bribe to a national of an Alliance member state, so that the foreign agent can appropriate the identity of the payee for the purpose of operating a social media account. In fact, U.S. citizens have accepted bribes from Russian agents to enable those agents to operate rental accounts.[4] Rental accounts differ from stolen and hacked accounts in that the owner of a stolen or hacked account is an unwitting victim, whereas the initial owner of a rental account is a willing participant in the fraud. The proposed regulatory system would impose criminal penalties on citizens or nationals of Alliance member states who accept money or any other thing of value from foreign agents to facilitate creation of rental accounts.

Fourth, Chinese and Russian cyber troops might register as Chinese or Russian nationals, while attempting to conceal the fact that they are state agents. The proposed regulatory system creates a rebuttable presumption to address this particular circumvention strategy. Specifically, the law would establish a rebuttable presumption that any person who registers as a Chinese or Russian national is presumed to be acting as a state agent, unless that person is a legal resident of an Alliance member state. Any person who registers as a Chinese or Russian national would have an opportunity to rebut that presumption by presenting evidence to show that he or she is not in fact a state agent. Chinese and Russian nationals who are not state agents would be subject to the disclaimer requirement, but they would not be banned from U.S. social media platforms.

Fifth, Chinese and Russian cyber troops might attempt to create *fake foreign national accounts*. A *fake foreign national account* is an account created by a Chinese or Russian agent who claims to be a citizen or national of some state other than China or Russia that is not an Alliance member state. Under the registration system, if a person claims to be a citizen of Venezuela, for example, his/her declaration of citizenship would not be subject to verification by the Venezuelan government, assuming that Venezuela is not an Alliance member state. Accounts registered to persons who claim to be nationals of nonmember states would be subject to disclaimer requirements, but would not be banned. Therefore, once the registration system is established, Russian and Chinese cyber troops would likely try to evade the ban by creating fake foreign national accounts that are not subject to the verification system operated by governments of Alliance member states. Social media companies and Alliance member states could develop technical measures (discussed later in this chapter) to detect fake foreign national accounts. However, Chinese and Russian cyber troops would likely be able to create and operate some fake foreign national accounts because they have the technical skills to evade even very sophisticated technical measures. Therefore, under the proposed regulatory system, this strategy would likely become a viable strategy for Chinese and Russian agents to circumvent the ban. To reiterate, though, fake foreign national accounts would still be subject to disclaimer requirements.

Sixth, Chinese and Russian agents might attempt to create bots or cyborg accounts. A "bot" is "a software tool that performs specific actions on computers connected in a network without the intervention of human users."[5] A "cyborg account" is an account that is either operated by a human being with assistance from a bot, or operated by a bot with assistance from a human being. Companies use a variety of "good bots" for legitimate business purposes. However, cyber troops can use bots or cyborg accounts to help spread disinformation on social media to large numbers of recipients. Russian cyber troops have made extensive use of bots to conduct information warfare.[6] The transnational regulatory system described later in this chapter includes specific provisions designed to prevent Chinese and Russian cyber troops from creating bots or cyborg accounts. It also includes special disclaimers to warn users when they receive messages generated by bots or cyborg accounts.

Finally, if the transnational regulatory regime applied only to U.S. social media platforms, Chinese and Russian cyber troops could exploit Tik-Tok or some other non-U.S. platform to engage in foreign influence operations. TikTok is an app that reportedly has about 800 million monthly active users, including about 344 million outside of China.[7] TikTok's large global user base and the Chinese government's control over the platform makes it a potentially attractive tool for Chinese agents engaged in information warfare. The proposed regulatory system addresses this issue by specifying that the rules apply to all social media platforms with more than 50 million monthly active users outside of Russia and China (see the appendix). Under this approach, TikTok would qualify as a regulated social media platform.

There is one other circumvention strategy that the proposed transnational regulatory system does not address: useful idiots. As discussed in the preface, the category of "useful idiots" includes people like Donald Trump who—in pursuing their own, individual political agendas—also happen to advance Russian (or Chinese) foreign policy goals, such as Russia's goal of undermining faith in American democracy. Technically, exploitation of useful idiots is not really a circumvention "strategy" because it does not require any strategic planning by Russia or China. From the perspective of Russia, it is simply a lucky accident that some U.S. citizens happen to advance Russia's foreign policy goals by pursuing their own political agendas. Thus, useful idiots who spread disinformation on social media are properly viewed as a species of domestic OSM rather than a tactic of information warfare. Of course, Donald Trump—who is the most notorious useful idiot—arguably poses a greater threat to American democracy than either Chinese or Russian information warfare. Even so, the regulatory proposal presented in this chapter does not address the threat posed by useful idiots because the proposal is designed to counter the threat posed by information warfare, not domestic OSM.

The remainder of this chapter describes and explains the key elements of a transnational regulatory system designed to mitigate the threat posed by Chinese and Russian cyber troops who exploit social media to conduct information warfare. Some elements of that transnational regulatory system could be incorporated into domestic laws and/or regulations in virtually identical terms in all Alliance member states. Other elements would require differential treatment in different states to accomplish the same broad objectives.

SCOPE AND DEFINITIONS

Laws and/or regulations in all Alliance member states should state explicitly that the rules apply to all social media platforms with more than fifty million monthly active users outside of Russia and China, including platforms operated by Russian or Chinese companies. This threshold requirement regarding the scope of the rules would capture TikTok, but exclude platforms such as Sina Weibo and VK, which operate primarily within China and Russia, respectively.[8] (Designing regulations in a way that makes sense for WeChat will pose special challenges, as discussed later in this chapter.[9]) The fifty-million threshold is intended to exclude smaller social media companies for whom regulatory compliance would be a significant operational burden. Russian and Chinese cyber troops could continue conducting foreign influence operations on smaller platforms, but the small number of users would limit the reach of such operations. Alliance member states should conduct fact-finding to determine whether a threshold greater or smaller than fifty million users is appropriate.

All Alliance member states should adopt a common definition of the term "social media platform," because that definition will determine which companies are covered by the regulation and which ones are excluded. The appendix includes a proposed definition that consists of three parts: a generic description of the term "social media platform," a list of specific platforms that are covered by the regulation, and a list of different types of websites and web applications that are specifically excluded from the definition.

All Alliance member states should also adopt a common definition of "public communication." Individuals and other entities who use social media exclusively for private communications should be exempt from the mandatory registration system, including the mandatory disclosure requirements. (They would still be subject to platform-specific account registration requirements established by social media companies.) People who use social media exclusively for private communication are not likely to be targets of Russian or Chinese influence operations, so application to them of mandatory disclosure requirements would serve little purpose. Since the proposed registration system requires social media users to disclose certain identifying information to governments, and some users may be reluctant to disclose that information, individuals should have the option of avoiding mandatory disclosure by creating an account that is solely for private communication. The appendix includes a proposed definition of the term "public communication."

AN ALLIANCE FOR DEMOCRACY

The federal executive branch should work with other democratic countries to create an Alliance for Democracy to accomplish the goals identified at the beginning of this chapter. Initially, the goals should be defined fairly narrowly: to protect Alliance member states from Chinese and Russian information warfare. Over time, if the Alliance works well, member states could work together to combat information warfare by other authoritarian states, and to protect Alliance member states from other types of foreign influence operations.

The central short-term purpose of the Alliance would be to create and maintain a system of regulatory harmonization among member states so that all member states regulate social media domestically in ways that are mutually reinforcing. The Nuclear Suppliers Group (NSG) provides a useful model. The NSG is a group of forty-eight nuclear supplier countries that work together to combat the threat of nuclear proliferation "through the implementation of two sets of Guidelines for nuclear exports and nuclear-related exports."[10] From the perspective of international law, the Guidelines are informal, nonbinding documents. However, NSG member states implement the Guidelines by enacting export control laws and regulations that have binding domestic legal force and that generally conform to the internationally agreed Guidelines. Much of the substantive content of the Guidelines is modeled on the Nuclear Nonproliferation

Act, a U.S. federal statute enacted in 1978.[11] Members of the proposed Alliance for Democracy could also choose to codify agreed rules in a legally binding treaty. Regardless of whether an international agreement takes the form of a treaty, or a more informal arrangement, most of the real work in implementing agreed rules will necessarily have to occur at the domestic level.

There are two main reasons why cooperation with other countries will be necessary if the United States decides to make a concerted effort to protect democracy from Chinese and Russian information warfare. First, one of the key goals should be to prevent, to the maximum extent feasible, Russian and Chinese agents from exploiting social media to exacerbate the problem of democratic decay in leading constitutional democracies around the world. Obviously, the United States cannot accomplish this goal by itself. It must cooperate with other leading democratic countries to achieve this goal. Hence, the need for an Alliance for Democracy.

Second, for reasons that will become apparent later in this chapter, the registration system and other anti-circumvention measures that constitute a critical part of a domestic U.S. statute will, in practice, be much more effective if other democratic countries enact similar rules. In short, if forty countries collaborate to enforce the rule banning Chinese and Russian agents from regulated social media platforms, it will be more difficult for foreign cyber troops to circumvent the ban.

Creating an Alliance for Democracy will also serve broader geopolitical objectives. For most of the post–World War II era, the United States cultivated its image as the "leader of the free world." During the presidency of Donald Trump, the United States lost its moral standing to claim that title because President Trump befriended dictators like Vladimir Putin and Kim Jong-un, while simultaneously weakening ties with many traditional, democratic allies. If President Biden decides to fight back against Chinese and Russian policies that are undermining democracy and supporting rising authoritarianism, he will need the support of key allies to have a fair chance of success. The Alliance for Democracy could potentially be a very valuable coalition to support the broader goals of protecting democratic governments and resisting creeping authoritarianism.

Which Countries Should Participate in Such an Alliance?

A good starting point to develop a list of potential Alliance members is to consider members of the Organization for Economic Cooperation and Development (OECD). The OECD is a group of thirty-seven mostly wealthy, mostly democratic countries.[12] There should be substantial overlap between OECD membership and Alliance membership. However, the Alliance for Democracy should include some states that are not OECD members and exclude some states that are OECD members. Two membership criteria are critical. First, member states must have competent, professional government bureaucracies. Second, they must be stable, liberal democracies.

The first criterion is important because the transnational regulatory system will rely on member state governments to block circumvention attempts by Chinese and Russian cyber troops. Suppose, for example, that Mexico becomes a member of the Alliance. Mexico is an OECD member state. However, it receives consistently low scores on the World Bank's "government effectiveness" indicator. That World Bank indicator is the single best available measure to determine whether states have competent, professional government bureaucracies.[13] Countries are scored on a scale from −2.5 (ineffective government) to +2.5 (effective government). Mexico's consistent poor scores show that Mexico's government bureaucracy lacks basic professional competence.[14] If Mexico was a member of the Alliance, and Mexican civil servants allowed Chinese or Russian cyber troops to register social media accounts as Mexican nationals—due either to government incompetence or corruption—then those cyber troops would gain unrestricted access to regulated social media platforms, thereby evading both the ban and the disclaimer requirements. This example illustrates the point that anti-circumvention measures implemented by member state governments are only as good as the weakest link. Therefore, it is important to limit membership in the Alliance to countries that have competent, professional government bureaucracies.

I reviewed the government effectiveness scores for all thirty-seven OECD member states between 2014 and 2018. Countries that received a score of .25 or better for at least four of those five years are deemed to satisfy the threshold test for government competence. Thirty-four of the thirty-seven OECD member states pass that test.[15] The three states that failed the test are Colombia, Mexico, and Turkey. I would exclude those countries from the Alliance. Their inclusion would threaten the integrity of the transnational regulatory system because Russian and Chinese cyber troops could take advantage of weak government bureaucracies in those countries to evade or circumvent the regulatory controls.

The second key criterion for membership in the Alliance is that member countries should be stable, liberal democracies. For present purposes, I use the v2x_regime_amb variable from the V-Dem database,[16] which is a variant of the v2x_regime variable discussed in earlier chapters. Recall that the v2x_regime variable groups countries into four categories: liberal democracies (LD), electoral democracies (ED), electoral autocracies (EA), and closed autocracies (CA). The v2x_regime_amb variable adds more nuance by including separate categories for LD minus, ED plus, ED minus, etc. Here, I classify countries as liberal democracies if they rank in the top three categories: LD, LD minus, or ED plus. A country qualifies as a stable, liberal democracy if it ranked in one of the top three categories for at least four of the five years from 2015 to 2019. Thirty-two of the thirty-four OECD member states that passed the government effectiveness test also pass the liberal democracy test. The two exceptions are Hungary and Poland. They should be excluded from the Alliance because they do not qualify as stable, liberal democracies under the aforementioned criterion.

The final step in creating a list of states eligible to participate in the Alliance for Democracy is to identify non-OECD states that satisfy both the government effectiveness test (a score of .25 or better on the World Bank indicator for at least four out of five years) and the liberal democracy test (ranking in the top three categories on v2x_regime_amb variable for at least four out of five years). Seven non-OECD countries pass both tests: Barbados, Botswana, Costa Rica, Cyprus, Mauritius, Uruguay, and Taiwan. (It is debatable whether Taiwan qualifies as a "state" under international law, but I treat Taiwan as a state for these purposes.[17]) If we add those seven countries to the thirty-two OECD member states that satisfy both eligibility criteria, initial members in the Alliance for Democracy would include the following thirty-nine states: Australia, Austria, Barbados, Belgium, Botswana, Canada, Chile, Costa Rica, Cyprus, Czech Republic, Denmark, Estonia, Finland, France, Germany, Greece, Iceland, Ireland, Israel, Italy, Japan, Latvia, Lithuania, Luxembourg, Mauritius, Netherlands, New Zealand, Norway, Portugal, Slovakia, Slovenia, South Korea, Spain, Sweden, Switzerland, Taiwan, the United Kingdom, the United States, and Uruguay.

The initial document creating the Alliance for Democracy—whether it is in the form of a treaty or a more informal arrangement—should address the issue of membership changes over time. The document should state explicitly the two key criteria for membership: member states must have competent, professional government bureaucracies and they must be stable, liberal democracies. Ideally, member states would agree on neutral criteria for measuring these two factors. States should not adopt a consensus requirement for adding or removing members because consensus is too hard to achieve. However, states should require a supermajority vote, perhaps a two-thirds or three-quarters voting rule, to remove existing members or to add new members. Member states could use the prospect of Alliance membership as a carrot to induce nonmembers to make domestic institutional reforms to improve good governance and enhance protections for individual rights.

THE DISCLAIMER REQUIREMENT

Social media companies should be required to attach disclaimers to all public communications on their platforms by citizens or nationals of nonmember states that qualify as "electoral speech." The requirement to attach disclaimers to certain election-related speech is a critical element of the transnational regulatory system. Disclaimers are warning labels attached to certain messages posted on social media. Each Alliance member state would develop its own definition of "electoral speech"; the main idea is that public communications on social media that relate to elections in Alliance member states qualify as "electoral speech." The disclaimers would say something like: "This message was posted by a person who is a citizen or national of a nondemocratic state." Thus, citizens of Alliance member states would receive warnings when they see or hear messages about elections in their home countries that are posted by persons from nonmember states.

Under the proposed regime, citizens and nationals of Alliance member states could post election-related messages about elections anywhere in the world without a disclaimer requirement. Similarly, citizens and nationals of nonmember states could post election-related messages about elections in nonmember states without a disclaimer requirement. However, disclaimers would be required whenever citizens or nationals of nonmember states transmit election-related messages about elections in Alliance member states.

It is important to apply the disclaimer requirement to all citizens and nationals of nonmember states to help reinforce the ban on Chinese and Russian agents. Once the registration system and the other anti-circumvention measures are in place, one of the simplest ways for Chinese and Russian agents to circumvent the ban will be to register as nationals of states that are not Alliance members. (Companies and member states can adopt technical measures to counter this circumvention strategy, but such technical measures will never operate perfectly.) Application of the disclaimer requirement to all citizens and nationals of nonmember states will ensure that any Chinese and Russian cyber troops who successfully register as nationals of non-member states will be subject to the disclaimer requirement, even if they manage to evade the ban.

National definitions of "electoral speech" and associated rules should be sufficiently precise that social media companies can apply algorithms to decide with almost 100 percent accuracy which messages require disclaimers. To illustrate the point, here is a proposed rule that Congress could incorporate into a U.S. federal statute:

- Companies that operate regulated social media platforms shall affix disclaimers to all public communications via social media[18] that (1) are transmitted by a person who is registered as a citizen or national of a state that is not a member of the Alliance, and that (2) encourage eligible voters not to vote.

- Companies that operate regulated social media platforms shall also affix disclaimers to all public communications via social media that are transmitted by a person who is registered as a citizen or national of a state that is not a member of the Alliance that (1) refer to a clearly identified candidate for federal office, and that (2) are transmitted within 120 days before an election for the office sought by the candidate.[19]
- The term "clearly identified" means that the name of the candidate involved appears; OR a photograph or drawing of the candidate appears; OR the identity of the candidate is apparent by unambiguous reference.[20]
- If a message was initially transmitted by a citizen or national of a nonmember state and a disclaimer was attached to that message, the disclaimer shall remain affixed to that message whenever a citizen or national of an Alliance member state shares the message with a third party.
- If a message was initially transmitted by a citizen or national of an Alliance member state and a disclaimer was not attached, the company shall affix a disclaimer if a citizen or national of a nonmember state resends the message in a manner that qualifies as a "public communication" under this statute.

Alliance member states should work with each other and with social media companies to develop common criteria for the design of disclaimers, including rules about font type, coloring, accompanying images, etc. The main point is that disclaimers should be designed to capture the attention of recipients. (Empirical research indicates that polymorphic warnings capture the attention of recipients more effectively than static warnings. Polymorphic warnings are warnings that change appearance to reduce habituation.[21]) Companies should not be subject to penalties for failing to affix a disclaimer to a message that constitutes electoral speech by a national of a nonmember state unless the company engages in a willful violation of the relevant rules.

BANNING CHINESE AND RUSSIAN AGENTS

The centerpiece of the proposed transnational regulatory system is a rule prohibiting Chinese and Russian agents from creating or operating accounts on regulated social media platforms. That rule would be implemented by appropriate domestic legislation and/or regulations in all Alliance member states. Domestic laws and regulations on this point should be substantially identical.

Readers may ask: "Why do we need a ban? Why not just require disclaimers for messages transmitted by Chinese and Russian agents?" Chapter 8 addresses this question in detail by analyzing three possible versions of a "disclaimer-only" system. For now, the key point is that there is no practical way to design a disclaimer-only regime that would be even minimally effective in combatting information warfare by Chinese and Russian cyber troops. Under my proposal, the ban and the disclaimer regime complement each other. The proposed ban applies to a broad class of speech (all speech on social media) by a small group of speakers: those who are acting as agents of the Chinese or Russian governments. In China's case, the ban should also apply to agents of the Communist Party. The proposed disclaimer regime applies to a narrow category of election-related speech transmitted by a much larger group of speakers: those who are registered as citizens or nationals of nonmember states.

One could argue that the ban should be extended to a much broader group of states. For example, the Oxford disinformation report (referenced in earlier chapters) identifies twenty-six authoritarian countries that are exploiting U.S. social media platforms domestically "to suppress fundamental human rights, discredit political opponents, and drown out dissenting opinions."[22] Myanmar is one such example. In 2017, the Myanmar military used Facebook as a tool to instigate a genocidal campaign of mass violence against the Rohingya minority group.[23] Whereas China and Russia exploit U.S. social media platforms primarily for the purpose of communicating with foreign audiences, Myanmar and many other authoritarian states exploit those platforms primarily for the purpose of communicating with domestic audiences.

Suppose that Alliance member states banned Myanmar government agents from regulated social media platforms. In that case, implementation of the ban would face an insuperable dilemma. It is difficult for Alliance member states to determine whether a person who registers as a citizen or national of Myanmar is, or is not, a government agent. If the term "agent" is applied narrowly, it would be trivially easy for government agents to evade the ban by posing as nonagents. Conversely, if the term "agent" is applied broadly, the ban would have the unwanted consequence of preventing many innocent social media users in Myanmar from speaking on regulated social media platforms. There is no good solution to this dilemma if the ban is applied to authoritarian states that exploit social media primarily for domestic purposes. However, as discussed below, there is a viable solution if the ban is applied only to states—such as Russia and China—that exploit regulated social media platforms to communicate with external audiences.[24]

The Oxford disinformation report identifies seven states that have used U.S. social media platforms to conduct foreign influence operations targeted at external audiences: China, India, Iran, Pakistan, Russia, Saudi Arabia, and Venezuela.[25] Alliance member states might wish to extend the ban to some of these states, in addition to China and Russia. Iran, in particular, might be a good target for a ban. However, I focus here on China and Russia because they are the two most powerful authoritarian states in the world today, and because they are the states with the most sophisticated foreign influence operations.

How to Distinguish between Agents and Nonagents?

The proposed ban applies only to individuals or entities who are acting as agents of the Chinese or Russian governments, or of the Chinese Communist Party. Limiting the ban to "agents" presents a potential operational difficulty: How can the governments of Alliance member states distinguish between a Chinese citizen who is a state agent and a Chinese citizen who is not a state agent?

The Articles on State Responsibility, promulgated by the International Law Commission, provide internationally agreed guidelines for determining when an individual is acting as a state agent.[26] Alliance member states could incorporate Articles 4 to 11, which address "attribution of conduct to a state," into domestic legal regulations to help guide decision-makers responsible for making case-by-case determinations about whether a particular person is acting as a state agent.

Domestic rules should also include two presumptions to facilitate application of those criteria. First, Chinese and Russian nationals who are legal residents of Alliance member states should be presumed *not* to be state agents. When they register for new social media accounts, the government of the country where they reside would review the registration information and confirm that the applicant is a legal resident of that state. Companies would register legal residents as nonagents, unless the government of the country where a person resides determines that he/she qualifies as a state agent under the established criteria. In the United States, the implementing statute should provide an opportunity for judicial review in cases where a person who claims not to be a state agent is classified as a state agent. A person who registers as a Chinese or Russian national, but is not classified as a state agent, would be subject to the disclaimer requirements discussed previously.

Second, any person who registers as a Chinese or Russian national who is not a legal resident of an Alliance member state would be presumed to be a state agent. Social media companies would be prohibited from opening accounts for such persons, absent express approval from responsible government authorities. Persons who want to create accounts on regulated social media platforms, and who claim to be Chinese or Russian nationals, would have the burden of proving they are not state agents. Alliance member states should create a small multinational staff that is responsible for reviewing applications from Chinese and Russian nationals who claim that they are not state agents. Such a multinational staff could be modeled on the UN Counter-Terrorism Committee created pursuant to Security

Council Resolution 1373. That resolution required states to "freeze without delay funds and other financial assets or economic resources of persons who commit, or attempt to commit, terrorist acts or participate in or facilitate the commission of terrorist acts."[27] Among other things, the Counter-Terrorism Committee reviews information relevant to decisions about which persons are subject to the freeze.[28]

Under the proposed presumption, some Chinese and Russian nationals who are not state agents would likely be classified incorrectly as state agents and would consequently be subject to the ban. However, the cost of incorrect classification in these circumstances is quite low. Major U.S. social media platforms, including Facebook and Twitter, are already banned in China. Moreover, as discussed previously, the term "regulated social media platform" will be defined to exclude VK, Sina Weibo, and other platforms that are used primarily for internal communications within Russia and China. Thus, Russian and Chinese nationals who want to use social media for internal communications will still be able to use VK and Sina Weibo, respectively. Those platforms are not very useful for foreign influence operations because those platforms are not used by very many people outside of Russia and China.[29]

Individuals inside China and Russia who want to use the internet to communicate with the outside world must be wary of government surveillance and censorship. The Open Technology Fund "is an independent non-profit organization . . . [that] supports projects focused on counteracting repressive censorship and surveillance, enabling citizens worldwide to exercise their fundamental human rights online."[30] According to the *New York Times:* "Over two billion people in 60 countries rely on tools developed and supported by the [Open Technology] fund . . . to connect to the internet securely and send encrypted messages in authoritarian societies."[31] Therefore, although the presumption that Chinese and Russian nationals are state agents would likely result in the erroneous classification of some nonagents as agents, those people would still have access to tools to communicate with the outside world. Moreover, the tools available through the Open Technology Fund are better for these purposes than Facebook or Twitter because they enable people to avoid government surveillance and censorship.[32]

WeChat poses a special problem for the proposed regulatory regime. WeChat is often described as the Chinese equivalent of Facebook, but it has a broader range of functions than Facebook. As of March 31, 2020, WeChat had about 1.2 billion monthly active users, including about 240 million monthly active users outside of China.[33] The number of users outside China places WeChat well above the proposed threshold of fifty million users. However, it would be totally impractical to apply the presumption that declared Chinese nationals are state agents to almost one billion WeChat users inside China. One option would be to craft a special rule to exclude WeChat from the regulatory regime. That option is problematic because, with 240 million active users outside China, a decision to exclude WeChat might function as an open invitation for Chinese cyber troops to exploit WeChat for information warfare. Another option would be to ban WeChat from Alliance member states. (As of this writing, the Trump administration had banned WeChat from the United States, a federal judge blocked enforcement of the ban, and the Biden administration decided to drop the ban.[34]) A third possible approach would be to persuade WeChat to divide the platform into a "domestic WeChat" that operates within China and a "foreign WeChat" that operates outside China. This is effectively what ByteDance has done with TikTok (outside China) and Douyin (inside China).[35] Ultimately, Alliance member states will need to collect more information about WeChat users and usage in order to craft sensible rules that inhibit China from exploiting WeChat for information warfare, but that do not interfere unnecessarily with WeChat's established user base outside of China.

Creating an Exemption for Benign State Agents

A small group of social media users who clearly qualify as Russian or Chinese agents post content on social media that arguably makes a positive contribution to the overall information environment. The Chinese state media companies discussed in chapter 4—and the Russian companies RT and Sputnik—might be included in this category. However, we saw in chapter 4 that China uses its state media companies, such as China Daily and People's Daily, to conduct foreign influence operations. Similarly, we saw in chapter 3 that Russia used RT and Sputnik to try to influence the Brexit vote in the United Kingdom and to spread anti-NATO propaganda in Sweden. In light of these considerations, Alliance members might reasonably conclude that the rule banning Chinese and Russian agents from regulated social media platforms should provide limited exemptions for state agents whose speech on social media makes a positive contribution to the global information environment.

The best way to handle such an exemption would be to require overt Chinese and Russian agents to apply directly to the multinational staff discussed previously. The multinational staff should have fairly broad discretion to decide which Chinese and Russian agents qualify for an exemption from the ban. To qualify, an applicant would have to persuade the staff that, on balance, its presence on social media would make a positive contribution to the global information environment. The regulations should require special disclaimers for Chinese and Russian agents who are granted an exemption to warn social media users that the message they are seeing (or hearing) was transmitted by an agent of the Chinese or Russian government.

The regulations should also empower the multinational staff to shut down accounts operated by exempt state agents if they use their social media accounts to disseminate disinformation, or to undermine democracy in any Alliance member state, or to exacerbate the problem of political polarization in any Alliance member state. The multinational staff could utilize the threat of closing accounts to induce Chinese and Russian agents to behave responsibly on social media. The regulations should grant decision-makers fairly broad discretion in exercising their power to grant exemptions and to shut down accounts.

In a purely domestic statute, such broad discretionary power would likely raise significant constitutional concerns in the United States. However, the U.S. Supreme Court decided in 1936 that it is permissible for Congress to delegate broader discretion to the president in the foreign policy realm than it would be for a purely domestic statute.[36] Hence, statutes that grant the president or subordinate executive officials broad discretionary authority of this type are quite common in the foreign policy area. For example, the Committee on Foreign Investment in the United States (CFIUS) has authority to recommend that the president block transactions involving foreign investment in the United States if the committee determines that such investment "threatens to impair the national security of the United States."[37] One scholar has documented the existence of more than one hundred federal statutes that delegate broad authority to the president or subordinate officials to issue findings or waivers that alter the operation of otherwise applicable rules related to foreign policy and/or national security.[38] The proposed delegation of authority to a multinational staff—rather than the president or a subordinate executive officer—does raise distinct issues. Even so, the proposed delegation would almost certainly survive constitutional scrutiny because the main parties affected would be Chinese and Russian agents, and the Constitution does not generally protect the rights of noncitizens outside the United States.[39]

THE REGISTRATION SYSTEM

The proposed registration system is designed primarily to address the twin problems of fictitious user accounts and newly created impostor accounts (i.e., those that are neither hacked nor stolen). Without a registration system, it is trivially easy for Chinese and Russian cyber troops to create fictitious user accounts, and only slightly more difficult to create impostor accounts. The case studies in Part One demonstrate that these two types of accounts are two of the most powerful weapons in the Chinese and Russian information warfare arsenals. Social media companies have taken some steps to make it more difficult for foreign cyber troops to create and operate fictitious user accounts and impostor accounts. However, the companies do not have the capacity to solve these problems by themselves. Regulatory harmonization among Alliance member states is necessary to address the twin problems of fictitious user accounts and impostor accounts. The proposed registration system consists of six key elements: a requirement to distinguish between master and subsidiary accounts; a distinction between public and private accounts; disclosure requirements for natural and artificial persons who want to create public accounts; protocols for information sharing between social media companies and the governments of Alliance member states; verification procedures to be implemented by companies and Alliance member states; and rules to protect informational privacy and data security. The following sections discuss these six elements.

Master Accounts and Subsidiary Accounts

Some social media platforms allow users to maintain multiple accounts. On Instagram, for example, a person may operate an organization page and a private account.[40] Twitter allows people to operate multiple accounts, provided that those accounts do not post "substantially similar" content or engage in similar activity simultaneously.[41] The regulations should allow natural persons to operate multiple accounts by creating a master account and one or more subsidiary accounts. People who currently operate multiple accounts would have to consolidate those accounts into a single master account and one or more subsidiary accounts when they update their accounts to conform to the new regulatory requirements. The individual would register a single master account with the required identifying information. During the account registration process, they would specify, for example, that they want to maintain two subsidiary accounts—one with their real name and one with a pseudonym. Individuals would be free to create additional subsidiary accounts at any time.

The regulations should prohibit both natural and artificial persons from creating more than one master account. This prohibition is similar to the provision in the REAL ID Act that bars people from obtaining driver's licenses in more than one U.S. state;[42] it is necessary to facilitate detection of impostor accounts. Recall that an impostor account is a social media account operated by a Chinese or Russian agent that is created in the name of a real person who is a citizen or national of an Alliance member state. If citizens of Alliance member states are permitted to create and operate multiple master accounts, it would be extremely difficult to distinguish between an impostor account and a duplicate account operated by a single person who is a national of an Alliance member state. The rule that bars creation of more than one master account facilitates detection of impostor accounts: if a foreign cyber warrior attempts to appropriate the identity of a real person by creating an account in that person's name, and that person has already created a master account, the attempt will trigger a warning that someone is trying to create a duplicate account. That warning will, in turn, trigger the application of the verification procedures discussed later in this chapter. Whenever there is an attempt to create a duplicate account, the verification procedures should enable governments and social media companies to determine which one of the two accounts is an impostor account.

Public and Private Accounts

The rules should specify that the mandatory disclosure requirements for social media users, and the requirement for social media companies to share account registration information with the governments of Alliance member states (discussed below), apply only to public accounts, not private accounts. Under this approach, individuals who fear disclosing personal identifying information to national governments could avoid disclosure by registering for a private account. However, individuals with private accounts would be barred from engaging in public communications. (Some individuals might, for example, choose to create a public account on Twitter and a private account on Snapchat. In such cases, the person could engage in public communications on Twitter, but not on Snapchat.)

Thus, citizens and nationals of Alliance member states would face a basic trade-off: comply with disclosure requirements to gain access to a broader audience, or refuse disclosure and gain access to a more limited audience. Individuals with private accounts would have to comply with platform-specific disclosure requirements set by companies, but they would not have to comply with national requirements established by law. Chinese and Russian cyber troops could evade detection by creating private accounts, but such accounts would be of limited utility for information warfare because they would be barred from engaging in public communication.

Currently, some social media platforms enable individual users to classify an account or profile as "public" or "private." Call these "Type A platforms." Twitter and Instagram are prominent examples of Type A platforms.[43] Other platforms—Type B platforms—do not enable individual users to classify all of the content that an account or profile posts or shares as "public" or "private." Facebook is the leading example of a Type B platform.[44] In order for the registration system to function effectively, the rules would require Type B platforms to modify their account creation processes so that individuals would have to decide at the account creation stage whether to make their accounts public or private.

Disclosure Requirements

Under current corporate policies, all major social media companies require users to provide some identifying information to open an account. However, different companies have different requirements. Natural persons who open a Facebook account must provide a real name, a date of birth, and a phone number or email address.[45] Twitter also requires users to provide a phone number or email address, but it does not require a date of birth or real name.[46] The regulations should establish mandatory disclosure requirements for all regulated social media platforms, including a requirement for all social media users with public accounts to disclose their real names and their nationalities. (Undocumented immigrants in the United States could register for public social media accounts as nationals of their home countries, or they could register for private accounts.) These disclosure requirements are necessary to prevent Chinese and Russian cyber troops from creating fictitious user accounts. Recall that a fictitious user account is a social media account created in the name of a nonexistent person who pretends to be a citizen or national of an Alliance member state. As long as social media users are permitted to create accounts without disclosing their real names and nationalities, it will continue to be trivially easy for foreign cyber troops to create fictitious user accounts. Conversely, if all users with public accounts are required to disclose real names, nationalities, and certain other identifying information at the account creation stage, then Alliance member states can implement a registration system that makes it virtually impossible for cyber troops to create fictitious user accounts.

In addition to real names and nationalities, the disclosure requirements must be sufficient to enable the governments of Alliance member states to determine that a person who claims to be a citizen or national of Canada, for example, is a real Canadian person, not a fictitious user. Thus, disclosure requirements will vary by country, because different countries have different systems for tracking the identities of their nationals. Disclosure requirements will also have to be different for natural persons and artificial persons. (The term "artificial person" refers to a legally recognized entity that is not a human being.) In the United States, for example, most artificial persons can be identified by an employer ID number. Most natural persons can be identified by a name, date of birth, and either a driver's license number or a passport number. Each country will need to determine for itself whether, and to what extent, it is permissible for resident noncitizens to claim the country of their residence as their "nationality" for the purpose of registering a social media account. The United States should allow legal permanent residents (LPRs) to claim U.S. nationality for this purpose.

Registration of minors poses special problems. Currently, a substantial percentage of active social media users are minors. Some minors may already have a unique ID number, such as a passport number, or a USCIS number. Minors who already have a unique ID number should be able to use that number to register for a social media account. However, many minors who already have social media accounts may not have any type of unique ID number, especially if they are too young to drive. In such cases, parents should be authorized to utilize their master accounts to create subsidiary accounts for their children. (It is important to note that Congress enacted a special statute in 1998 to protect the privacy of minors who use the internet.[47] The Federal Trade Commission has promulgated rules to implement the statute.[48] The proposed registration system is entirely consistent with existing rules.)

According to a leading scholarly study, "at least 170 of the world's nearly 200 countries have some kind of national ID card or are implementing one. Included in this number are twenty-eight of the thirty-four" OECD countries.[49] (As of this writing, there are thirty-seven OECD members, compared to thirty-four at the time of that study.) In Alliance member states that issue such cards, disclosure of a legal name, nationality, date of birth, and ID card number would be sufficient for government authorities to determine whether a natural person is a fictitious user. Social media users should also be required to disclose either a phone number or an email address so that companies and relevant government officials can contact them if a problem arises.

In countries such as the United States that do not have national identification cards, the task of developing appropriate disclosure requirements would be slightly more complicated. Table 6 lists proposed disclosure requirements for natural persons who want to register as U.S. citizens or nationals. The basic idea is that all LPRs can be identified by a USCIS number and virtually all adult citizens can be identified by either a passport number or a state-issued ID number linked to an ID card that complies with the REAL ID Act.[50] (As of September 2020, all fifty states are in full compliance with the REAL ID Act.[51]) Therefore, under these requirements, substantially all U.S. citizens and legal permanent residents who want to create public accounts could register as U.S. nationals. U.S. residents who are not citizens or LPRs could register as nationals of their home countries. The requirements shown in table 6 would enable government authorities to determine whether a natural person who attempts to register as a U.S. national is a fictitious user.

For any given country that is an Alliance member state, the disclosure requirements should be the same for all regulated social media companies. Such mandated uniformity is necessary to enable Alliance member states to detect fictitious users. Companies should be free to adopt their own registration requirements for people who claim to be citizens or nationals of states that are not Alliance members, except that all social media users with public accounts must be required to disclose their real names and nationalities, regardless of whether they are nationals of Alliance member states or nonmember states.

TABLE 6. Disclosure requirements to register a public account as a U.S. national. Created by author.

Adult citizen	• Legal name, AND • Date of birth, AND • Phone number or e-mail address, AND • Declaration of U.S. citizenship, AND • Passport number OR identification number from a state driver's license or state ID card that complies with the requirements of the REAL ID Act
Legal permanent resident (LPR) (adult or minor child)	• Legal name, AND • Date of birth, AND • Phone number or e-mail address, AND • Declaration of LPR status, AND • USCIS number
Minor child	*Option One (for citizens or legal permanent residents)* • Parent or legal guardian with master account creates subsidiary account for minor child. *Option Two (for citizens only)* • Legal name, AND • Date of birth, AND • Phone number or e-mail address, AND • Declaration of U.S. citizenship, AND • Passport number OR identification number from a state driver's license or state ID card that complies with the requirements of the REAL ID Act

The regulations should give existing account holders a reasonable period of time, perhaps three or six months, to update their accounts by providing the necessary account registration information. Companies should be obligated to suspend the accounts of any existing users who fail to provide the required disclosures within the specified time period.

In sum, a mandatory disclosure regime for public accounts is necessary to enable Alliance member states to detect and block fictitious users. The required disclosures will vary by country and by the type of social media user—e.g., natural persons versus artificial persons and minors versus adults. Despite these variations, every Alliance member state should establish disclosure requirements that are sufficient to enable its government to determine that any person who claims to be a national of that state is indeed a national of that state, and not a fictitious user.

Information Sharing Protocols

The term "account registration information" refers to the information that social media users disclose to companies when they apply to open an account. Since all existing users will be required to update their accounts, "account registration information" also refers to information that existing users disclose to companies when they update their accounts. Regulations should require social media companies to share account registration information for all public accounts with the relevant government entities when a new user applies to open an account, or when an existing user updates his account. The required information sharing should apply only to master accounts. The regulations should prohibit companies from revealing to governments information about the number or types of subsidiary accounts linked to a particular master account, because users have a valid interest in protecting the privacy of such information, and governments do not need that information to detect impostor accounts or fictitious user accounts. Similarly, the regulations should prohibit companies from revealing information about private accounts to national governments, except insofar as other national laws require disclosure.

If a user claims to be a national of an Alliance member state, the regulations should require companies to share the account registration information with the government of the state where that person claims to be a national to enable the government to confirm that the person is not creating a fictitious user account or an impostor account. In the United States, legislation should delegate authority to the FBI to confirm that a person who claims to be a U.S. national is not a fictitious user or an impostor. To ensure that the FBI has access to information necessary to perform this task, the legislation should grant FBI officials access to the database of USCIS numbers maintained by the Department of Homeland Security, and the database of passport information maintained by the Department of State, and the state motor vehicle databases maintained by all fifty states under the REAL ID Act.[52] It would arguably be more efficient to create a single national database for this purpose, but a proposal to create such a database would likely generate substantial political opposition.[53]

If a user claims to be a Chinese or Russian national who is not a resident of an Alliance member state, the regulations should require companies to share the account registration information with the multinational staff discussed previously so that the staff can determine whether the person should be classified as a state agent, and if so whether that agent is entitled to an exemption. If a user claims to be a national of a state other than Russia or China that is not an Alliance member state, the primary concern is that the applicant may be a Chinese or Russian cyber warrior who is attempting to create a fake foreign national account. Specific measures to address the problem of fake foreign national accounts are discussed later in this chapter.

To protect the security of account registration information, all communications between social media companies and the governments of Alliance member states should be transmitted via a secure, dedicated data link. Data should be encrypted to make it difficult for potential hackers to decipher any information that they are able to intercept. For social media users who choose to remain anonymous, domestic regulations should prohibit social media companies from sharing information with governments that would enable governments to link pseudonyms to the real names disclosed in the account registration process.

Verification Procedures

For the purpose of this section, let us assume that a natural or artificial person is attempting to create a public account and to register as a national of an Alliance member state. In that case, the regulations will require companies to share the account registration information with the government of the state where that person claims to be a national so that the government can confirm that the person is not creating a fictitious user account or an impostor account. Before reporting account registration information to national governments, companies must first determine whether a newly registered account is a "duplicate account." A duplicate account is a new or updated account with registration information that is identical to, or almost identical to, the account registration information associated with a preexisting account on that platform. After checking for duplicates, the company would report all account registration information to the relevant national government, marking each account either as a duplicate or a nonduplicate.[54]

Responsible government authorities would review all nonduplicate accounts to determine whether the person registering is a fictitious user. In the vast majority of cases, governments should be able to determine quickly and easily whether an account is a fictitious user account by comparing the account registration information to existing government databases. Domestic rules should establish fairly tight timelines for government review of nonduplicate accounts, perhaps on the order of 48–72 hours. If the government determines that a nonduplicate account is not a fictitious user account, the government would notify the company and the account would be activated. If the government determines that a particular account is a fictitious user account, the government would notify the company and the company would block the account. If a person is classified incorrectly as a fictitious user, that person should be able to contest that determination in a quick, simple administrative procedure.

If a newly created account is classified as a duplicate, three explanations are possible: (1) someone made an innocent mistake; (2) the preexisting account is an impostor account and the person creating the new account is the person he/she claims to be; or (3) the newly created account is an impostor account and the person who created the prior account told the truth. Relevant government authorities should conduct an initial screening in every case to determine which of the three scenarios is more likely.

In some cases, the available evidence may indicate that the duplication is probably the result of an innocent mistake.[55] In such cases, the company should work with the person to correct the mistake. In cases where the evidence suggests that one of the duplicate accounts is an impostor account, government officials may want to monitor both accounts for a while to gather additional information. If the available evidence supports a high-confidence conclusion as to which account is the impostor account, government officials may prefer to close that account immediately. The potential permutations are sufficiently varied that it is difficult to establish detailed rules in advance. Therefore, the regulations should facilitate communication and coordination between governments and social media companies, while preserving flexibility to address each duplicate account on a case-by-case basis. The regulations should also establish a time limit for government review of duplicate accounts and provide for judicial review of contested decisions.

The most difficult detection problem concerns foreign agents who register nonduplicate accounts as impostor accounts. To appreciate the magnitude of the problem, consider the following scenario. The 2017 Equifax data breach compromised the personal information of 143 million American consumers.[56] It is fair to assume that Chinese and Russian agents already have, or could easily obtain, most of that information. Moreover, foreign cyber troops could use that information to create new accounts with identifying information that matches actual U.S. persons. Assume, conservatively, that the Equifax breach gave Chinese and Russian agents sufficient information to create 20 million accounts with identifying information matching actual U.S. persons. If 99 percent of those accounts are duplicates, and 1 percent are not duplicates, then foreign agents could create 200,000 impostor accounts (1 percent of 20 million) that would evade the initial screening procedures for duplicate accounts.

Chapter 7 considers the implications of this analysis for the overall effectiveness of the transnational regulatory regime. For now, suffice it to say that the registration system, if implemented effectively, would make it almost impossible for Chinese and Russian cyber troops to create fictitious user accounts. The system would also make it much more difficult, but not impossible, to create impostor accounts.

Privacy and Data Security

For the transnational regulatory scheme to function effectively, innocent social media users must have confidence that the identifying information disclosed during account registration will be protected. Accordingly, domestic regulations in all Alliance member states should require both social media companies and governments to manage account registration information in accordance with the requirements of the EU General Data Protection Regulation.[57] Additionally, domestic regulations should require companies to store account registration information on a secure, dedicated server that is isolated from other information by a firewall. Employee access to account registration information should be restricted on a need-to-know basis. U.S. legislation should require the FBI to establish a secure, dedicated data link to permit encrypted transmission of account registration information between the FBI and social media companies. The FBI should also be required to store the information on a secure, dedicated server that is protected by a firewall. Access by FBI employees should also be restricted on a need-to-know basis. Other Alliance member states should adopt similar regulatory measures to protect both informational privacy and data security.

Existing rules to protect user privacy limit the power of governments in most Alliance member states to monitor the social media accounts of their own citizens. Those rules should be expanded to prevent government monitoring of social media accounts registered to nationals of other Alliance member states. Additionally, government employees should be prohibited from using account registration information for any purpose other than to facilitate detection of fictitious user accounts and impostor accounts. Finally, the system should include strict limits on data retention that require governments to destroy records obtained during the account registration process after a relatively brief time period.

To provide added security, domestic regulations should require both companies and government entities to use data hashing to store account registration information. Hashing is "a special cryptographic function to transform one set of data into another of fixed length by using a mathematical process. . . . In the context of security, it is virtually impossible to reconstruct the input data from the output, even if the hash function is known."[58] If governments and companies use hashing to store account registration information, then the data would remain secure, even if an unauthorized person hacked into the system where the information is stored.

Most social media companies currently allow an individual to communicate publicly by using a pseudonym, without revealing his or her true identity. The regulations should explicitly permit social media users to maintain anonymity with respect to the public and with respect to governments by creating pseudonymous subsidiary accounts. Assume, for example, that David Sloss creates a master Twitter account in his own name, with a subsidiary account in the name of "Doctor J." Some Twitter employees would need to know that Doctor J is really David Sloss. However, the governments of Alliance member states do not need to know that Doctor J is David Sloss. Indeed, if governments had information linking pseudonyms to real names, and if social media users knew that governments collected such information, there would likely be a significant chilling effect on free speech. In the United States, rules that have such a chilling effect raise First Amendment concerns.[59] Therefore, for social media users who choose to remain anonymous, domestic regulations should prohibit social media companies from sharing information with governments that would enable governments to link pseudonyms to the real names disclosed in the account registration process. Moreover, for social media users who elect anonymity, the domestic rules should require companies to implement need-to-know restrictions to limit dissemination within companies of information linking pseudonyms to real names.

ANTI-CIRCUMVENTION MEASURES

Many of the detailed provisions that constitute the proposed registration system are properly characterized as "anti-circumvention measures," because the registration system as a whole is designed to make it difficult and costly for Russian and Chinese cyber troops to evade the ban and disclaimer requirements. In addition to the registration system, though, the transnational regulatory system should include three other anti-circumvention measures.

First, Alliance member states should enact laws to impose criminal penalties on any person who accepts money or some other thing of value to facilitate the creation of a rental account. Recall that a *rental account* is a specific type of impostor account in which a foreign agent pays a bribe to a national of an Alliance member state so that the foreign agent can appropriate the identity of that person for the purpose of operating a social media account. Each Alliance member state should make such criminal laws applicable to its own citizens and nationals, as well as nonnationals who reside in its territory. States could also attempt to impose criminal penalties on foreign agents who pay bribes, but such penalties are unlikely to be effective because foreign agents who violate the law can easily avoid the jurisdiction where they would potentially be subject to criminal prosecution. In contrast, applying criminal law to the recipients of bribes will likely have a greater deterrent effect because bribe recipients will generally be within the jurisdiction of an Alliance member state.

Second, Alliance member states should work cooperatively with social media companies to address the problem of fake foreign national accounts. Recall that a *fake foreign national account* is an account created by a Chinese or Russian agent who claims to be a citizen or national of some state other than China or Russia that is not an Alliance member state. The registration system will not detect fake foreign national accounts: when a person registers as the national of a state that is not an Alliance member, his declaration of nationality is not subject to verification by any government. Therefore, although Chinese and Russian cyber troops have not previously utilized fake foreign national accounts, we can expect them to adopt this tactic as a circumvention technique when Alliance member states implement a registration system.

Social media companies have developed sophisticated technical measures to detect fake accounts. Facebook's community standards "require people to connect on Facebook using the name they go by in everyday life."[60] Any attempt to create an account in violation of Facebook's misrepresentation policy is designated as a "fake account." Facebook claims "that our detection systems help us prevent millions of attempts to create fake accounts every day."[61] Facebook disabled about 1.7 billion fake accounts in the first quarter of 2020.[62] Facebook has provided very little public information about how it detects fake accounts because that type of public disclosure would help foreign cyber troops and others figure out how to evade its detection procedures. Even so, one can fairly assume that Facebook is relying heavily on artificial intelligence and automated software to detect and block fake accounts. That software could be adapted to detect and block fake foreign national accounts. Alliance member states and social media companies should establish a joint government-industry technical working group for these purposes. No system will ever be perfect. However, over time, Alliance member states and social media companies should be able to develop automated software that can detect and block most attempts to create fake foreign national accounts. In cases where cyber troops successfully create fake foreign national accounts, all electoral speech from those accounts will be subject to disclaimers to alert readers that the message is transmitted by a person who is a citizen or national of a nondemocratic state.

Third, Alliance member states should include in their domestic laws and regulations specific provisions to address the threat posed by *bots and cyborg accounts*. Regulation of bots is tricky because experts agree that there are "good bots" and "bad bots," but there is no clear line to distinguish the two. Assuming that Alliance member states implement a registration system along the lines I have suggested, the following set of rules could be utilized to address the issue of bots and cyborg accounts:

- Consistent with the overall design of the registration system, all master accounts must be registered in the name of a real person who declares his/her nationality. That declaration of nationality will be subject to verification if the person claims to be a citizen or national of an Alliance member state. All bot and/or cyborg accounts must be registered as subsidiaries to a master account that is a public account established in the name of a real person. These requirements will effectively prevent Russian and Chinese cyber troops from operating bot or cyborg accounts insofar as the ban on Russian and Chinese agents is enforced effectively, because the ban prohibits them from establishing public master accounts.

- If a natural or artificial person who has established a master account intends to use a subsidiary account as a bot or cyborg account, he/she must declare that fact to the company operating the relevant social media platform. The company will then register the subsidiary account as a bot or cyborg account. Domestic laws should require companies to shut down any subsidiary account operated as a bot or cyborg account without the required declaration. Companies can utilize sophisticated bot detection software to identify undeclared bot or cyborg accounts with a high degree of accuracy and reliability.[63]

- Messages disseminated by bots or cyborg accounts should be accompanied by a disclaimer to alert the recipient to the fact that the message is coming from a bot or cyborg account. The disclaimer requirement should apply to all bot and cyborg accounts associated with master accounts that are registered to a citizen or national of a nonmember state. Social media companies should be responsible for attaching disclaimers to messages transmitted from subsidiary accounts that have been declared as bots or cyborg accounts.

- Accounts operated as either bots or cyborg accounts should be prohibited from engaging in electoral speech. This prohibition should apply to nationals of nonmember states, but not to nationals of Alliance member states.

The proposed rules for bots and cyborg accounts require little explanation or justification, but one point merits additional comment. Given the general policy favoring unrestricted free speech, readers might ask: "Why ban electoral speech by bots associated with accounts registered to nationals of nonmember states? Why not simply require disclaimers?" Indeed, California recently enacted a law that requires disclaimers for bots used "to influence a vote in an election."[64] The short answer is that most of the documented cases of "good bots" do not involve electoral speech.[65]

A ban on electoral speech by bots associated with accounts registered to nationals of nonmember states will block some malicious bots but will not interfere with the broad range of benign bot applications.

This chapter has presented a fairly detailed proposal for a new transnational regulatory system. Clearly, much work would be required to negotiate a multilateral agreement on the basis of these ideas and then to translate any such agreement into concrete domestic laws and regulations. Even so, the proposal developed in this chapter has sufficient detail to permit both a policy analysis and a constitutional analysis of the proposed system. The next chapter presents a policy analysis, weighing the likely costs and benefits of the proposed regulatory system. The final chapter addresses potential First Amendment objections that would likely be raised in the United States.

CHAPTER SEVEN

POLICY ANALYSIS
Weighing Costs and Benefits

THE LAST CHAPTER PRESENTED a proposal for transnational regulation of social media to protect Western democracies from Chinese and Russian information warfare. This chapter contends that, on balance, the benefits of the proposed transnational regulatory regime outweigh the costs. The analysis assumes that the proposed system—if implemented into U.S. law by means of appropriate legislation—would be constitutionally valid.

Two key assumptions underlie the cost-benefit analysis in this chapter. First, I assume that the problem of democratic decay is a significant problem. Chapter 1 defended that assumption, but it is impossible to prove the truth of that claim. Readers who do not accept the first assumption would likely conclude that the costs of the proposed transnational regulatory system outweigh the benefits. Second, I assume that foreign threats to liberal democracy—and, in particular, the threats posed by China and Russia—are significant factors contributing to the problem of democratic decay. Previous chapters defended that assumption. It bears emphasis that many causal factors contribute to the problem of democratic decay and there is no good way to measure the relative contribution of different factors. Readers who believe that domestic threats to liberal democracy are far more salient than foreign threats might also conclude that the costs of the proposed transnational regulation outweigh the benefits. (As discussed in the preface, the insurrection at the Capitol on January 6, 2021, tends to strengthen the argument that domestic threats are more salient than foreign threats.)

Accordingly, the argument in this chapter is directed toward a target audience who agree that democratic decay is a significant problem and that foreign threats to liberal democracy are significant causal factors contributing to that problem. If those two assumptions are correct, it follows almost inexorably that Chinese and Russian information warfare constitutes a significant threat to liberal democracy. Clearly the category of foreign threats to liberal democracy is broader than just information warfare (see figure 3 in chapter 1). Nevertheless, there is a broad consensus among relevant experts that Chinese and Russian information warfare is one of the most salient foreign threats—if not the most salient foreign threat—to liberal democracy. This chapter assumes that the expert consensus is correct. The analysis of costs and benefits proceeds from that premise.

The argument unfolds as follows. First, I contend that exclusive reliance on industry self-regulation is a misguided approach and that government regulation of social media is essential to protect Western democracies from Chinese and Russian information warfare. Next, I explain why government regulation, to be even minimally effective, must address organic posts on social media—not just paid advertisements—and must be preventative, not merely reactive. The subsequent section demonstrates that the rule banning Chinese and Russian agents from regulated social media platforms, and the associated disclaimer rules, would yield substantial benefits with very few offsetting costs. The chapter then evaluates the proposed social media registration system, focusing first on the potential benefits of that system. The last two sections analyze the potential downsides of the registration system, including the concern that implementation would be too administratively burdensome, and the argument that the system invites abuse because governments would take advantage of registration information to infringe the privacy rights of social media users.

THE NEED FOR GOVERNMENT REGULATION

Libertarians may argue that the proposed transnational regulatory system is undesirable because all government regulation of speech is bad. This argument does not withstand close scrutiny. Consider the classic example of a person who yells "fire" in a crowded theater. That type of speech is subject to criminal prosecution in almost every country because it poses a clear danger to the other people in the theater. The criminal prohibition on such speech is a type of government speech regulation that is universally accepted as beneficial. More broadly, as Cass Sunstein has demonstrated, government regulation of speech is pervasive in the United States. In his words: "Government is permitted to regulate computer viruses, unlicensed medical advice, attempted bribery, perjury, criminal conspiracies . . . threats to assassinate the president, blackmail . . . criminal solicitation . . . child pornography, violations of the copyright law, false advertising . . . and much more."[1] Reasonable people may disagree about how to draw the line between good and bad regulation, but government regulation of speech will not disappear.

Internet libertarians may concede this point. They argue that the internet is different from other communications media and that government regulation of cyberspace is unwarranted.[2] Again, this claim does not withstand close scrutiny. First, it bears emphasis that cyberspace, and in particular social media, is already heavily regulated. In 1996, Congress added section 230 to Title 47 of the U.S. Code.[3] Section 230 created new legal rules for companies that operate "interactive computer services." In particular, the statute grants social media companies immunity from civil liability for content that social media users post on their platforms.[4] Many internet libertarians approve of section 230 because it limits the liability of large technology companies.[5] Like it or not, though, there can be no dispute that section 230 qualifies as government regulation of the internet.

Although the government regulates internet speech with a fairly light touch, private regulation of speech on social media is pervasive. Jack Goldsmith and Andrew Woods note that "significant monitoring and speech control are inevitable components of a mature and flourishing internet."[6] Facebook promulgates "community standards" that regulate speech on Facebook.[7] Similarly, Twitter has enacted "Twitter rules and policies"[8] and YouTube has developed "community guidelines."[9] These are all forms of speech regulation. They are functionally equivalent to laws enacted by the government because they involve general rules governing the conduct of private parties.[10] The most significant difference between Facebook's community standards and government regulation of speech on social media is the identity of the lawmaker. Thus, arguments for or against regulation of speech on social media miss the point. Properly framed, the key question is: What is the appropriate mix of private regulation and government regulation?

In addressing this question, it is helpful to distinguish between rulemaking and rule implementation. First, consider rulemaking. The United States Constitution establishes a system of democratic self-governance, in which "We the People" make the laws that govern our conduct through our elected representatives. Lawmaking by elected legislators is consistent with fundamental principles of democratic self-governance because democratically elected legislators are accountable to the people. In contrast, lawmaking by private companies like Facebook and Twitter is antithetical to basic principles of democratic self-governance because the corporate executives and employees who formulate "community standards" and "Twitter rules" are neither democratically elected nor accountable to the people who are governed by their "platform laws."[11] Therefore, insofar as internet libertarians prefer private lawmaking to public lawmaking, their position is antithetical to the core principles of democratic self-governance that lie at the heart of our constitutional order. Of course, the choice between public and private lawmaking is not an all-or-nothing proposition. Even if Congress enacts additional legislation to regulate social media, the companies are free to supplement federal laws with their own platform laws. As a general rule, though, public lawmaking is preferable to private lawmaking because democratically elected legislators are accountable to the people.

Note that the preceding argument is *not* an argument against industry self-regulation. The platform laws enacted by Facebook, Twitter, and YouTube differ fundamentally from traditional forms of industry self-regulation. Rules promulgated by the New York Stock Exchange (NYSE), for example, govern companies listed on the NYSE,[12] but they do not directly govern every individual who buys and sells stock. In contrast, social media companies do not enact platform laws to regulate themselves: they enact platform laws to regulate the billions of social media users who use their products. Hence, with respect to the targets of regulation, platform laws have more in common with laws enacted by governments than they do with traditional forms of industry self-regulation.

Some people may contend that rulemaking by private companies is preferable because companies are not constrained by the First Amendment, whereas government regulators are constrained by the Constitution. The idea is that private companies may be able to create more socially beneficial rules because they are not hamstrung by constitutional limitations. I will say more about the First Amendment in the next chapter. At present, suffice to say that an interpretation of the First Amendment that prevents Congress from enacting socially beneficial laws to regulate social media is constitutionally suspect. The First Amendment should not be construed to create a constitutional straitjacket that prevents Congress from regulating social media because Congress, unlike private companies, is accountable to the American people, and the Framers adopted the Constitution for the express purpose of empowering the federal government to enact laws to "promote the general welfare."[13]

If we shift our focus from rulemaking to rule implementation, the picture is more complex. Any practical system for regulating harmful content on social media necessarily involves public-private collaboration. To quote Goldsmith and Woods again, social media "platforms have engaged in strategic collaboration with the federal government, including by sharing information, to fight foreign electoral interference."[14] After revelations emerged about Russian interference in the 2016 presidential election, Facebook created an information operations team that is "tasked with detecting, and then thwarting, coordinated disinformation campaigns" that originate from foreign countries.[15] The team includes "several dozen former intelligence operatives." They rely partly on current government officials to provide "tip-offs about suspect behavior." When making decisions about how best to respond to foreign disinformation campaigns, Facebook considers the "geopolitical impact" of its decisions.

The information operations team "regularly passes information on to law enforcement and governments."[16]

Thus, when it comes to rule implementation, the current system for defending against information warfare involves a substantial amount of public-private collaboration. Companies engage in such collaboration because they know that the effort to counter information warfare has significant foreign policy implications, and they recognize that governments have greater expertise and greater institutional competence regarding foreign policy than do social media companies. However, the current ad hoc system is not very effective in countering foreign threats to democracy because it is largely reactive, not proactive. Absent an effective registration system, foreign cyber troops will continue to be able to create fictitious user accounts more quickly and inexpensively than social media companies can block and detect such accounts: it is a game of whack-a-troll that the companies cannot win.[17]

In addition to the whack-a-troll problem, the current system of informal, public-private collaboration creates three substantial problems. First, because the system lacks transparency, we do not know the extent to which information sharing between companies and governments infringes the privacy rights of social media users. Second, although Facebook collaborates with the U.S. government to address threats to American democracy, it is unclear whether, or to what extent, Facebook and other companies engage in similar collaboration with France, Germany, Italy, and other constitutional democracies to address foreign threats to their countries. Third, the current system relies heavily on the goodwill of private companies, some of which are much less willing to devote their resources to fighting disinformation. For example, after the 2020 presidential election, alternative social media sites like Parler attracted users by promising that they would *not* follow Facebook's and Twitter's examples of labeling false claims by outgoing president Trump.[18]

The proposed transnational regulatory system would ameliorate all of these problems. It would solve the whack-a-troll problem by shifting the attack/defense ratio in favor of defenders. It would provide clear, transparent rules for information-sharing between companies and governments in all Alliance member states. It would replace the current hodge-podge of ad hoc practices that vary by platform with an agreed set of rules that apply equally to all regulated social media platforms. It would codify protections for data security and informational privacy to protect social media users. Finally, domestic legislation and regulations implementing the transnational rules could help structure the appropriate division of labor between governments and industry based on considerations of comparative expertise and comparative institutional competence.

WHAT KIND OF GOVERNMENT REGULATION?

The federal government's primary response to Chinese and Russian information warfare has been to impose sanctions on individuals and on the Russian government. Sanctions have an expressive value in conveying U.S. condemnation of information warfare activities by foreign cyber troops. However, sanctions have very little value in deterring or preventing future information warfare activities. Members of Congress have introduced legislation to regulate paid political advertisements on social media. Such legislation, if enacted, could be helpful, but it does not address the root of the problem. As discussed previously, paid political advertisements are merely the tip of the iceberg. During the 2016 U.S. presidential election, "the most far reaching IRA activity [was] in organic posting, not advertisements."[19]

Assuming that Chinese and Russian information warfare poses a significant threat to liberal democracy, neither government sanctions nor regulation of paid political advertisements is an adequate response. We need transnational regulation of organic posts on social media, along the lines discussed in the last chapter. This section highlights the shortcomings of both government sanctions and legislative proposals to regulate paid political advertisements.

Government Sanctions

The Trump administration filed criminal charges against numerous Chinese defendants for cyber-espionage and related offenses.[20] However, as of this writing, the U.S. government has not filed any criminal charges against Chinese individuals for exploiting social media to conduct information warfare. Accordingly, this section focuses on sanctions against Russian defendants.

In December 2016, President Obama announced a set of tough sanctions in response "to significant malicious cyber-enabled activities . . . in view of the increasing use of such activities to undermine democratic processes."[21] The executive order froze the assets of five named Russian entities and four named Russian individuals. The order also delegated authority to the secretary of the treasury to freeze the assets of other persons responsible for cyber-enabled activities that, among other things, have "the purpose or effect of interfering with or undermining election processes or institutions."[22] Congress subsequently enacted legislation that made it difficult for President Trump to remove those sanctions.[23] After President Obama imposed sanctions, activity on social media by Russia's Internet Research Agency (IRA) actually "increased and covered a widening range of public policy issues."[24] Indeed, "[t]he highest peak of IRA ad volume on Facebook is in April 2017." Moreover, "IRA posts on Instagram and Facebook increased substantially after the [2016 presidential] election, with Instagram seeing the greatest increase in IRA activity."[25] Thus, it is clear that sanctions imposed by President Obama did not deter or prevent Russian cyber troops from conducting information warfare.

In his capacity as special counsel, Robert Mueller filed three separate indictments charging a total of twenty-six Russian individuals and three Russian entities with various federal crimes. In February 2018, a federal grand jury "returned an indictment charging 13 Russian nationals and three Russian entities . . . with violating U.S. criminal laws in order to interfere with U.S. elections and political processes."[26] One of the Russian entities entered an appearance to contest the charges. However, according to the Mueller report, "the other defendants remain at large."[27] In July 2018, the government charged twelve Russian military intelligence officers with computer hacking and related offenses. According to the Mueller Report: "As of this writing, all 12 defendants remain at large."[28] In June 2018, the government also charged a Russian national named Konstantin

Kilimnik as a co-defendant of Paul Manafort.[29] According to ABC News, as of February 2019, "Kilimnik has not entered a plea, and remains out of reach of U.S. officials."[30] In sum, virtually all of the Russian defendants indicted by Robert Mueller are beyond the jurisdictional reach of U.S. criminal process. Moreover, it is very unlikely that any of them will actually be punished because Russia has little or no incentive to extradite Russian citizens to the United States. The threat of criminal punishment is not an effective deterrent because Russian cyber troops have high confidence that their government will not allow them to be subjected to criminal punishment in the United States.

Next, consider sanctions targeted at the Russian government. After Russia illegally annexed Crimea in March 2014 (which was legally recognized as Ukrainian territory), the United States joined with other Western democracies to impose tough multilateral sanctions on Russia.[31] Most international relations experts agree that multilateral sanctions are more effective than unilateral sanctions. Nevertheless, there is virtually no chance that Ukraine will regain control over Crimea in the foreseeable future, because Russia has evidently decided that the benefits of annexation outweigh the cost of sanctions.

Although Russian cyber troops have engaged in information warfare directed against several western European countries,[32] neither the EU nor any individual EU country has imposed sanctions on Russia in response to Russia's information warfare activities. (The EU did impose sanctions on six senior Russian officials in response to the poisoning of Alexei Navalny.[33]) The United States imposed unilateral sanctions against Russia in response to Russian information warfare activities in the United States.[34] However, those sanctions have had no discernible effect in deterring or preventing Russia from continuing to engage in information warfare. If the United States could persuade European allies to join in imposing multilateral sanctions for information warfare, those sanctions might be more effective. However, it seems unlikely that multilateral sanctions for information warfare would be any more effective than multilateral sanctions related to the annexation of Crimea because—as in the case of Crimea—Vladimir

Putin probably believes that the benefits of information warfare outweigh the cost of sanctions.

Proposals to Regulate Paid Political Advertisements

Several members of Congress have introduced legislation to regulate paid political advertisements on social media. For example, in May 2020, Congresswoman Anna Eshoo introduced the "Banning Microtargeted Political Ads Act."[35] The draft legislation is laudable for several reasons, but it does not specifically address the problem of Chinese and Russian information warfare.

The most significant proposal that specifically addresses information warfare is the "Honest Ads Act," first introduced by Senators Klobuchar, Warner, and McCain in October 2017.[36] (Senators Klobuchar, Graham, and Warner reintroduced the Honest Ads Act in May 2019.[37]) The stated purpose of the draft legislation is "to enhance the integrity of American democracy and national security by improving disclosure requirements for online political advertisements."[38] The legislation purposefully builds on the 2002 Bipartisan Campaign Reform Act, which established "disclosure requirements for political advertisements distributed from a television or radio broadcast station or provider of cable or satellite television."[39] The Honest Ads Act, if enacted, would constitute a helpful first step in protecting American democracy from Chinese and Russian information warfare. However, the scope of the legislation is excessively narrow because it focuses exclusively on paid advertisements and ignores the much bigger problem of organic posts on social media.

According to a finding in the Honest Ads Act, "between June 2015 and May 2017, Russian entities purchased $100,000 in political advertisements, publishing roughly 3,000 ads linked to fake accounts associated with the Internet Research Agency."[40] Compare these figures to the data on organic posts. In 2017, the IRA had an operational budget of $12.2 million.[41] In the context of the 2016 U.S. presidential election, the IRA generated more than 8 million posts on Twitter, more than 116,000 posts on Instagram, and more than 67,000 posts on Facebook.[42] The IRA's organic posts on Instagram "garnered almost 185 million likes."[43] In sum, "[t]he most far reaching IRA activity is in organic posting, not advertisements."[44] In military jargon, the IRA uses organic posts as "force multipliers" to magnify the harmful effects of its information warfare activities.

Legislation to regulate paid political advertisements, without also regulating organic posts, is like performing surgery on the finger of a heart attack victim. Even if the victim hurt his finger as a result of the heart attack, surgery on the finger will not address the root cause of the problem. Similarly, legislation that targets paid political advertisements does not address the root cause of the harm resulting from information warfare. To provide meaningful protection from Chinese and Russian information warfare, legislation and regulations must directly confront organic posting activity by blocking creation of fictitious user accounts and impostor accounts.

THE BENEFITS (AND COSTS) OF THE PROPOSED BAN AND DISCLAIMER REGIME

Under the transnational regulatory system described in the previous chapter, the ban and the disclaimer regime complement each other. The proposed ban applies to a broad class of speech (all speech on social media) by a small group of speakers: those who are acting as agents of the Chinese or Russian governments, or the Chinese Communist Party. The proposed disclaimer regime applies to a narrow category of election-related speech transmitted by a much larger group of speakers: those who are registered as citizens or nationals of states that are not Alliance members.

Recall that disclaimers would say something like: "This message was posted by a person who is a citizen or national of a nondemocratic state." The benefit of such disclaimers is both obvious and noncontroversial. U.S. citizens have a clear interest in knowing that a social media post related to a U.S. election was posted by a citizen or national of a nondemocratic state. Similarly, citizens of other liberal democracies have a clear interest in knowing that a social media post related to an election in their countries was posted by a citizen or national of a nondemocratic state. By providing information about the source of a message, disclaimers help people evaluate the reliability and persuasiveness of the claims made in that message.

Readers may question whether disclaimers are effective. The evidence is mixed. After the 2020 U.S. presidential election, BuzzFeed News reported that "the labels Facebook has been putting on false election posts from President Donald Trump have failed to slow their spread across the platform."[45] However, the evidence acquired from long experience with cigarette warning labels is more reassuring. The federal government has required warning labels on cigarette packages since 1965.[46] Congress mandated new labels in 1984 and again in 2009 because then-current data indicated that the old labels "had little effect on public awareness . . . and that a new informational remedy may now be necessary."[47] The prevalence of smoking in the United States has decreased markedly since 1965. One scholar reports: "The empirical evidence on graphic warning labels— though mixed—suggests that they may be reasonably effective. Studies have found that graphic warning labels may reduce overall rates of smoking."[48] Some people will invariably ignore disclaimers attached to messages on social media. Even so, the evidence from cigarette warnings indicates that disclaimers would have some positive effect in warning social media users about the dangers of information warfare. As noted in the last chapter, warnings that change appearance to reduce habituation capture the attention of recipients more effectively than static warnings.[49]

Readers may ask: "If we have disclaimers, why do we need a ban? Couldn't we just require disclaimers for messages transmitted by Chinese and Russian agents?" The next chapter addresses this question in detail by analyzing three possible variants of a "disclaimer-only" system. The analysis demonstrates that there is no practical way to design a disclaimer-only regime that would be even minimally effective in combatting information warfare by Chinese and Russian cyber troops. Both bans and disclaimers require a registration system: if social media users do not register by nationality, then it is not possible to apply either a ban or a disclaimer that is based on nationality. Creation and implementation of a transnational registration system in which social media users register by nationality will be costly and administratively cumbersome. To justify the cost and

administrative burden, the system must be reasonably effective in countering Chinese and Russian information warfare. "Reasonably effective"
means that the system significantly reduces the effectiveness of Chinese
and Russian information warfare tactics by altering the attack/defense
ratio. A "disclaimer-only" system would not pass that test.

Evaluating whether the "disclaimer plus ban" system is reasonably effective requires a two-level analysis. The first level of analysis is tactical:
to what extent would the combination of a ban and disclaimers reduce
the effectiveness of Chinese and Russian information warfare tactics? That
analysis hinges on the effectiveness of the registration system and associated anti-circumvention measures, which are designed to make it more
costly and time-consuming for Chinese and Russian cyber troops to create fake accounts. The second level of analysis is strategic: to what extent
would an effective defense against information warfare help halt or reverse
democratic decay? Even if the "disclaimer plus ban" system reduced the
effectiveness of Chinese and Russian information warfare tactics to zero
(which is an unrealistic goal), the benefits would not justify the costs unless the regulatory system actually helped halt or reverse democratic decay.
Let us consider each level of analysis separately.

Tactical Analysis: Reducing the Effectiveness of Information Warfare

Part One demonstrated that Chinese and Russian cyber troops utilize
social media both overtly and covertly to conduct information warfare.
Blocking overt uses of social media is easy. The ban on Chinese and Russian agents would be almost 100 percent effective in blocking overt uses
of social media—that is, cases in which the operator of a social media
account identifies himself as a Chinese or Russian agent at the account
creation stage. The exemption for benign state agents would allow some
Chinese and Russian agents to operate overt accounts, but only if Alliance
members decide to grant an exemption. Moreover, the exemption would
be revocable at any time if the account is misused.

The previous chapter identified seven distinct circumvention strategies
that Chinese or Russian agents could employ in an effort to operate covert accounts and evade the regulatory system.[50] Consider each technique

separately. Without a registration system, the cheapest and easiest strategy for foreign cyber troops is to create *fictitious user accounts*. Facebook reports that its automated "detection systems help us prevent millions of attempts to create fake accounts every day."[51] Facebook reports that it blocked 1.7 billion attempts to create fake accounts in the first quarter of 2020 and 1.5 billion attempts in the second quarter of 2020.[52] Unfortunately, Facebook's reporting does not distinguish among bots, fictitious user accounts, and impostor accounts. Even so, it is fair to assume that the vast majority of fake accounts blocked by Facebook and other social media companies are bots, because it is much easier for companies to identify bots than it is to identify impostors or fictitious users.[53] Facebook tacitly admits that it is not very good at identifying impostors or fictitious users: "We estimate that fake accounts represented approximately 5% of our worldwide monthly active users (MAU) on Facebook during Q2 2020."[54] Five percent of 2.7 billion monthly active users is 135 million fake accounts. The vast majority of those 135 million fake accounts are probably fictitious user accounts because, under the current system, it is essentially cost-free for cyber troops to create fictitious user accounts.

Assuming that Alliance member states have complete and accurate information about their own citizens and nationals, the registration system would make it virtually impossible for foreign cyber troops to create fictitious user accounts because governments would detect and block those accounts before they are created. (It is fair to assume that Alliance member states do have complete, accurate information about their own nationals because most OECD countries, and most countries in the world, have a national ID card.[55]) The registration system has two potential loopholes in this respect. Foreign cyber troops could potentially bribe government officials to get them to approve a fictitious user account. Or, government officials could mistakenly approve a fictitious user account by relying on inaccurate information, or just by doing sloppy work. Regardless, the registration system would make it much more costly and time-consuming for Chinese and Russian cyber troops to create fake accounts by making it almost impossible to create fictitious user accounts. Cyber troops would presumably respond by creating other types of fake accounts. However, for the reasons explained in the following paragraphs, the other options available to them are either less effective or more costly and difficult to implement.

Next, consider *impostor accounts* and *rental accounts*. Chinese cyber troops have created numerous impostor accounts by hacking and/or stealing accounts initially created by other people.[56] They have also created rental accounts by purchasing accounts from other people.[57] The registration system includes specific provisions to address duplicate accounts.[58] Those provisions would make it much more difficult for Chinese and Russian cyber troops to create impostor accounts from scratch. The proposed regulatory system does *not* include features that would make it more difficult to hack or steal accounts initially created by others. (The best way to address that tactic is to induce ordinary social media users to implement improved cybersecurity measures.) However, when cyber troops create hacked or stolen accounts they often leave an electronic trail that increases the risk of detection. The proposed regulatory system addresses the problem of rental accounts by imposing criminal penalties on citizens or nationals of Alliance member states who rent or sell their accounts to others. If such penalties are enforced effectively, they will make it much more difficult for Chinese and Russian cyber troops to obtain rental accounts because the threat of criminal punishment will greatly reduce the number of people who are willing to rent or sell their accounts.

Assuming that Chinese and Russian cyber troops succeed in creating some impostor and rental accounts, they can operate those accounts in precisely the same way that they currently operate fictitious user accounts. In particular, insofar as impostor or rental accounts are registered under the nationality of an Alliance member state, they will not be subject to disclaimers. Even so, the system as a whole would make it much more costly and difficult for Chinese and Russian cyber troops to create fake accounts because: (1) under the current system, it is much cheaper and easier to create fictitious user accounts than it is to create impostor or rental accounts; (2) the registration system effectively blocks the creation of fictitious user accounts, thereby forcing foreign cyber troops to pursue the more costly and time-consuming alternative of establishing impostor or rental accounts; and (3) the attempt to create impostor and/or rental accounts, whether successful or not, will expose foreign cyber troops to an increased risk of detection.

If Alliance member states implement a regulatory system along the lines described in the previous chapter, it would still be fairly easy and inexpensive for Chinese and Russian cyber troops to create *fake foreign national accounts*. However, governments and social media companies could adopt technical measures to help detect fake foreign national accounts. Moreover, such accounts would be subject to disclaimer requirements for electoral speech. With disclaimers attached, fake foreign national accounts would be relatively ineffective weapons in the information warfare arsenal, compared to fictitious user, impostor, and rental accounts.

Cyber troops could try to evade the ban on Chinese and Russian agents by providing truthful information about their nationalities when they register for social media accounts, but claiming falsely that they are not state agents. However, as discussed previously, any person who registers as a Chinese or Russian national who is not a legal resident of an Alliance member state would be legally presumed to be a state agent.[59] That presumption is rebuttable, but the presumption would effectively block this particular circumvention strategy.

The proposed transnational regulatory system includes special rules that would make it very difficult for Chinese and Russian cyber troops to utilize bots to conduct information warfare.[60] All accounts operated as bots would have to be registered as a national of either an Alliance member state or a nonmember state. To operate a bot account registered as a national of a member state, cyber troops would have to successfully create an impostor account or a rental account. For the reasons discussed previously, the proposed regulatory system makes that difficult (but not impossible). If cyber troops manage to register successfully as a national of an Alliance member state, the account would still have to be declared as a bot account. Bots registered to nonmember states would be subject to special disclaimers (for all messages) and would be prohibited from engaging in electoral speech. In the aggregate, these rules would significantly impair the ability of Chinese and Russian cyber troops to exploit bots to conduct information warfare.

The final circumvention strategy available to Chinese and Russian cyber troops is to create social media accounts on platforms that do not qualify as "regulated social media platforms." The proposed regulatory system addresses this issue by defining a "regulated social media platform" to include all social media platforms with more than fifty million monthly active users outside of Russia and China. Platforms below that threshold are poor vehicles for information warfare because messages disseminated on such platforms have limited reach. As discussed previously, WeChat presents special problems for the proposed regime. In working out the details of the regulatory system, Alliance member states would have to confront squarely the trade-offs between capturing WeChat as a regulated platform or excluding it from the regime. A decision to exclude WeChat would mean that Chinese and Russian agents could exploit the platform to conduct information warfare.

In sum, assuming that Alliance member states do a reasonably competent job implementing the proposed transnational regulatory system, the system would significantly reduce the effectiveness of Chinese and Russian information warfare tactics by substantially increasing the cost and difficulty involved in exploiting social media to conduct information warfare.

Strategic Analysis: Information Warfare and Democratic Decay

Assuming that the proposed regulatory system would significantly impair the effectiveness of Chinese and Russian information warfare tactics, the benefits would still not justify the costs unless the regulatory system actually helped halt or reverse democratic decay. The evidence summarized in Part One demonstrates that Chinese and Russian information warfare contributes to the problem of democratic decay. Unfortunately, though, there is no analytically rigorous way to measure the degree to which information warfare contributes to democratic decay. Instead, this section summarizes a variety of anecdotal evidence suggesting that Chinese and Russian information warfare makes a substantial contribution to the problem.

Let us begin with an analogy. Chapter 5 demonstrated that organized social media manipulation (OSM) contributes to democratic decay because OSM is used to spread disinformation and to heighten both cognitive and affective polarization. Disinformation and polarization are analogous to chicken pox for the body politic. If a person has chicken pox, scratching the rash spreads the infection. When Chinese and Russian cyber troops engage in information warfare, they are scratching the itch and spreading the "pox" of disinformation and polarization. Foreign cyber troops did not create those problems. Even if China and Russia never conducted information warfare, Western democracies would still be afflicted by the twin problems of disinformation and polarization. Ultimately, to solve those problems, we must address the underlying causes. However, just as it is hard for a person to cure his chicken pox if a third person is repeatedly scratching his sores, it is difficult for liberal democracies to address the twin problems of disinformation and polarization if foreign actors are exacerbating those problems by repeatedly scratching the sores. Banning Chinese and Russian cyber troops from regulated social media platforms would make it much more difficult for them to scratch the itch, thereby making it easier for liberal democracies to address the homegrown sources of disinformation and polarization.

Assuming that the proposed regulatory regime would significantly reduce the effectiveness of Chinese and Russian information warfare tactics, would that regime also help halt or reverse democratic decay? Chapter 2 contended that an impartial observer could reasonably conclude that it is more likely than not that, absent Russian information warfare, Hillary Clinton would have won the 2016 election. If Russian information warfare did indeed help elect Donald Trump as president, then Russia clearly had a significant impact on democratic decay in the United States. As president, Donald Trump has disseminated a huge amount of disinformation about a variety of topics.[61] He has also personally contributed to increased polarization in the United States. The U.S. score on V-Dem's liberal democracy ("libdem") index dropped dramatically from .814 in 2016 to .700 in 2019. After the 2016 election, *The Economist* downgraded the United States from a "full democracy" to a "flawed democracy."[62] Even if the

Russians did not swing the election in favor of Donald Trump, information warfare clearly weakens democracy in the United States by increasing doubts about the integrity of the electoral process. According to a survey conducted in 2020, "77% of Americans expect that a foreign country will spread false information about candidates this year . . . [and] six in 10 of them say it's hard to tell the difference between what's true and what isn't."[63] If liberal democracies institute an effective ban on Russian and Chinese cyber troops, we could avert or mitigate these types of harms in future electoral cycles.

Chapter 3 demonstrated that Russian information warfare has adversely affected European democracies. The Bakamo study of French social media indicates that almost one-quarter of the French electorate inhabits its own informational echo chamber that is heavily influenced by Russian disinformation. The cognitive polarization of French social media users poses a significant long-term threat to the health of French democracy. Russia has also used information warfare and other foreign influence operations to support the rise of far-right political parties in France, Sweden, and other European democracies.[64] The growing political strength of far-right parties poses a threat to liberal democracy domestically; it also threatens the liberal internationalist project of European integration. RT and Sputnik's advocacy for the Leave campaign—using both traditional media and social media—may have had a significant impact on the Brexit vote in the United Kingdom.[65] Moreover, the Brexit campaign "exacerbated the social and cultural division about the merits of EU membership that already existed in British society" before the referendum.[66] An effective ban on Russian cyber troops could help reduce polarization within European countries and counter the growth of far-right political parties who threaten both liberal democracy and liberal internationalism. An effective ban could also help preserve popular support for both NATO and the EU: two institutions that are essential building blocks for the liberal international order.

As discussed in chapter 4, the Chinese Communist Party (CCP) places great value on its "discourse power." Chinese state media companies have developed a huge presence on Facebook and Twitter (see table 3).

Those companies make a substantial contribution to the CCP's growing discourse power, which it deploys to undermine the liberal international order. China exploits its control over WeChat to extend its surveillance system to the Chinese diaspora community and to censor communications between politicians in liberal democracies and their ethnic Chinese constituents.[67] China has exploited Facebook to conduct information warfare and interfere with democratic elections in Taiwan. Moreover, many China analysts agree that Chinese information warfare will pose a greater threat in the future as Chinese cyber troops become increasingly sophisticated in using covert social media accounts to conduct information warfare. Banning Chinese agents from regulated social media platforms would help counter China's growing discourse power and mitigate the threat that Chinese information warfare poses to liberal democracy and the liberal international order.

The main costs associated with banning Chinese and Russian agents from regulated social media platforms are the costs of the registration system, which is necessary to make the ban effective. Implementation of the transnational regulatory system involves significant administrative costs, both for governments and for companies. If ongoing Chinese and Russian information warfare is an important causal factor contributing to democratic decay, then the benefits of the ban and related measures outweigh the costs. However, if the main causes of democratic decay lie elsewhere—and Chinese and Russian information warfare is, at most, a minor contributing factor—then the costs of the proposed transnational regulatory system probably outweigh the benefits. To reiterate, the insurrection at the Capitol on January 6, 2021, shows that domestic OSM is a significant factor contributing to democratic decay, but it does not prove that Chinese and Russian information warfare is an insignificant factor.

THE BENEFITS AND COSTS OF A SOCIAL
MEDIA REGISTRATION SYSTEM

When I speak with people about the idea of creating a registration system for social media users, some people claim that the very idea is "fascist" or "anti-American." In fact, though, licensing and registration systems are neither illiberal nor anti-democratic: they are pervasive in the United States and in other modern liberal democracies. Most countries in the world—including most liberal democracies—already operate national registration systems because they issue national ID cards.[68] In the United States, all fifty states and the District of Columbia operate licensing/registration systems for barbers and cosmetologists.[69] Similarly, all fifty states and the District of Columbia operate licensing/registration systems for city bus drivers, emergency medical technicians, pest control applicators, school bus drivers, truck drivers, and vegetation pesticide applicators.[70] Governments require licenses for these and many other professions to protect the public from the potential dangers posed by unlicensed bus drivers, barbers, etc.

Like bus drivers and barbers, the job of "internet troll" or "information warrior" has now become a routinized profession. "Like many jobs, these positions come with pay scales, performance bonuses, organizational hierarchies, office politics, and paper work to fill out."[71] China reportedly employs as many as two million people in its so-called "50-cent party." Collectively, they generate about 448 million social media posts per year (most of which are intended primarily for domestic consumption).[72] Between about 2013 and 2017, Russia's Internet Research Agency "employed and trained over a thousand people to engage in round-the-clock influence operations."[73] In light of everything we know about Chinese and Russian information warfare, it is clear that the risks associated with unlicensed cyber troops are much greater than the risks associated with unlicensed barbers or bus drivers. (Granted, poor bus drivers can potentially kill people, but cyber troops cause ongoing, widespread harm to our entire political system.) Therefore, given that the main benefit of government licensing and registration systems is to protect the public from danger, the potential benefits of an effective social media registration system (measured by the risks averted) are much greater than the benefits associated with state-run professional licensing systems.

Of course, a comprehensive registration system for social media users would have to cover billions of people around the globe. The overall scope of the project would be comparable to India's Aadhaar cards, which the

Unique Identification Authority of India has issued to more than 1.25 billion people.[74] Hence, the costs associated with a global social media registration system are much greater than the costs associated with state professional licensing requirements in the United States. Broadly speaking, those costs can be divided into three categories: administrative costs and burdens; risks to the privacy of social media users; and potential infringement of free speech rights. While the next chapter will address free speech issues, the next section of this chapter addresses privacy issues. This section addresses administrative costs and burdens. First, though, this section analyzes the benefits of a social media registration system.

The Benefits of a Social Media Registration System

The primary benefit of a social media registration system is clear. The registration system, together with the ban and disclaimer regime, would provide Western democracies a reasonably effective preventative defense against information warfare. Conversely, without a social media registration system, liberal democracies cannot and will not have an effective, preventative defense against information warfare. None of the available alternatives comes close to providing the type of preventative defense that a properly functioning registration system would offer. Government sanctions against foreign cyber troops will not deter or prevent continued information warfare because those cyber troops are beyond the reach of the criminal jurisdictions of Western democracies. Government sanctions against foreign countries will not deter or prevent information warfare because Russia, China, and other states have determined that the benefits of information warfare outweigh the rather small cost of sanctions. Media literacy efforts have achieved notable success in some countries.[75] However, in the United States—where roughly 30 percent of the population gets most of its news from the "right-wing media ecosystem"[76]—even a very successful media literacy campaign will have limited utility as long as Fox News, Breitbart, and others continue to disseminate disinformation to millions of people. Government sanctions and media literacy efforts can provide valuable complements to a social media registration system, but they are not viable substitutes.

Social media companies—especially Facebook and Twitter—have made admirable efforts to provide the United States with a national defense against information warfare.[77] (It is unclear whether, or to what extent, those U.S. companies have performed a similar public service for other Western democracies.) Judging by the early reports from the 2020 U.S. elections, it appears that the companies' efforts have been at least partially successful. Facebook has arguably done more than any other major social media company to combat information warfare. Even so, as Facebook itself admits, "fake accounts represented approximately 5% of our worldwide monthly active users (MAU) on Facebook during Q2 2020."[78] Five percent of 2.7 billion monthly active users is 135 million fake accounts. A system that permits 135 million fake accounts to remain operational does not provide an effective, preventative defense against information warfare.

In contrast, the transnational regulatory system described in the last chapter—of which the registration system is an essential component—would provide a reasonably effective defense against information warfare, assuming that governments implement the system in a competent fashion. The system as a whole would virtually eliminate fictitious user accounts. Chinese and Russian cyber troops would not be able to operate bots overtly because the ban would preclude them from registering as Chinese or Russian agents. Foreign cyber troops could operate fake foreign national accounts, but all electoral speech on such accounts would be subject to disclaimers. Foreign cyber troops could also operate bots as subsidiary accounts linked to fake foreign national accounts. However, such bot accounts would be barred from engaging in electoral speech, and other (nonelectoral) speech would be subject to disclaimers to warn social media users that they are receiving a bot-generated message. Chinese and Russian cyber troops could evade disclaimer requirements by creating impostor accounts or rental accounts. However, compared to the current system of purely private regulation, the proposed transnational regulatory system would make it much more difficult and costly for cyber troops to create and operate impostor accounts and rental accounts.

In addition to providing an effective, preventative defense against information warfare, the proposed transnational regulatory system would offer two other significant benefits. Recall that information warfare is an activity that lies at the intersection of foreign influence operations (FIOs) and organized social media manipulation (OSM). The proposed Alliance for Democracy, once established, would provide a useful institutional framework for Alliance member states to cooperate to address threats posed by other types of FIOs—such as covert financing of political parties and political candidates—that do not depend on social media.[79] Similarly, the proposed registration system, once established, would provide an essential building block for countering the threat posed by domestic OSM campaigns that spread disinformation.[80] Both FIOs and domestic OSM campaigns undermine democracy and contribute to the problem of democratic decay. Thus, the registration system and the Alliance for Democracy would help liberal democracies protect themselves from other threats to democracy, in addition to the threat of information warfare.

Administrative Costs and Burdens

Some readers may wonder whether the challenge of negotiating a multilateral agreement among forty countries poses an insurmountable obstacle, given the technical complexity of the subject matter. I can say from personal experience that I have participated in the successful negotiation of other multilateral agreements involving matters of comparable technical complexity. Strong U.S. leadership and political will are the keys to successful negotiation.

The idea of creating a global registration system for all social media users seems, at first glance, to entail an unimaginably complex administrative challenge. However, given the private registration systems operated by all social media companies, the national ID systems operated by most national governments, and the more decentralized ID system that currently exists in the United States, we already have the essential building blocks of a comprehensive, global registration system for social media users. The additional administrative steps needed to implement the proposed system are fairly simple and not terribly burdensome.

To assess the level of administrative burden, it is helpful to consider three groups separately: governments with national ID cards, governments without national ID cards, and private companies. As of 2017, "at least 170 of the world's nearly 200 countries have some kind of a national ID card or are implementing one. Included in this number are twenty-eight of the thirty-four" OECD countries.[81] The vast majority of OECD countries are liberal democracies.[82] Thus, most of the national governments in the world, including most of the countries that qualify as liberal democracies, already operate national registration systems. As a practical matter, the existence of those national registration systems means that it would be an extremely simple administrative task for most Alliance member states to check the identifying information provided by social media users who register as nationals of their states to confirm that they are not fictitious users.

Although the United States does not operate a national registration system, the REAL ID Act of 2005 requires every state to maintain a "State motor vehicle database" with identifying information about all residents with driver's licenses or other state ID cards. It also requires all fifty states to "provide electronic access to all other States to information contained in the motor vehicle database of the State."[83] As of September 10, 2020, "all 50 states are now in full compliance" with the REAL ID Act.[84] Thus, although the statute does not create a national database or a national registration system, the network of fifty state databases that now exists as a result of the REAL ID Act means that, as a practical matter, it is a very simple administrative task to create a system that would enable the FBI to check the identity of all social media users who register as U.S. citizens or nationals to confirm that they are not fictitious users. (I recognize that many critics fear the privacy implications of the REAL ID Act. I address those concerns in the next section.)

As discussed previously, a federal statute creating the registration system would need to grant FBI officials access to the database of USCIS numbers maintained by the Department of Homeland Security, and the database of passport information maintained by the Department of State, and the database of state driver's license numbers maintained by all fifty states under the REAL ID Act. Although it would be more administratively efficient to create a single national database, a proposal to create such a database would likely generate substantial political opposition. I assume that other Alliance member states that do not have national ID cards could develop a similar decentralized approach so that those governments could efficiently and effectively screen account registration information to identify fictitious users.

For all governments—including those with and without national ID systems—the process of investigating accounts that appear initially as duplicate accounts would be slightly more cumbersome than the process of screening for fictitious users.[85] However, the task of investigating duplicate accounts would be no more difficult or time-consuming than the current, informal process of public-private collaboration that governments and social media companies use to identify fake accounts. For all governments, the most costly element of the system would be the installation of secure, dedicated communication links to permit rapid, secure transmission of data between governments and social media companies. Even so, the cost of installing such communication links is a tiny fraction of the money that most governments spend on national security.

What about the burden on private companies? The registration system would require companies to collect user information, check for duplicate accounts, report account registration information to national governments, and block fictitious user accounts identified by national governments. These steps can be easily automated; the burden on companies would be very slight. Companies would need to process appeals from users who claim that they were mistakenly identified as fictitious users; such appeals may impose a modest burden on companies. However, companies are already handling similar appeals and there is no reason to believe that the system would increase the number or frequency of such appeals. The enhanced data protection requirements described in the previous chapter—in particular, the requirement to use data hashing to store account registration information—would impose a greater burden on companies. However, that burden is justified because data hashing will protect personally identifiable information in cases where hackers gain unauthorized access to a company database with account registration information.

Undoubtedly, the most burdensome requirement for companies is the requirement to attach disclaimers to election-related speech. Every

Alliance member state would need to develop its own definition of "electoral speech." Assuming that the definitions might refer to something like a "clearly identified candidate" for elective office,[86] the application of those definitions would change with each electoral cycle. Thus, to identify the electoral speech that is subject to disclaimers, companies would need to develop different algorithms for each Alliance member state and update those algorithms for each new electoral cycle. The task of developing and updating those algorithms would clearly entail a substantial amount of work. However, the time and effort needed to perform those tasks would likely be a fraction of the time and effort companies currently devote to content moderation functions.[87] Moreover, the registration system would successfully block many "bad" users at the account creation stage. Thus, assuming that a relatively small number of bad users create a disproportionately large amount of work for content moderators, the system could potentially yield substantial savings for companies by reducing the amount of time and effort companies devote to moderating content posted by bad users.

The proposed regulatory system would require all social media platforms to enable individual users to classify their accounts or profiles as "public" or "private" at the account creation stage. As discussed earlier, Type A platforms already do this, so the proposed rule would not impose any new burden on them. (See pp. 66–67 on the distinction between Type A and Type B platforms.) However, the rule would require Type B platforms, including Facebook, to make some operational changes. In order for the registration system to function effectively, Type B platforms would have to modify their account creation procedures so that individuals would decide at the account creation stage whether to make their accounts public or private. This requirement would impose a modest cost on Facebook and other Type B platforms.

Finally, critics may object that the burden of regulatory compliance will weigh most heavily on small social media companies that do not have the resources available to Google and Facebook. My proposal addresses this objection by restricting application of the rules to social media platforms with more than fifty million registered users. The threshold of fifty million users will ensure that the system does not create unrealistic demands for small companies that do not have sufficient resources to implement the regulatory requirements.

PRIVACY AND ANONYMITY

Almost every month, it seems, we receive more news about how governments and technology companies are invading our privacy. In June 2013, the *Guardian* published a story based on information leaked by Edward Snowden, which disclosed that Verizon was providing the National Security Agency (NSA) "on an ongoing daily basis . . . all call detail records . . . created by Verizon for communications (i) between the United States and abroad; or (ii) wholly within the United States, including local telephone calls."[88] In March 2018, we learned that Cambridge Analytica "harvested private information from the Facebook profiles of more than 50 million users without their permission" and exploited that data to support Donald Trump's 2016 election campaign.[89] In January 2020, the *New York Times* reported: "Every minute of every day, everywhere on the planet, dozens of companies—largely unregulated, little scrutinized—are logging the movements of tens of millions of people with mobile phones and storing the information in gigantic data files."[90]

Perhaps most troubling are reports that federal, state, and local law enforcement authorities exploit social media to target disfavored groups. Al Jazeera reported in fall 2020 that the U.S. military was "purchasing private information gathered from apps around the world," with a special emphasis on apps that are popular among Muslims.[91] U.S. Customs and Border Protection (CBP) "continuously monitors social media sites using web-based platforms." CBP created a "surveillance target list . . . [that] featured journalists, activists, social media influencers and lawyers working on immigration issues."[92] It is not hard to imagine how the Trump administration might have used such a list to target its perceived political enemies. In summer 2020, when protests erupted in response to police killings of black men and women, an artificial intelligence firm named Dataminr "helped law enforcement digitally monitor the protests that swept the country . . . tipping off police to social media posts with the latest whereabouts and actions of demonstrators."[93]

In light of these examples, critics might object: "Why do you want to create a social media registration system that would explicitly authorize companies and the federal government to collect even more data about social media users? Given widespread concerns about violations of privacy rights, we should be limiting the amount of data they collect, not expanding data collection programs."

This is a powerful objection to the proposal to create a social media registration system. In response, I would emphasize three key points. First, the proposed registration system offers substantial benefits, as explained previously. Second, the system is designed to provide the greatest possible protection for data security and user privacy. Existing threats to user privacy are troubling. The proposed registration system would not exacerbate any of those threats and could potentially ameliorate some of the problems associated with the current system. Third, critics may be concerned that the government will simply violate statutory or regulatory rules that restrict government access to user data. Granted, in the past, government agents have exploited legal ambiguities and loopholes to pursue very aggressive data collection efforts.[94] The best way to mitigate that problem is to draft rules that establish clear, bright-line limits on the government's authority to retain and utilize data disclosed to the government under the social media registration system. If the rules are ambiguous, government agents will construe their authority broadly. If the rules establish clear limits, the vast majority of government officers will respect those limits, and those who violate clear statutory rules can be held accountable.

The remainder of this section addresses, separately, concerns about violation of privacy rights (1) by social media companies and (2) by government actors. First, though, let us briefly consider the right to anonymous speech on social media.

The Right to Anonymous Speech

Many social media users prefer to speak anonymously. The Supreme Court has stated that "an author's decision to remain anonymous . . . is an aspect of the freedom of speech protected by the First Amendment."[95] Critics may object that the proposed rules infringe the individual right to speak anonymously. In fact, the rules would not impose any restrictions on the right to speak anonymously in the public sphere, although they would require individuals to disclose more detailed personal information to social media companies (and indirectly to the government).

Under current rules, social media users who want to communicate anonymously must disclose identifying information to social media companies to create an account. An Instagram customer, for example, who chooses to appear publicly as "Doctor J," must provide certain identifying information to create the account.[96] The proposed rules would still allow that individual to appear publicly on Instagram as "Doctor J." The individual would be required to provide more detailed personal information to Facebook when the account is created, but disclosure of information to the company would not affect the individual's right to communicate anonymously with other Instagram users. Moreover, the proposed rules explicitly preclude companies from sharing information with the government that would enable the government to ascertain Doctor J's true identity.[97] Therefore, social media users who want to preserve anonymity in relation to the government would be able to do so.

Violation of Privacy Rights by Social Media Companies

The proposed rules would affect users' privacy by requiring disclosure of more detailed personal information to social media companies. However, it bears emphasis that technology companies already collect huge amounts of information about social media users.[98] As the *New York Times* reports: "Personal data has become the most prized commodity of the digital age, traded on a vast scale by some of the most powerful companies in Silicon Valley and beyond.[99] Given the nature of modern digital technology, companies may already know more about customer "John Doe" than some of his closest friends know about him. In light of the vast quantity of personal information already collected by social media companies, the additional disclosure of nationality, passport numbers, and/or driver's license numbers would have at most a negligible impact on user privacy.

Granted, the risk that hackers may gain unauthorized access to private information held by social media companies is a serious concern. However, the proposed rules, if enacted, would substantially reduce that risk by requiring companies to implement enhanced data security measures—including data hashing—to protect account registration information. Therefore, the proposed rules would actually enhance protection for personally identifiable information retained by social media companies.

Notwithstanding the enhanced data security measures, some social media users may still be reluctant to disclose personally identifiable information. Under the proposed rules, social media users could avoid such disclosure by registering for a private account rather than a public account. Individuals with private accounts could still use social media to communicate with friends and family. Hence, social media users who place a high value on privacy could protect their privacy by opting to create private accounts.

Violation of Privacy Rights by Governments

Perhaps the biggest concern about the proposed registration system is the fear that governments will exploit account registration information to monitor the social media activity of innocent social media users. In the United States, the Electronic Communications Privacy Act (ECPA) addresses this concern by limiting the government's power to intercept electronic communications[100] or to gain unauthorized access to electronic communications after they have been stored.[101] The proposed regulations would add several additional protections for people who register as citizens or nationals of Alliance member states. These include: a rule requiring governments to destroy account registration information after they have confirmed that a particular account is neither a fictitious user account nor an impostor account; a rule prohibiting governments from using account registration information for any purpose other than to determine whether a particular account is a fictitious user account or an impostor account; a rule prohibiting companies from disclosing information to governments that would enable governments to determine the true identity of a person who operates an account under a pseudonym (subject to other applicable laws); and a rule that bars companies from sharing information with governments about subsidiary accounts or private accounts. With these rules in place, it is difficult to imagine how governments could exploit account registration information to spy on innocent social media users. Granted, nothing in the proposed rules bars government access to public communications by social media users who operate accounts under their real names. In that respect, though, the proposed rules merely preserve the status quo.

In the majority of countries that already operate national ID systems, governments would not gain access to any personally identifiable information beyond what they already have stored in their national ID databases. Governments would learn one new piece of information about their citizens—that Jane Doe, for example, has a Facebook account. Even so, given the rules summarized in the preceding paragraph, it is difficult to see how that additional piece of information raises any legitimate privacy concerns.

In the United States, the FBI would gain access to personally identifiable information beyond what is authorized under current laws and regulations. In order to perform its verification functions, the FBI would need access to (1) the database of USCIS numbers maintained by the Department of Homeland Security, for noncitizens who register as U.S. nationals; (2) the database of passport information maintained by the Department of State, for citizens who choose to disclose their passport numbers; and (3) the various state motor vehicle databases maintained by all fifty states under the REAL ID Act, for citizens who choose to disclose their driver's license numbers (see table 6 in the previous chapter).

Privacy advocates are likely to object, in particular, to rules granting the FBI access to state motor vehicle databases.[102] Under current law, the Driver's Privacy Protection Act (DPPA) prohibits "a State department of motor vehicles, and any officer, employee, or contractor thereof," from knowingly disclosing "personal information . . . about any individual obtained by the department in connection with a motor vehicle record."[103] This prohibition bars state officers from disclosing personal information to federal officers, but there is an exception that authorizes disclosure "for use by any government agency [including a federal agency] . . . in carrying out its functions."[104] Rules implementing the proposed registration system would effectively override the prohibition on disclosing personal information to the FBI by mandating disclosure in certain cases. Even so, for the reasons noted previously, the safeguards built into the registration system would effectively preclude FBI officers from exploiting that information to infringe the legitimate privacy rights of innocent social media users.

Under the Trump administration, some states resisted sharing information about undocumented immigrants from state motor vehicle databases with federal agencies responsible for immigration enforcement.[105] Under the proposed registration system, undocumented immigrants could register for public social media accounts as nationals of their home countries, or they could register for private accounts. In neither case would social media companies be required or authorized to share account registration information with the FBI, so there would be no occasion for the FBI to query state databases about undocumented immigrants. Moreover, the REAL ID Act explicitly envisions that states may issue "a driver's license or identification card that does not satisfy the requirements of" the act.[106] As of this writing, thirteen states have taken advantage of this provision to authorize issuance of driver's licenses for undocumented immigrants that do not comply with the REAL ID Act.[107] Although the statute is not entirely clear on this point, it appears that states are free to store information about noncompliant licenses separately from the motor vehicle databases that they are required to maintain under the REAL ID Act. Thus, even if federal agents searched state motor vehicle databases in ways that the social media registration system did not authorize, states could prevent them from discovering information about undocumented immigrants by storing that information separately.

Finally, as discussed earlier in this chapter, the current system for detecting covert social media accounts operated by foreign cyber troops relies heavily on informal information sharing between the FBI and social media companies.[108] Under the current informal system, we simply do not know whether, or to what extent, the personal information of innocent social media users is being compromised, because the entire information-sharing process lacks transparency. The proposed registration system could potentially enhance protection for user privacy by formalizing the rules governing disclosure of personal information to the FBI, and codifying statutory protections for the personally identifiable information of social media users who register as nationals of Alliance member states.

CHAPTER EIGHT

THE FIRST AMENDMENT

THIS CHAPTER ASSUMES THAT Congress will enact a statute to implement the transnational regulatory system described in chapter 6. For convenience, I will refer to that hypothetical statute as the Defending American Democracy Act, or simply DADA. I assume that DADA would (1) prohibit Chinese and Russian agents from creating or operating accounts on regulated social media platforms (the "ban"), subject to exemptions for benign state agents; (2) require disclaimers for all public communications on regulated social media platforms that qualify as "electoral speech" and that are transmitted by citizens or nationals of states that are not Alliance members; and (3) create a registration system requiring social media users to register their accounts, declare their nationalities, and provide identifying information to social media companies, and requiring companies to share account registration information with the U.S. government for all users with public accounts who claim U.S. nationality.[1]

Given Donald Trump's current power within the Republican Party, and his disdain for those who fear foreign interference in U.S. elections, it seems unlikely that many Republicans would support DADA in the near term. However, Trump will not control the Republican Party forever, and DADA's main purpose aligns well with more traditional Republican foreign policy positions. Therefore, although congressional enactment of DADA seems unlikely in the near term, a First Amendment analysis of DADA is not merely of academic interest.

This chapter demonstrates that DADA is constitutionally defensible. Current Supreme Court doctrine is shaped by deep divisions between what I call Madisonian and libertarian theories of the First Amendment.[2] The chapter begins by outlining the key differences between Madisonian and libertarian perspectives. To be transparent, I acknowledge that my sympathies lie with the Madisonian theory. Among other things, that theory is consistent with the original understanding of the Constitution, as reflected in the writings of James Madison. However, the Court's recent First Amendment jurisprudence has moved in a decidedly libertarian direction. The Court's libertarian tendencies are tempered by a respect for precedent and a commitment to the principle that "[p]roper respect for a coordinate branch of the government requires that we strike down an Act of Congress only if the lack of constitutional authority to pass the act in question is clearly demonstrated."[3] Although doctrinaire libertarians would certainly argue that the proposed ban is unconstitutional, the more moderate libertarians who sit on the Supreme Court might well be persuaded to uphold its validity.

After explaining key differences between Madisonian and libertarian theories, the chapter briefly considers the question: Whose constitutional rights are at stake? Then, the remainder of the chapter presents a First Amendment analysis of DADA in three parts. Those three parts, respectively, address the disclaimer provisions, the registration system, and the ban on Russian and Chinese agents. Each part discusses key Supreme Court precedents that advocates on both sides might invoke when debating the constitutionality of specific features of DADA. The analysis shows that all three elements of DADA would pass constitutional muster if one views the Court's First Amendment doctrine through a Madisonian lens. If one views that doctrine through a libertarian lens, the outcome of constitutional litigation is more difficult to predict. The Court's moderate libertarian justices would almost certainly uphold the disclaimer requirements and would probably uphold the registration system. Finally, there are sound constitutional arguments the government could advance that might, or might not, persuade moderate libertarian justices that the ban is constitutionally valid.

MADISONIAN AND LIBERTARIAN THEORIES

The following sketch of Madisonian and libertarian theories presents ideal types. None of the current Supreme Court justices fits precisely into either the Madisonian or libertarian mold, although former justice Kennedy was fairly consistent in his libertarian leanings, and Justice Breyer's jurisprudence fits well with the Madisonian model. Leading Madisonian First Amendment scholars, such as Robert Post and Cass Sunstein, may not agree with every position I ascribe to the Madisonian theory. Leading libertarian scholars, such as Randy Barnett, may not agree with every position I ascribe to the libertarian theory. Nevertheless, this contrast between Madisonian and libertarian theories helps frame the terms of the constitutional arguments that would likely be presented if Congress enacted legislation along the lines I have proposed.

Madisonians and libertarians disagree about four key issues that influence their views about the First Amendment. First, they disagree about the central purpose of the First Amendment. Madisonians believe that the central purpose of the Constitution as a whole is to establish a system of democratic self-government rooted in the principle of popular sovereignty. The First Amendment, in their view, is designed to promote and facilitate active participation by citizens in the system of democratic self-government. In the words of Robert Post, the First Amendment was designed to promote democratic self-governance by helping "to forge a living connection between the people and their representatives" and by establishing "a chain of communication . . . to sustain the popular conviction that representatives spoke for the people whom they purported to represent."[4] In the words of Ashutosh Bhagwat, "the Speech, Press, Assembly, and Petition Clauses [of the First Amendment] together enable a form of active, participatory citizenship" that he calls "democratic citizenship."[5]

In contrast to this positive view of First Amendment rights, libertarians emphasize the negative function of the First Amendment as a constraint on governmental power. From a libertarian perspective, "[f]reedom of speech is based in large part on . . . a distrust of governmental determinations of truth and falsity, an appreciation of the fallibility of political leaders, and a somewhat deeper distrust of governmental power in a more general sense."[6] Libertarian scholar Randy Barnett argues that "We the People" who adopted the Constitution "is not a collective entity, but an aggregate of particular individuals."[7] In his view, the Bill of Rights, which includes the First Amendment, was intended to prevent the government from interfering with the natural, pre-political rights of individuals. In sum, Madisonians believe that individual liberty flourishes when people participate actively in a political community. Libertarians believe that individual liberty flourishes when the government steps aside and avoids interfering in the private sphere.

The second key distinction between Madisonians and libertarians relates to trust in our elected representatives. Madisonians generally trust the legislative process to produce good laws that promote the public welfare. In Federalist Number 10, Madison extolled the virtues of a legislative body composed of elected representatives "whose wisdom may best discern the true interest of their country and whose patriotism and love of justice will be least likely to sacrifice it to temporary or partial considerations."[8] Of course, Madisonians recognize that elected legislators are not infallible. However, they believe we should generally trust the government to promote the common good because the Constitution protects individual liberty by dividing power between the federal government and the states, by limiting the powers of all three branches of the federal government, and by preserving the right of citizens to choose their elected representatives in periodic elections. In contrast, libertarians have a much more skeptical view of the wisdom and altruism of elected legislators. They tend to see governments—including legislative bodies composed of elected representatives—as a threat to the liberty of individual citizens. From a libertarian perspective, courts provide an essential check on the unfortunate tendency of elected legislators to enact laws that impose unwarranted restrictions on the natural rights of citizens, which are enshrined in the Bill of Rights.[9]

The third key difference between Madisonian and libertarian theories relates to the division of power over "constitutional construction." Courts and other actors engage in constitutional interpretation when they examine the semantic meaning of constitutional text to answer questions of constitutional law. They engage in "constitutional construction" when they look beyond the semantic meaning of the text because they have a practical need to answer a disputed question of constitutional law, and the text is too vague or ambiguous to provide a definitive answer.[10] Libertarians generally favor a system of "judicial supremacy," in which the federal courts are the final decision-makers regarding contested constitutional issues, including disputes about the proper construction of the First Amendment. Libertarians ultimately place their faith in the judicial branch to settle disputed questions of constitutional law by engaging in constitutional construction.[11]

In contrast, Madisonians are wary of vesting too much power in unelected judges to settle contested questions of constitutional construction. In Madison's words, "the Judicial Department also may exercise or sanction dangerous powers beyond the grant of the constitution; and consequently . . . the ultimate right of the parties to the constitution, to judge whether the compact has been dangerously violated, must extend to violations . . . by the judiciary, as well as by the executive or the legislature."[12] Madison's view that the "parties to the constitution" have the "ultimate right" to settle disputed questions of constitutional construction is consistent with the modern theory of "popular constitutionalism."[13] In contrast to judicial supremacists, who think courts should have the final say, popular constitutionalists believe that "We the People" should have the final say regarding disputed constitutional issues because the Constitution vests ultimate sovereignty in the people of the United States.[14] According to Larry Kramer, the leading academic proponent of popular constitutionalism, "We the People" decide contested questions of constitutional construction through our elected representatives in the legislative and executive branches.[15] Thus, whereas libertarians place their faith in unelected judges to settle contested questions of constitutional construction, popular constitutionalists believe that the power of constitutional construction is, or should be, divided among the legislative, executive, and judicial branches. The view that all three branches share responsibility for constitutional interpretation and constitutional construction is known as "departmentalism."

Doctrinally, the distinction between judicial supremacy and departmentalism manifests as a tension between more and less deferential forms of judicial review. Courts generally distinguish between three tiers of scrutiny: rational basis review, intermediate scrutiny, and strict scrutiny. If a law is subject to strict scrutiny, the government must prove that it is "narrowly tailored to achieve a compelling interest."[16] If a law is subject to intermediate scrutiny, the government must show that the law is "substantially related to the achievement of important governmental objectives."[17] If a law is subject to rational basis review, the government need only show that it is "rationally related to a legitimate government interest."[18] Libertarians tend to favor more aggressive judicial review—namely, strict scrutiny—in part because they trust the judiciary and distrust the legislature.[19] Madisonians tend to favor more deferential judicial review—either intermediate scrutiny or rational basis—especially with respect to laws that are intended to enhance the process of democratic self-government, in part because they trust the legislature and distrust the judiciary.[20]

The final key distinction between Madisonians and libertarians relates to the marketplace of ideas. In his famous dissenting opinion in *Abrams v. United States*, Justice Holmes said: "But when men have realized that time has upset many fighting faiths, they may come to believe . . . that the ultimate good desired is better reached by free trade in ideas—that the best test of truth is the power of the thought to get itself accepted in the competition of the market."[21] Holmes himself was no libertarian. In fact, he was a leading critic of the libertarian philosophy that shaped the Supreme Court's Fourteenth Amendment jurisprudence (but not its First Amendment doctrine) in the early twentieth century.[22] Even so, modern libertarians have appropriated Holmes's "marketplace of ideas" metaphor to develop and defend a constitutional vision based on the assumption that truth will prevail over falsehood in an unregulated marketplace of ideas. Based partly on this assumption, libertarian judges have construed the Constitution generally, and the First Amendment specifically, in a manner that shields private markets from unwanted government regulation.[23]

In contrast to libertarians, modern Madisonians are skeptical about claims that truth inevitably prevails over lies in an unregulated marketplace of ideas. They worry that foreign interference, malicious lies spread to promote a partisan political agenda, and disparities in wealth and power among various groups of speakers tend to distort the marketplace of ideas in ways that systematically weaken deliberative democracy and prevent the triumph of truth over falsehood. Therefore, Madisonians believe that government regulation is necessary to help correct systemic defects in the marketplace of ideas.[24]

WHOSE CONSTITUTIONAL RIGHTS ARE AT STAKE?

It is well established that foreigners outside the United States have no constitutional rights. As early as 1891, the Supreme Court ruled that the Constitution "can have no operation in another country."[25] Although the Court has extended constitutional protections to U.S. citizens residing in foreign countries,[26] it reaffirmed in 2020 that it is "settled as a matter of American constitutional law that foreign citizens outside U.S. territory do not possess rights under the U.S. Constitution."[27] In *Boumediene v. Bush*, the Court recognized a very narrow exception for aliens detained at the U.S. naval base in Guantanamo Bay, Cuba.[28] However, Russian and Chinese agents located outside the United States cannot seriously maintain that the First Amendment protects their right to speak on social media.

On the other hand, numerous Supreme Court decisions dating back several decades support the proposition that the First Amendment protects the right of U.S. citizens and residents to receive information from foreign speakers.[29] For example, in *Stanley v. Georgia*, the Court asserted that the "right to receive information and ideas, regardless of their social worth, is fundamental to our free society."[30] Justice Marshall's opinion in *Stanley* cited, among other cases, *Lamont v. Postmaster General*, where the Court affirmed the First Amendment right of citizens to receive "communist political propaganda" sent from a foreign country.[31] The right of citizens to receive information from foreigners is not so broad that it requires the government to admit foreigners into the United States,[32] but allowing speech and permitting physical entry are two very different things.

In light of the above, the answer to the question "whose rights are at stake" depends upon which aspect of DADA is under consideration. The disclaimer regime primarily affects the First Amendment rights of U.S. companies because it requires companies to attach disclaimers to certain messages. The registration system primarily affects the First Amendment rights of U.S. citizens as speakers because it requires them to disclose identifying information to the government and to obtain government permission before they can operate public social media accounts. The ban on Chinese and Russian agents primarily affects the rights of U.S. citizens as listeners because the First Amendment does not protect the rights of Chinese and Russian agents as speakers—at least, not those located outside the United States. The exemption for benign state agents protects the First Amendment rights of U.S. listeners by enabling them to receive the speech of some Chinese and Russian agents, while also avoiding bombardment by Chinese and Russian cyber troops engaged in information warfare.

ARE DISCLAIMERS CONSTITUTIONAL?

DADA's disclaimer rule would require regulated social media companies to attach disclaimers to all public communications on their platforms sent by citizens or nationals of nonmember states that qualify as "electoral speech." In the United States, "electoral speech" would be defined to include two types of messages: (1) those that encourage eligible voters not to vote; and (2) those that refer to a "clearly identified" candidate for federal office that are transmitted within 120 days before the relevant election. Under current federal election law, the term "clearly identified" means that "the name of the candidate involved appears; a photograph or drawing of the candidate appears; or the identity of the candidate is apparent by unambiguous reference."[33] The required disclaimers would say something like: "This message was posted by a person who is a citizen or national of a nondemocratic state."

The requirement for social media companies to attach disclaimers to electoral speech is a type of compelled speech. The Supreme Court has consistently held that the First Amendment protects "both the right to speak freely and the right to refrain from speaking at all."[34] Hence, social media companies could potentially challenge the disclaimer requirement on the grounds that it infringes their First Amendment right "to refrain from speaking." The disclaimer rule also constitutes a form of compelled speech for citizens and nationals of nonmember states, because disclaimers would be attached to their messages. However, foreign nationals outside the United States are not entitled to First Amendment protections. Therefore, the constitutional challenge would have to come from U.S. social media companies.

In light of existing precedent, the Supreme Court would almost certainly affirm the constitutional validity of the disclaimer requirement. Disclaimer requirements in federal election laws typically require "candidates and other actors in the campaign finance system to disclose their identity in a communication, such as a TV advertisement, mailer, or billboard."[35] In *Citizens United v. Federal Election Comm'n*,[36] plaintiffs challenged the disclaimer and disclosure provisions of the Bipartisan Campaign Reform Act of 2002 (BCRA).[37] BCRA section 201 requires every person who spends more than $10,000 in a calendar year on "electioneering communications" to file a detailed disclosure statement with the Federal Election Commission.[38] BCRA section 311 is a disclaimer requirement. It provides that any "electioneering communication" on radio or television that is *not* authorized by a candidate must include an audio statement specifying that "_____ is responsible for the content of this advertising" and that the blank must "be filled in with the name of the political committee or other person paying for the communication."[39] The Supreme Court in *Citizens United*, by an 8–1 vote, rejected plaintiffs' First Amendment arguments and affirmed the validity of sections 201 and 311.[40]

To understand why the *Citizens United* Court upheld BCRA's disclaimer and disclosure provisions, we must begin with the earlier decision in *Buckley v. Valeo*.[41] The plaintiffs in *Buckley* raised First Amendment challenges to the Federal Election Campaign Act of 1971 (FECA), as amended in 1974. FECA involved detailed disclosure requirements, but did not include disclaimer requirements. The *Buckley* plaintiffs conceded that FECA's disclosure requirements were not "per se unconstitutional."[42] However, they argued that specific disclosure requirements were unconstitutional as applied to certain persons. The *Buckley* Court decided that FECA's disclosure requirements merited more "exacting scrutiny" than mere rational basis review, but did not require strict scrutiny. Instead, the appropriate constitutional test was that FECA's disclosure requirements must bear a "substantial relation" to a "sufficiently important" government interest.[43] The Court in *Citizens United* applied this same test to the disclaimer requirements in BCRA.[44] (This test is functionally equivalent to intermediate scrutiny, but the Court has not applied the term "intermediate scrutiny" to disclosure and disclaimer requirements.)

For present purposes, the key issue in *Buckley* relates to section 434(e), which required "every person (other than a political committee or candidate) who makes contributions or expenditures aggregating over $100 in a calendar year . . . to file a statement with the [Federal Election] Commission."[45] The Court agreed that section 434(e) "raises serious problems of vagueness,"[46] because it required disclosure of "expenditures" and the statutory definition of expenditures was quite broad. A different section of FECA defined "expenditures" to include "the use of money or other valuable assets *'for the purpose of . . . influencing'* the nomination or election of candidates for federal office."[47] The Court emphasized that the ambiguity of the italicized phrase posed constitutional difficulties. However, it avoided those difficulties by adopting a narrowing construction of the statute. Specifically, the Court said: "To insure that the reach of section 434(e) is not impermissibly broad, we construe 'expenditure' for purposes of that section . . . to reach only funds used for communications that *expressly advocate the election or defeat of a clearly identified candidate.*"[48] After *Buckley*, commentators began referring to the distinction between "issue advocacy" and "express advocacy." An advertisement that expressly advocates the election or defeat of a candidate is "express advocacy." Other political advertisements that take stands on policy issues, but that do not expressly advocate the election or defeat of a particular candidate, constitute "issue advocacy."

Congress made comprehensive amendments to FECA in the 2002 Bipartisan Campaign Reform Act (BCRA). BCRA introduced a new term to federal election law. It defined the term "electioneering communication" to mean "any broadcast, cable, or satellite communication which refers to a clearly identified candidate for Federal office," if that communication also satisfies other statutory requirements (discussed below).[49] BCRA included both disclosure and disclaimer provisions that applied to "electioneering communications." The term "electioneering communication," as defined in BCRA, clearly encompassed both express advocacy and some issue advocacy, as those terms were understood after *Buckley*. In *McConnell v. Federal Election Comm'n*, plaintiffs argued that "Congress cannot constitutionally require disclosure of . . . 'electioneering communications' without making an exception for those 'communications' that do not meet *Buckley's* definition of express advocacy."[50] The Court rejected that argument, emphasizing that "*Buckley* makes clear that the express advocacy limitation . . . was the product of statutory interpretation rather than a constitutional command."[51] The Court added that it was not persuaded "that the First Amendment erects a rigid barrier between express advocacy and so-called issue advocacy."[52]

The *McConnell* plaintiffs also challenged the disclaimer provision in BCRA section 311. After the Supreme Court decided *Buckley*, Congress enacted the Federal Election Campaign Act Amendments of 1976 (FECA).[53] The 1976 amendments added disclaimer requirements for political advertisements that constituted "express advocacy," as defined in *Buckley*.[54] BCRA expanded the class of communications for which disclaimers are required by using the term "electioneering communication" to delimit the scope of the disclaimer requirement. Plaintiffs argued that expansion of the disclaimer requirement was unconstitutional for essentially the same reasons that they argued it was unconstitutional to require disclosures for electioneering communications beyond the scope of express advocacy. The Court summarily rejected plaintiffs' challenge to BCRA's disclaimer requirement, referring back to its previous analysis of BCRA's disclosure requirements.[55] The Court emphasized that the disclaimer requirement "bears a sufficient relationship to the important governmental interest of shedding the light of publicity on campaign financing."[56]

Just seven years after its decision in *McConnell*, the Court revisited many of the same issues in *Citizens United v. Federal Election Comm'n*.[57]

In *McConnell*, the Court affirmed the constitutional validity of a statutory rule that prohibited corporations and unions from using "general treasury funds to finance electioneering communications."[58] *Citizens United* overruled that aspect of the *McConnell* decision, holding that corporations have First Amendment rights, and that the ban on corporate expenditures for electioneering communications violated those rights.[59] However, the Court in *Citizens United* reaffirmed *McConnell*'s holding that BCRA's disclosure and disclaimer provisions are constitutionally valid.[60]

The rationale of *McConnell* and *Citizens United*—insofar as those decisions address disclaimer rules—strongly supports the constitutional validity of DADA's disclaimer requirement for foreign nationals who engage in electoral speech on social media. Justice Kennedy, writing for the Court in *Citizens United*, said that "[t]he disclaimers required by § 311 provide the electorate with information and insure that voters are fully informed about the person or group who is speaking."[61] He added that the disclaimer regime "enables the electorate to make informed decisions and give proper weight to different speakers and messages."[62] The same rationale applies to DADA's disclaimer requirement for foreign nationals. When U.S. citizens see a message on social media that refers to a clearly identified candidate for federal office, they deserve to know if that message was transmitted by a citizen or national of a nondemocratic state. By providing that information, the disclaimer requirement enables the electorate to make informed decisions and give proper weight to different speakers. The warning that the message was transmitted by a national of a nondemocratic state helps insure that voters are properly informed about the person or group who is speaking.

If social media companies challenged the DADA disclaimer rule, they might note several distinctions between the BCRA disclaimer rules—which the Court has consistently upheld—and the proposed disclaimer rule in DADA. First, the BCRA disclaimer rule applies only to paid political advertisements.[63] In contrast, the DADA disclaimer rule applies not just to paid political advertisements but also to organic posts on social media. Challengers might argue that the attempt to expand disclaimer requirements to cover organic posts on social media violates the

First Amendment. However, as explained previously, paid political advertisements are merely the tip of the iceberg when it comes to Russian and Chinese information warfare on social media.[64] It is difficult to quantify the relative importance of the two types of messages, but it is fair to say that organic posts constitute at least 90 percent of the problem, whereas paid political advertisements constitute less than 10 percent of the problem. If Congress made a specific factual finding that a rule covering only paid ads, and not organic posts, would fail to address the primary problem—and Congress supported that finding with expert testimony—the Court would lack the institutional competence to second-guess such a finding.

Second, BCRA's disclaimer rule imposes the burden of compliance on candidates, political committees, and others who buy political advertisements, not on the newspapers, television stations, and other media outlets that carry those advertisements.[65] In contrast, the DADA disclaimer rule imposes the burden of compliance on social media companies. The Fourth Circuit Court of Appeals recently held that a Maryland election law violated the First Amendment because it imposed disclosure and disclaimer requirements on "neutral third-party platforms" rather than "direct participants in the political process."[66] One could argue that the proposed DADA rule violates the First Amendment for similar reasons.

This argument might make sense if applied exclusively to paid advertisements. However, it makes little sense when applied to organic posts on social media by foreign nationals, most of whom are not physically present in the United States. The U.S. government has no power to enforce a disclaimer requirement against foreign nationals outside the United States. If the burden of compliance was placed exclusively on them, they could violate the rule with impunity. If Congress has the power to create a disclaimer requirement—which it clearly does—then it must have the power to frame the rule in a manner that is capable of enforcement. Here, the only practical mechanism is to impose the disclaimer requirement on the social media companies themselves. As discussed in the previous chapter, companies could make a reasonable policy argument that the disclaimer requirement imposes an undue administrative burden on social media companies. However, if they fail to persuade Congress on that score, and Congress decides that the public policy benefits of such a requirement outweigh the private burden on social media companies, then a First Amendment argument that the burden outweighs the benefit is unlikely to succeed in court.

Third, the DADA rule requires disclaimers for messages that encourage eligible voters not to vote. Neither FECA nor BCRA includes any comparable provision. Thus, one could argue, the proposed DADA rule is unconstitutional because it expands the scope of disclaimer requirements beyond the BCRA definition of "electioneering communication." However, the Constitution does not prohibit Congress from developing novel solutions to novel problems. During the 2016 presidential election campaign, the Russians made a concerted effort to persuade potential Clinton voters not to vote.[67] There are grounds to believe that Russia's voter suppression effort may have helped swing the election in favor of President Trump in a few key swing states.[68] In light of that evidence, Congress is clearly entitled to protect American democracy by creating statutory rules to counter voter suppression efforts by foreign nationals. The disclaimer rule in DADA, like other disclaimer requirements, is constitutionally valid because it "impose[s] no ceiling on campaign-related activities" and does "not prevent anyone from speaking."[69]

In addition to disclaimers for messages that encourage eligible voters not to vote, the DADA rule also requires disclaimers for messages that refer to a "clearly identified candidate for federal office" that are transmitted within 120 days before the relevant election. The quoted language is copied verbatim from the BCRA definition of "electioneering communication."[70] However, the BCRA rule adds one qualifying limitation that is not included in the proposed DADA rule. Under BCRA, disclaimers are required only for messages that are "targeted to the relevant electorate."[71] A communication is "targeted to the relevant electorate" if it "can be received by 50,000 or more persons" in the state or district the candidate seeks to represent.[72] Thus, challengers might argue that the DADA disclaimer requirement is overbroad, and therefore violates the First Amendment, because it fails to incorporate the targeting requirement.

BCRA's targeting requirement cannot easily be applied to messages transmitted on social media because disclaimers must be applied before a message is sent, not after it has been received. If one views the situation *ex ante*, before a message is sent, then every public communication on social media "can [potentially] be received by 50,000 or more persons" in the relevant state or district: that is simply the nature of the technology. Nevertheless, the proposed DADA rule that disclaimers are required only for "public communications" is functionally similar to BCRA's targeting requirement. Both rules restrict the application of the disclaimer regime so that disclaimers are not required for messages with limited circulation. Therefore, courts would almost certainly reject a First Amendment challenge to DADA based on the idea that DADA fails to incorporate BCRA's targeting requirement.

One final distinction between BCRA and the proposed DADA rule also merits a brief comment. BCRA's disclaimer requirement applies only to communications made within "60 days before a general, special, or runoff election" or "30 days before a primary or preference election, or a convention or caucus of a political party that has authority to nominate a candidate."[73] The specific 60/30 rule is clearly not constitutionally mandated. Nevertheless, to avoid potential First Amendment problems, and to ease the burden on social media companies, it would be advisable for Congress to incorporate some sort of time limitation into the DADA disclaimer requirement. In chapter 6, I suggested a simple 120-day rule for DADA (see p. 158). Regardless of whether DADA includes a 60/30 rule like BCRA, or a simpler 120-day rule, courts would be unlikely to find a constitutional violation as long as Congress places a reasonable time limitation on the disclaimer requirement.

In sum, despite the libertarian trend in recent First Amendment jurisprudence, Supreme Court decisions in *Buckley*, *McConnell*, and *Citizens United* virtually compel the conclusion that the proposed DADA disclaimer regime is constitutionally valid.

THE REGISTRATION SYSTEM AND COMPELLED DISCLOSURE

Recall that DADA's registration system includes: a distinction between master and subsidiary accounts; a distinction between public and private accounts; mandatory disclosure requirements for all public accounts; a requirement for social media companies to share account registration information with relevant government officials (but only for master accounts and only for public accounts); procedures for government officials to verify that newly registered accounts are neither fictitious user accounts nor impostor accounts; and various privacy and data security measures. I believe the DADA registration system would survive a First Amendment challenge. However, the constitutional argument in favor of the registration system is not a slam dunk. This section analyzes the constitutionality of the registration system as applied to adult natural persons who are U.S. citizens because they would likely have the strongest First Amendment claims against DADA.

The Supreme Court has held that the First Amendment protects the right of individuals to speak anonymously. For example, in *McIntyre v. Ohio Elections Comm'n*, the Court invalidated an Ohio election law that prohibited the circulation of anonymous leaflets related to political campaigns.[74] The Court said that "an author's decision to remain anonymous, like other decisions concerning omissions or additions to the content of a publication, is an aspect of the freedom of speech protected by the First Amendment."[75] Challengers might argue that DADA's registration system violates the First Amendment right to speak anonymously by requiring individuals to disclose their names and other identifying information directly to companies and indirectly to the federal government. However, that argument would fail. DADA protects anonymous speech by segregating account registration information from other information, limiting information sharing between companies and the federal government so that the government sees only account registration information, and restricting the government's authority to use that information for anything other than a narrowly defined purpose. In fact, DADA strengthens federal protection for the right to speak anonymously. Under current law, social media companies are free to make their own rules, and some companies prohibit anonymous speech on their platforms.[76] In contrast, DADA would require companies to allow individuals to use pseudonyms for public communications on social media.

Although DADA fully protects the right to anonymous speech, DADA's mandatory disclosure requirements raise a different issue. The Court has long recognized that compelled disclosure of the type required by DADA, "has the potential for substantially infringing the exercise of First Amendment rights."[77] In *Nat'l Assoc. for the Advancement of Colored People v. Alabama*, the Court held that Alabama violated the rights of individual NAACP members by ordering the association "to reveal to the State's Attorney General the names and addresses of all its Alabama members and agents."[78] Crucial to the Court's reasoning was the finding that "on past occasions revelation of the identity of its rank-and-file members has exposed these members to economic reprisal, loss of employment, threat of physical coercion, and other manifestations of public hostility."[79]

Building on this precedent, plaintiffs in *Buckley v. Valeo* challenged the compelled disclosure requirements in the Federal Election Campaign Act (FECA) "as they apply to minor parties . . . because the . . . danger of significant infringement on First Amendment rights is greatly increased" when minor parties are compelled to disclose information.[80] As noted previously, the Court held that the law would survive constitutional scrutiny if the government demonstrated a "substantial relation" between the compelled disclosure requirements and "sufficiently important" government interests.[81] The Court identified three important government interests, two of which are particularly relevant for present purposes. "First, disclosure provides the electorate with information as to where political campaign money comes from and how it is spent."[82] Second, "record-keeping, reporting, and disclosure requirements are an essential means of gathering the data necessary to detect violations" of other FECA rules.[83] The Court conceded that there could be a future case, similar to *NAACP v. Alabama*, "where the threat to the exercise of First Amendment rights is so serious and the state interest furthered by disclosure so insubstantial that the Act's [compelled disclosure] requirements cannot be constitutionally applied."[84] However, the Court said, "no appellant in this case has tendered record evidence of the sort proffered in *NAACP v. Alabama*." Therefore, "on this record, the substantial public interest in disclosure . . . outweighs the harm generally alleged."[85]

Six years after *Buckley*, the Court reconsidered the application of compelled disclosure rules to a different minor party. In *Brown v. Socialist Workers '74 Campaign Committee*, the Socialist Workers Party challenged the disclosure requirements of the Ohio Campaign Expense Reporting Law.[86] The Ohio law required "every political party to report the names and addresses of campaign contributors and recipients of campaign disbursements."[87] The Court said that "the First Amendment prohibits the government from compelling disclosures by a minor political party" if that party "can show a reasonable probability that the compelled disclosures will subject those identified to threats, harassment, or reprisals."[88] In *Brown*, the Socialist Workers Party presented "substantial evidence of both governmental and private hostility toward and harassment of SWP members and supporters."[89] Therefore, the Court concluded, "in light of the substantial evidence of past and present hostility . . . against the SWP, Ohio's campaign disclosure requirements cannot be constitutionally applied to the Ohio SWP."[90] Three decades later, in *Doe v. Reed*, the Court rejected a First Amendment challenge to a Washington state law because plaintiffs failed to demonstrate a sufficient risk that the law's disclosure requirements would "subject them to threats, harassment, or reprisals."[91]

With this background in mind, let us now consider Madisonian and libertarian arguments for and against DADA's compelled disclosure requirements.

The Madisonian Argument in Favor of Compelled Disclosure

From a Madisonian perspective, *Buckley*'s rationale—which the Court later affirmed in both *McConnell* and *Citizens United*—applies fully to DADA's compelled disclosure requirements. First, *Buckley* said that "disclosure requirements are an essential means of gathering the data necessary to detect violations" of other FECA rules.[92] Similarly, DADA's disclosure requirements are an essential means of gathering the data necessary to ensure that Russian and Chinese agents do not create fictitious user accounts or impostor accounts. Without compelled disclosure requirements for all public accounts on social media, it will continue to be trivially easy for foreign agents to evade detection by creating fictitious user accounts and impostor accounts. Second, *Buckley* said that "disclosure provides the electorate with information" relevant to political campaigns.[93] Similarly, DADA's disclaimer requirement provides the electorate with relevant information: that the speaker is a citizen or national of a nondemocratic state. Moreover, the disclosure requirements are an essential means of gathering the data necessary to apply disclaimers to the appropriate messages. Absent compelled disclosure of nationality, it would be impossible for social media companies to know which messages require disclaimers.

The Court in *Brown* said that "the First Amendment prohibits the government from compelling disclosures" if a person "can show a reasonable probability that the compelled disclosures will subject [that person] to threats, harassment, or reprisals."[94] DADA incorporates numerous safeguards to minimize the risk that any U.S. citizen or national would be subject to "threats, harassment, or reprisals" as a result of compelled disclosure. Compelled disclosure is required only for master accounts and only for public accounts. Companies are required to share account registration information with the government, but they are barred from sharing other information with the government, unless required to do so by some other law. The government is prohibited from using account registration information for any purpose other than to detect fictitious user accounts and impostor accounts. DADA specifically protects the right of individuals to use pseudonyms and prohibits companies from sharing information with the government that would enable the government to link pseudonyms to account registration information. Finally, individuals have the right to avoid compelled disclosure entirely by creating private accounts rather than public accounts. In these circumstances, as the Court said in *Buckley*, "any serious infringement of First Amendment rights brought about by the compelled disclosure . . . is highly speculative."[95]

Additionally, DADA promotes important governmental interests beyond those at stake in *Buckley* and its progeny. First, "[f]oreign interference in the American political system was among the gravest dangers feared by the Founders of our nation and the Framers of our Constitution."[96] In Federalist Number 22, Alexander Hamilton said: "One of the weak sides of republics, among their numerous advantages, is that they afford too easy an inlet to foreign corruption."[97] Similarly, in his farewell address to the nation at the end of his presidency, George Washington warned that "foreign influence is one of the most baneful foes of republican government."[98] The DADA registration system gives the federal government the information it needs to combat foreign interference in our political system. Given the Framers' fears about foreign interference in our democracy, and given that the political branches have greater institutional competence than the judiciary to address threats from hostile foreign powers, Madisonians would argue that the Court should be very hesitant to invalidate a federal law designed to protect the integrity of our democratic system from the threat of foreign interference.

DADA is also designed to promote an important foreign policy objective: helping U.S. allies defend their constitutional democracies against the threat posed by Russian and Chinese information warfare. When Congress and the president cooperate to enact legislation designed to promote important foreign policy goals, the Court has traditionally been extremely hesitant to invalidate that legislation on constitutional grounds. Hence, the Court has often emphasized that, "where foreign affairs is at issue," there is a "practical need for the United States to speak with one voice and act as one."[99] This argument applies with even greater force when—as is the case with DADA and the Alliance for Democracy—the legislation is designed to fulfill the nation's commitments under an international agreement, because a judicial decision invalidating such legislation would embarrass the nation in the conduct of its foreign policy.

The Libertarian Argument against Compelled Disclosure[100]

At least since Edward Snowden revealed details about the National Security Agency's PRISM program in 2013,[101] U.S. citizens have rightly feared that the government is exploiting the internet and associated technologies to conduct surveillance of innocent Americans. Recent reports that a private company funded by Twitter and the CIA "helped law enforcement digitally monitor" Black Lives Matter protesters after the killing of George Floyd reinforce the point that fears of government surveillance are well founded.[102] In light of these fears, DADA's compelled disclosure rules— which require social media companies to share account registration information with the federal government—would likely induce many social media users to opt for private accounts, or close their accounts entirely, to avoid supplying private information to the government that can be used for mass surveillance. If large numbers of social media users close their accounts, or switch to private accounts, the public sphere would be deprived of their voices on important public policy issues. That result would be directly contrary to the core First Amendment goal of ensuring that we have a robust, open marketplace of ideas.

The Court in *Buckley* noted that First Amendment violations can occur "even if any deterrent effect on the exercise of First Amendment rights arises, not through direct government action, but indirectly as an unintended but inevitable result of the government's conduct in requiring disclosure."[103] In *Packingham v. North Carolina*, the Court proclaimed that "the Internet in general, and social media in particular," is one of "the most important places . . . for the exchange of views."[104] Libertarians may argue that DADA's compelled disclosure requirements will inevitably deter millions of Americans from exercising their First Amendment right to engage in public communication on social media. Moreover, a law that has the unintended but inevitable consequence of deterring millions of Americans from engaging in public communication on social media violates the First Amendment, even if the deterrent effect is merely an unintended consequence of a law designed to promote other objectives.

DADA's requirement for social media users to disclose their nationalities is reminiscent of the controversy about the Trump administration's decision to reinstate a citizenship question on the 2020 census questionnaire.[105] In evaluating that decision, the Supreme Court noted that "the Census Bureau and former Bureau officials have resisted occasional proposals to resume asking a citizenship question of everyone, on the ground that doing so would discourage noncitizens from responding to the census."[106] Similarly, libertarians may argue, DADA's requirement for all social media users to disclose their nationalities would have a disproportionate deterrent effect on noncitizens and immigrant communities in the United States, because they are especially fearful of government surveillance. Even if DADA explicitly authorizes legal permanent residents to claim U.S. nationality when they register their social media accounts, the compelled disclosure requirement would induce millions of undocumented immigrants to close their social media accounts, or switch to private accounts, to avoid the registration requirement. Thus, the DADA registration system would interfere substantially with the First Amendment rights of immigrants, including U.S. citizens who are friends and family members of undocumented immigrants.

Additionally, libertarians may argue, if other Alliance member states enact laws similar to DADA, then millions of citizens of Alliance member states will also opt for private accounts, or close their social media accounts entirely, because they also fear government surveillance. Indeed, Europeans have generally been more protective of electronic privacy than Americans.[107] The Supreme Court has long held that the First Amendment protects the right of U.S. citizens and residents to receive information from foreign speakers.[108] If millions of Europeans exit U.S. social media platforms, that would interfere with the First Amendment right of U.S. citizens to hear European perspectives on important public policy issues.

Finally, from a libertarian perspective, the First Amendment "is based in large part on . . . an appreciation of the fallibility of political leaders, and a somewhat deeper distrust of governmental power in a more general sense."[109] The combined effect of DADA's compelled disclosure requirements for U.S. nationals—plus the anti-circumvention measures related to fake foreign national accounts, and the rules designed to enable the government to distinguish between "agents" and "nonagents" of the Chinese and Russian governments—would give the U.S. government information about billions of social media users from numerous foreign countries. Information is power. Libertarians would argue that the Court should be deeply skeptical of a law that gives the U.S. government such a huge quantity of information about billions of innocent social media users throughout the world.

Would the Supreme Court Invalidate DADA's Compelled Disclosure Rules? Although the libertarian argument against DADA's compelled disclosure requirements is fairly persuasive, I think the Supreme Court would probably uphold DADA's registration system against a First Amendment challenge—especially if litigants try to prevent implementation before the law takes effect. First, as the Court said in *Buckley*, DADA's "disclosure requirements are an essential means of gathering the data necessary" to implement the disclaimer regime.[110] For the reasons explained previously, DADA's disclaimer regime is almost certainly constitutionally valid. Moreover, it would be impossible to implement the disclaimer regime without collecting information about the nationality of every social media user with a public account because the disclaimer requirement applies only to citizens and nationals of states that are not Alliance members. The Court should be extremely hesitant to invalidate a disclosure requirement that is absolutely necessary to implement an admittedly valid disclaimer regime.

Second, in prior Supreme Court cases, the central concern about disclosure requirements has been that compelled disclosure might expose some people to "threats, harassment, or reprisals."[111] Given all the safeguards that are built into DADA's registration system, the risk that compelled disclosure will expose anyone to threats, harassment, or reprisals is exceedingly low. Moreover, the Court could address that problem by considering an as-applied challenge to DADA after the registration system takes effect (as it did in *Brown*), rather than invalidating the entire law based on mere speculation about the likely effect of the law before it is even implemented. Considering the magnitude of the government interests at stake—especially the government's interest in preventing hostile foreign powers from interfering with American democracy—the Court should, and likely would, be exceedingly reluctant to invalidate DADA up front, before the law is implemented, without giving the system a chance to operate to see what actually happens.

Third, DADA's disclosure requirements are very similar to compelled disclosure requirements that the Court upheld against a First Amendment challenge in *Meese v. Keene*.[112] *Meese* involved a challenge to the Foreign Agents Registration Act (FARA),[113] which "requires registration, reporting, and disclosure by persons engaging in propaganda on behalf of foreign powers."[114] Keene was a member of the California State Senate who wanted to show three Canadian films that the Department of Justice (DOJ) identified as "political propaganda" under FARA. Since the DOJ classified the films as political propaganda, FARA required Keene to register as an agent of a foreign government before showing the films, and to file a detailed registration statement to satisfy the statute's extensive disclosure requirements. Keene argued that FARA's registration and disclosure provisions violated his First Amendment rights. The Court rejected that argument, holding that FARA's registration and disclosure requirement "serves rather than disserves the First Amendment" because the purpose is "to inform recipients of advocacy materials produced by or under the aegis of a foreign government of the source of such materials."[115] Similarly, DADA's registration and disclosure requirements serve the purpose of the First Amendment by informing social media users that certain messages are disseminated by citizens or nationals of nondemocratic governments.

Fourth, although libertarian fears about chilling constitutionally protected speech are not unwarranted, the actual chilling effect on the exercise of First Amendment rights will depend, to a large extent, on the public communication strategy that accompanies the initial rollout of the DADA registration system. If the federal government and major social media companies, acting in unison, can persuade the American people that they need not fear DADA's registration system because the system incorporates numerous safeguards to minimize the potential risk that information will be used for government surveillance, then the number of Americans who self-censor by exiting social media would be quite small. From the Court's perspective, it is impossible to know the extent to which DADA's registration system would deter the exercise of First Amendment rights, and induce U.S. citizens to refrain from engaging in public communication on social media, without first giving the system a chance to operate. Thus, the

Court would likely rebuff attempts to block implementation of the law up front, while also preserving the opportunity to consider First Amendment challenges based on the actual effects of implementation.

Additionally, it bears emphasis that the federal government collects information from individuals through a variety of other mechanisms, including tax collection forms and passport applications. (As of January 2018, 42 percent of Americans held passports.[116]) The disclosure requirements for tax returns and passport applications are more extensive than DADA's disclosure requirements for social media accounts. Thus, as a practical matter, the vast majority of data that DADA requires individuals to disclose to the federal government is information that the government has already obtained by other means. Although DADA's compelled disclosure requirements would probably have the unintended consequence of inducing some people to refrain from engaging in public communication on social media, it seems unlikely that the Court would invalidate a law that—to a large extent—merely requires people to tell the federal government what it already knows.

Granted, DADA's registration system would enable the federal government to ascertain which U.S. citizens are using social media. However, people who are currently using their real names to post messages publicly on social media have already disclosed that information to the government. And DADA is designed to ensure that individuals who fear government monitoring of their social media accounts can avoid that outcome by using pseudonyms, or by setting up private accounts.

IS A BAN CONSTITUTIONAL?

The centerpiece of the proposed legislation is a rule prohibiting Russian and Chinese agents from creating or operating accounts on regulated social media platforms. This section evaluates arguments for and against the constitutionality of that rule. In *Citizens United v. Fed'l Election Comm'n*, the Court emphasized that the First Amendment protects the "open marketplace of ideas" by securing listeners' access to a wide range of "information, knowledge, and opinion."[117] The Court stated in dicta that the First Amendment prohibits "restrictions distinguishing among different speakers, allowing speech by some but not others."[118] If taken literally, this statement would bar rules that apply specifically to Chinese and Russian agents. However, the statement should not be read too literally because the Court also said: "We need not reach the question whether the Government has a compelling interest in preventing foreign individuals or associations from influencing our Nation's political process."[119]

The proposed ban on Chinese and Russian agents covers three broad categories of speech: speech directed primarily at a U.S. audience; speech directed at audiences in other Western liberal democracies; and speech directed at audiences in the global South. Since the Constitution does not confer rights on foreigners abroad—either in terms of speaker interests or listener interests—the proposed ban does not raise any significant constitutional issues insofar as it restricts speech by foreign agents directed at non-U.S. audiences overseas. However, in light of First Amendment protections for U.S. citizens to receive information, ideas, and opinions, DADA's ban is potentially vulnerable to a constitutional challenge that focuses on the interests of listeners in the United States.

Should Speech by Chinese and Russian Agents be Classified as Unprotected Speech?

The Supreme Court has previously recognized several categories of speech that are not protected by the First Amendment, including incitement, fighting words, obscenity, and child pornography.[120] The Court distinguishes obscenity from other types of sexually explicit speech—which are constitutionally protected—on the grounds that obscenity "lacks serious literary, artistic, political or scientific value."[121] Like obscenity, speech on social media by Russian and Chinese agents lacks any redeeming social value. From a Madisonian perspective, information warfare by Russian and Chinese agents is even less deserving of constitutional protection than other forms of unprotected speech because the purpose of such speech is antithetical to the central purpose of the First Amendment. The Founders adopted the First Amendment to enhance the effective operation of our constitutional system of democratic self-governance.[122] However, Russian agents, in particular, engage in speech on social media with the intent to undermine our system of democratic self-governance.[123] Therefore, in terms of Madisonian theory, there is a powerful argument that speech on social media by Russian and Chinese agents does not merit any First Amendment protection.

Even so, the current Supreme Court would likely reject the argument that speech on social media by Russian and Chinese agents should be classified as unprotected speech. Almost forty years have passed since the last Supreme Court decision establishing a new category of speech that is unprotected by the First Amendment.[124] In a pair of cases decided in 2010 and 2011, the Court made clear that it is very reluctant to add new categories of harmful speech to the already recognized, existing categories of speech that are unprotected by the First Amendment.[125] Over the past few decades, the Court's First Amendment doctrine has trended in a more libertarian direction, based on a general mistrust of government speech regulation, including regulation of what might be deemed "low value speech." Moreover, with the rise of the internet, the Court has often extolled the virtues of cyberspace as an important forum for speech. For example, in *Packingham v. North Carolina*, Justice Kennedy, writing for the Court, proclaimed that "the Internet in general, and social media in particular," is one of "the most important places . . . for the exchange of views."[126] In *Packingham*, the Court affirmed the constitutional right of a registered sex offender—hardly a sympathetic defendant—to access social media. Given that registered sex offenders have a constitutional right of access to social media, the Court would likely hold that the First Amendment offers at least some protection for U.S. citizens who want to communicate with Russian and Chinese agents via social media.

Intermediate Scrutiny or Strict Scrutiny?

We saw previously that DADA's disclosure and disclaimer requirements are subject to a special constitutional test that is functionally equivalent to intermediate scrutiny: the government must establish "a substantial relation between the disclosure [and disclaimer] requirement[s] and a sufficiently important governmental interest."[127] That test is not applicable to DADA's ban on Russian and Chinese agents. Hence, in litigation challenging the constitutional validity of the ban, the Court would have to decide whether the ban is subject to intermediate scrutiny or strict scrutiny. Madisonians would argue for intermediate scrutiny; libertarians would argue for strict scrutiny. It is unclear how the Court would rule on this question.

Libertarians might cite this passage from *Citizens United* to support their view that the ban on Chinese and Russian agents should be subject to strict scrutiny:

> Laws that burden political speech are subject to strict scrutiny . . . Premised on mistrust of governmental power, the First Amendment stands against attempts to disfavor certain subjects or viewpoints. Prohibited, too, are restrictions distinguishing among different speakers, allowing speech by some but not others. As instruments to censor, these categories are interrelated: Speech restrictions based on the identity of the speaker are all too often simply a means to control content.[128]

Like the federal election law at issue in *Citizens United*, the proposed ban on Chinese and Russian agents burdens political speech. Like *Citizens United*, where the law distinguished between corporations and other speakers, the proposed ban distinguishes between foreign agents and other speakers. Finally, like the law in *Citizens United*, the speaker-based restriction in this case is clearly "a means to control content." Therefore, libertarians would argue, the ban on Chinese and Russian agents should be subject to strict scrutiny.

Nevertheless, two competing arguments weigh in favor of intermediate scrutiny, which entails a more deferential approach to judicial review. First, as noted previously, "[f]oreign interference in the American political system was among the gravest dangers feared by the Founders of our nation and the Framers of our Constitution."[129] Given the Framers' fears about foreign interference in our democracy, and given the fact that the political branches have greater institutional competence than the judiciary to address threats from hostile foreign powers, Madisonians would argue that the Court should adopt a more deferential standard of review (i.e., intermediate scrutiny) when presented with a law designed to protect the integrity of democratic self-government from the threat of foreign interference.

Aside from the threat of foreign interference with American democracy, the proposed statute is also designed to promote an important foreign policy objective: helping key U.S. allies protect their constitutional democracies from the threat posed by Russian and Chinese information warfare. When Congress and the president cooperate to enact legislation designed to promote foreign policy goals, and litigants challenge that legislation on constitutional grounds, the Court has historically adopted a deferential approach to judicial review.[130] Ganesh Sitaraman and Ingrid Wuerth contend that Supreme Court decisions over the past couple of decades manifest a trend away from traditional foreign affairs deference.[131] Other scholars contest that claim.[132] Regardless, if Congress enacted a statute to ban speech by Russian and Chinese agents on regulated social media platforms, and litigants challenged that ban in court, the government would certainly argue for judicial deference to the political branches. Some justices would likely be persuaded to apply traditional foreign affairs deference and evaluate the law under an intermediate scrutiny standard.

In evaluating arguments for strict scrutiny versus intermediate scrutiny, the Court should consider the primary goals that the First Amendment is designed to promote. Affirmatively, the First Amendment is said to promote democratic self-government, the search for truth, and individual self-fulfillment.[133] Given what we know about speech on U.S. social media platforms by Chinese and Russian agents, the Court might reasonably conclude that such speech does not advance any of these goals, especially if Congress makes explicit legislative findings that speech on social media by Russian and Chinese agents undermines democratic self-governance and does not advance the search for truth or individual fulfillment. These considerations weigh strongly in favor of intermediate scrutiny. However, the First Amendment also serves the important goal of constraining government power.[134] Justices who focus primarily or exclusively on the limiting function of the First Amendment would be inclined to apply strict scrutiny rather than intermediate scrutiny.

The argument about whether DADA's ban on Chinese and Russian agents should be subject to intermediate or strict scrutiny is reminiscent of the arguments advanced by litigants in *Holder v. Humanitarian Law Project*.[135] In that case, plaintiffs raised a First Amendment challenge to a statute that makes it a federal crime to "knowingly provide material support or resources to a foreign terrorist organization."[136] The government emphasized the national security context of the law and argued that the Court should apply intermediate scrutiny. The Court rejected that argument—despite the fact that the statute at issue was designed to address threats from foreign terrorist organizations—and decided that the law should be subject to strict scrutiny.[137] In light of *Holder*, I will assume that the Court would apply strict scrutiny to evaluate the constitutionality of DADA's ban on Chinese and Russian agents.

Applying Strict Scrutiny

Gerald Gunther coined the oft-quoted phrase that strict scrutiny is "strict in theory, but fatal in fact."[138] However, the Court has stated explicitly that it seeks to "dispel the notion that strict scrutiny is . . . fatal in fact."[139] During John Roberts's tenure as chief justice, the Court has decided two First Amendment cases where it upheld the constitutional validity of laws subject to strict scrutiny: *Williams-Yulee v. Florida Bar*[140] and *Holder v. Humanitarian Law Project*.[141]

Holder is especially instructive here. When applying strict scrutiny in *Holder*, the Court manifested substantial deference to factual findings by the political branches on empirical questions. For example, the Court noted that the question of "whether foreign terrorist organizations meaningfully segregate support of their legitimate activities from support of terrorism is an empirical question" about which "Congress made specific findings."[142] The Court accepted Congress's factual findings on that empirical question. Similarly, the Court said: "In analyzing whether it is possible in practice to distinguish material support for a foreign terrorist group's violent activities and its nonviolent activities . . . we have before us an affidavit stating the Executive Branch's conclusion on that question."[143]

The Court added that the "evaluation of the facts by the Executive, like Congress's assessment, is entitled to deference."[144]

Holder provides a road map for the political branches to enact a ban on Chinese and Russian agents that could survive strict scrutiny. Congress would need to include detailed factual findings in the legislation, supported by expert testimony at congressional hearings. The executive branch would need to provide expert testimony during trial on key factual issues. That approach would not guarantee that the Court would uphold DADA's ban against a First Amendment challenge, but it would offer a reasonable prospect of success, because the Court would likely defer to factual findings by the political branches.

Assuming that the Court applies strict scrutiny, the government would have to show that DADA's ban is narrowly tailored to achieve a compelling government interest. The law is designed to promote three objectives: protect American democracy from information warfare; protect key U.S. allies from the threat that information warfare poses to constitutional democracy in their countries; and tilt the playing field in the ongoing geopolitical competition with China in favor of democratic self-government and against authoritarian governance models. Let us assume that neither of the foreign policy goals qualifies as a compelling interest. In that case, strict scrutiny analysis would focus on the U.S. interest in protecting American democracy from Chinese and Russian information warfare.

In *Citizens United*, the Supreme Court declined to "reach the question whether the Government has a compelling interest in preventing foreign individuals or associations from influencing our Nation's political process."[145] If pressed, though, the Court would almost certainly agree that the government has a compelling interest in protecting American democracy from powerful foreign adversaries. However, litigants who challenge DADA's ban might argue that the question, properly framed, is whether the government has a compelling interest in preventing Chinese and Russian agents from operating accounts on U.S. social media platforms. If litigants persuade the Court that the interest at stake should be framed in these narrower terms, it is unclear whether the government interest would qualify as "compelling."

If Chinese and Russian activity on social media constitutes a tiny fraction of the broader class of foreign threats to American democracy, then the interest at stake, narrowly defined, may not be compelling. On the other hand, if Chinese and Russian activity on social media constitutes a significant subset of the broader class of foreign threats to American democracy, then the government interest in blocking that activity would qualify as a compelling interest. Ultimately, it is an empirical question whether Chinese and Russian information warfare on social media is a tiny fraction, or a significant subset, of the broader class of foreign threats to American democracy. The Supreme Court is uniquely unqualified to answer that empirical question. Accordingly, if the legislation includes a congressional finding that Chinese and Russian information warfare on social media constitutes a significant threat to American democracy, the Court would almost certainly defer to the judgment of the political branches on that question. In that case, the government interest at stake would qualify as "compelling."

Assuming that the government has a compelling interest in protecting American democracy from Chinese and Russian information warfare, the government would still have to show that DADA's ban on Chinese and Russian agents is "narrowly tailored" to achieve that goal. Libertarians might argue that the ban is not narrowly tailored because the ban is a form of censorship, and censorship is the very opposite of narrow tailoring. Libertarians could cite Supreme Court decisions related to campaign finance laws where the Court has invalidated bans, while upholding disclaimers.[146] From a Madisonian perspective, though, use of the word "censorship" in this context is misleading. The First Amendment clearly prevents the government from censoring political speech by members of the American political community. However, Russian and Chinese agents are not members of our political community: the First Amendment does not protect their rights as speakers. If the First Amendment invalidates DADA's ban, it can only be because the First Amendment protects the right of U.S. citizens and residents to hear what Russian and Chinese agents want to say.

Libertarians may argue that DADA's ban fails the narrow tailoring requirement because Congress could achieve its objectives in a manner that imposes fewer restrictions on constitutionally protected speech by eliminating the ban and instead requiring disclaimers for all speech on social media by Chinese and Russian agents. Here, it is helpful to consider three possible versions of a "disclaimer-only" system. One approach would be to apply disclaimers to a narrowly defined category of "electoral speech." The problem with this approach is that it addresses only a very small portion of the harmful speech on social media by Chinese and Russian cyber troops. As documented in detail in Part One, Chinese and Russian cyber troops have disseminated a wide variety of messages on social media that do not involve electoral speech (narrowly defined), but that have the purpose and/or effect of undermining democracy in the United States and other liberal democracies. In light of the evidence summarized in Part One, Congress could reasonably conclude that a disclaimer regime that focuses exclusively on a narrowly defined category of electoral speech would be utterly ineffectual in addressing the global threat to democracy presented by Chinese and Russian cyber troops. As in *Holder*, if Congress includes such a finding in the legislation, the Supreme Court would be unlikely to second-guess that congressional finding.[147]

A second possible approach to a disclaimer-only regime would be to require disclaimers for a much broader category of speech on social media. For example, Congress could require social media companies to apply disclaimers to any message transmitted by Chinese or Russian agents that *has the purpose or effect of increasing political polarization in an Alliance member state* or, perhaps, any message that *has the purpose or effect of eroding the quality of democratic governance in an Alliance member state*. There are two fundamental problems with this approach to a disclaimer-only regime. First, in contrast to the disclaimer regime discussed in chapter 6—which focuses on a narrowly defined category of electoral speech—it would be practically impossible for social media companies to develop algorithms to identify accurately speech that is subject to disclaimer requirements under these broader categories. The broad categories are simply too vague to be applied in a consistent, predictable way by companies whose platforms handle billions of messages per day.

Second, even if the companies could figure out how to operationalize a disclaimer regime that targets a much broader class of political speech, the disclaimers would be much less effective if they were applied to such a broad range of speech. Empirical research shows that the target audience for disclaimers develops an increasing tendency to ignore warnings if they see or hear those warnings too many times. Social scientists refer to this phenomenon as the "repetition suppression effect."[148] If disclaimers apply to a broad class of political speech, social media users will see (or hear) those disclaimers frequently. In that case, they would likely become so habituated to the warnings that they would simply ignore them. In contrast, if the disclaimers apply only to a narrow category of electoral speech, social media users would see or hear the disclaimers much less frequently. In that case, the warnings are likely to be more effective in alerting social media users to the danger of electoral speech on social media by citizens of nondemocratic countries. If Congress obtains testimony from people with expertise in social psychology and communication studies, and the legislation includes specific factual findings based on that testimony, the Court would be ill equipped to second-guess those factual findings.

A third possible approach to a disclaimer-only regime would be to require disclaimers for all public communications on social media by Chinese and Russian agents, regardless of the content of those messages, but require disclaimers only for a narrowly defined category of "electoral speech" by other citizens or nationals of nonmember states. Under this approach, the broad disclaimer requirement for Chinese and Russian agents would effectively replace the proposed ban. Social media companies could easily develop algorithms to implement these rules because disclaimers for Chinese and Russian agents would be based exclusively on the identity of the speaker, not the content of the messages.

If disclaimers were required for all public communications by Chinese and Russian agents, however, we could expect Chinese and Russian cyber troops to flood the system with millions of trivial messages requiring disclaimers. Indeed, under this version of a disclaimer-only regime, China and Russia would not need to employ any of the anti-circumvention strategies discussed in chapter 6. They could defeat the system by hiring hundreds or thousands of cyber troops whose only job is to transmit innocuous messages that trigger disclaimers. In that case, social media users from Alliance member states would soon become so habituated to seeing the disclaimers that they would simply ignore all such disclaimers, and the disclaimer rule would be completely ineffective.[149] Therefore, Congress could reasonably conclude that a broad disclaimer rule that applies to all public communications on social media by Chinese and Russian agents would be much less effective than a rule prohibiting Chinese and Russian agents from creating or operating accounts on regulated social media platforms. As in *Holder*, if the legislation includes specific factual findings to that effect, the Court would be ill equipped to second-guess those findings.

The lower court decision in *Bluman v. Fed'l Election Comm'n* supports the Madisonian argument that the proposed ban on Chinese and Russian agents should survive strict scrutiny.[150] *Bluman* involved a First Amendment challenge to a federal law that prohibits foreign nationals "from contributing to candidates or political parties; from making expenditures to expressly advocate the election or defeat of a political candidate; and from making donations to outside groups when those donations in turn would be used to make contributions to candidates or parties or to finance express-advocacy expenditures."[151] Judge Kavanaugh—writing for a three-judge panel before he was elevated to the Supreme Court—declined to decide whether the statute should be subject to strict scrutiny or more deferential review "because we conclude that § 441e(a) passes muster even under strict scrutiny."[152] The Supreme Court affirmed the lower court decision in *Bluman* by issuing a summary decision without a published opinion.[153]

The proposed ban on Chinese and Russian agents is substantially narrower than the statute in *Bluman* inasmuch as the statute in *Bluman* applied to all foreign nationals, whereas the DADA ban applies to a small subset of foreign nationals. However, the Court in *Bluman* adopted a narrowing construction of the statute, interpreting some of its provisions so that they applied only to express advocacy, not issue advocacy.[154]

In contrast, the ban on Chinese and Russian agents is vulnerable to a First Amendment challenge because it covers a much broader range of content, including both express advocacy and issue advocacy. Still, the court expressed the central principle animating the decision in *Bluman* as follows: "It is fundamental to the definition of our national political community that foreign citizens do not have a constitutional right to participate in, and thus may be excluded from, activities of democratic self-government."[155] Justice Kavanaugh's endorsement of this principle, and the fact that the Supreme Court affirmed *Bluman* without a published opinion, suggest that the current Supreme Court might be persuaded that the ban on Chinese and Russian agents is sufficiently narrowly tailored to survive strict scrutiny.

One other feature of DADA's ban also supports the Madisonian argument that DADA is narrowly tailored. As discussed previously, DADA's ban on Chinese and Russian agents includes an exemption for benign state agents. That exemption, if implemented in good faith, will protect the right of U.S. citizens and residents to receive information via social media from Chinese and Russian agents. Moreover, as discussed earlier in this chapter, the right of U.S. citizens and residents to receive information is the only First Amendment right at stake, because the First Amendment does not protect the rights of Chinese and Russian agents outside the United States.

In sum, Madisonians will argue that DADA's ban is narrowly tailored to accomplish the precise objective it is designed to accomplish. The ban does not apply to all foreign states, or even to all authoritarian states. It applies only to two powerful states that are the United States' principal adversaries in the world today. Moreover, the ban does not apply to all Russian and Chinese nationals: it applies only to people and organizations acting as state agents, and it includes an exemption for benign state agents. Finally, it does not apply to all speech by those state agents: it applies specifically to speech on regulated social media platforms. For the reasons explained previously, a disclaimer-only regime would utterly fail to accomplish the primary goal that DADA is intended to accomplish:

namely, protecting American democracy from Chinese and Russian information warfare. Therefore, although the Court has generally preferred disclaimers to bans in the context of campaign finance regulation, the Court might be persuaded that DADA's ban satisfies the narrow tailoring requirement because it restricts no more speech than necessary to accomplish the statute's primary objective.

GLOSSARY

Bots are automated accounts that are programmed to disseminate messages via social media without the need for human intervention.

Cyber troops are employees or contractors who act as agents of governments or political parties to engage in information warfare or other types of organized social media manipulation.

A *cyborg account* is an account that is either operated by a human being with assistance from a bot, or operated by a bot with assistance from a human being.

Data mining involves collecting large volumes of information about individuals from social media and other sources and aggregating that information in proprietary databases. Those databases facilitate the use of social media for microtargeting.

Digital authoritarianism is a set of laws, policies, and technical practices that empower authoritarian governments to exploit social media and other digital technologies for surveillance, censorship, and online content manipulation.

Disinformation is false or misleading information that is purposefully crafted and strategically placed to achieve a political goal. Disinformation is a subset of misinformation. The term "disinformation" is broader than OSM in that it includes information disseminated through social media and information disseminated by other means. The term "disinformation" is narrower than OSM in that OSM can include the dissemination of truthful information.

Fake accounts are social media accounts operated by someone who adopts a false identity for the purpose of misleading other social media users about the identity of the person operating the account. Fake accounts include fake foreign national accounts, fictitious user accounts, hacked accounts, impostor accounts, rental accounts, and stolen accounts.

A *fake foreign national account* is an account created by a Chinese or Russian agent who claims to be a citizen or national of some state other than China or Russia that is not an Alliance member state.

Fictitious user accounts are fake accounts created in the name of a nonexistent person who pretends to be a citizen or national of an Alliance member state.

Foreign influence operations are activities conducted by agents of governments and/or political parties that are designed to influence domestic electoral, political, or policy processes in foreign countries, or to influence deliberative processes in international organizations.

Hacked accounts are fake accounts where cyber troops have hacked into existing accounts created by real people and taken control of those accounts.

Impostor accounts are fake accounts in which cyber troops misappropriate the identity of a real person without that person's knowledge or consent. The term "impostor accounts" includes hacked accounts, rental accounts, and stolen accounts.

Information operations are actions by government or political party employees or contractors involving the dissemination of information through any means—including print or broadcast media, social media, traditional diplomacy, and public diplomacy—that is directed toward a foreign audience or is intended to promote a foreign policy objective.

Information warfare is OSM that is directed toward a foreign audience or is intended to promote a foreign policy objective. Alternatively, information warfare can be defined as the exploitation of social media by state agents to conduct foreign influence operations.

Microtargeting is the process of preparing and delivering customized messages to voters or consumers via social media. Commercial advertisers, political strategists, and cyber troops exploit information acquired from data mining to refine the practice of microtargeting.

Misinformation is false or misleading information. The term "misinformation" includes information disseminated through social media and information disseminated by other means.

Organized social media manipulation (OSM) involves the use of government or political party employees or contractors to manipulate public opinion online for political purposes. OSM includes disinformation, but it can also include the dissemination of truthful information that is purposefully crafted and strategically placed to achieve political goals.

A *rental account* is a specific type of impostor account in which a foreign agent pays a bribe to a national of an Alliance member state so that the foreign agent can appropriate the identity of the payee for the purpose of operating a social media account.

A *stolen account* is a hacked account that has been sold to a third party without the knowledge or consent of the account's true owner.

APPENDIX
Proposed Statutory Text

SCOPE

This statute applies to all social media platforms with more than fifty million monthly active users outside of Russia and China.

DEFINITIONS

Except as provided in subparagraph (b), the term "social media platform" means any public-facing website, web application, or digital application that is used for electronic communication of words or images and that is purposefully designed to enable users to share content by finding and connecting with other users who have common interests.

(a) The term "social media platform" includes, without limitation, Facebook, Twitter, Instagram, YouTube, LinkedIn, Reddit, Tumblr, Pinterest, Medium, Vine, Gab, and TikTok.

(b) The term "social media platform" does not include the following types of websites or web applications:

(1) web applications whose primary function is to transmit e-mail communications;

(2) web-based database software;

(3) web-based financial management or accounting software;

(4) search engines;

(5) blogs, except for blogs embedded in other social media platforms;

(6) online gaming platforms;

(7) online dating sites;

(8) websites operated by newspapers or television stations with national or global readership or viewership, such as the *New York Times* or CNN;

(9) web applications whose primary purpose is to facilitate the online purchase of goods or services, or to provide ratings or recommendations for different vendors of goods or services; or

(10) websites or applications whose primary purpose is something other than sharing content by finding and connecting with other users who have common interests.

The term "public communication" means any communication posted to an account or profile that is registered as public, unless the user tags a particular message as "private." A private message may not be transmitted to more than 500 recipients.

BAN ON PUBLIC COMMUNICATIONS BY PRIVATE ACCOUNTS

Social media companies shall ensure that any communication posted to an account registered as a private account may not be transmitted directly to or immediately accessible to more than 1,000 registered users. If a social media user with a public account receives a message from a user with a private account, the user with the public account shall be entitled to share the message in a manner that constitutes public communication.

NOTES

PREFACE

1. See Snyder, "The American Abyss," 30.
2. See, e.g., Menn, "QAnon Received Earlier Boost."
3. See United States v. Alvarez, 567 U.S. 709 (2012); see also Goodyear, "Priam's Folly."
4. Agency for Int'l Development v. Alliance for Open Society Int'l, Inc., 140 S. Ct. 2082 (2020).
5. See chapter 8.
6. Fearnow, "82 Percent of Trump Voters."
7. See Dwoskin and Timberg, "The Unseen Machine."
8. See chapter 6 for a detailed explanation of the proposed registration system.
9. See Menn, "QAnon Received Earlier Boost."

CHAPTER ONE: INFORMATION WARFARE AND DEMOCRATIC DECAY

1. Berkes, "Eternal Vigilance."
2. V-Dem Institute, "Autocratization Surges," 4.
3. Polyakova, "Introduction," 6.
4. See chapters 2 and 3.
5. See chapter 4.
6. Rosenberger, "Making Cyberspace Safe," 146–47.
7. See chapter 4.
8. TheGlobalEconomy.com, "Percent of World GDP: Country Rankings," https://www.theglobaleconomy.com/rankings/gdp_share/ (last visited September 6, 2021).
9. See Barlow, "A Declaration."
10. See, e.g., Sullivan, "The Revolution Will be Twittered."
11. See Morozov, *The Net Delusion.*
12. See Balkin, "Free Speech Is a Triangle"; Klonick, "The New Governors."
13. Newton, "Interface with Casey Newton."
14. See Lührmann, Tannenberg, and Lindberg, "Regimes of the World."
15. Ibid., 61.

16. The V-Dem database and codebook are available at https://www.v-dem.net/en/data/data-version-10/.

17. See Fukuyama, *The End of History.*

18. The variable "v2x_regime_amb," which is a variant of the "v2x_regime" variable, ranks states on a scale from 0 to 9, with 9 being the best score. See V-Dem Institute, "V-Dem Codebook," 266–67. Using that scale, Hungary dropped dramatically from 9 to 4 between 2009 and 2018; Poland dropped from 9 to 6 between 2012 and 2016; Turkey dropped from 6 to 3 between 2013 and 2014; Philippines dropped from 6 to 4 between 2015 and 2019; South Africa dropped from 8 to 6 between 2012 and 2017; and India dropped from 6 to 5 between 2016 and 2017.

19. See V-Dem Institute, *Autocratization Turns Viral*, 31.

20. See, e.g., Abrams, "American Leadership"; Haass, "Foreign Policy"; Kundnani, "Foreign Interference."

21. Agency for Int'l Development v. Alliance for Open Society Int'l, Inc., 140 S. Ct. 2082 (2020).

22. See Rid, *Active Measures.*

23. Bradshaw and Howard, *The Global Disinformation Order.*

24. See Howard, *Lie Machines.*

25. See Hamilton and Ohlberg, *Hidden Hand.*

26. See Rudolph and Morley, "Covert Foreign Money."

27. This definition is a variant of the definition offered by Philip Howard. See Howard, *Lie Machines*, 172–73.

28. See chapter 2.

29. Bradshaw and Howard, *The Global Disinformation Order*, 2.

30. See Douek, "The Free Speech Blind Spot."

31. See Gray, *International Law*, 134–36.

32. See Akram and Johnson, "Race, Civil Rights, and Immigration Law."

33. See Ginsburg, "Authoritarian International Law?"

34. Benkler, Faris, and Roberts, *Network Propaganda.*

35. Statista, "Number of Monthly Active Facebook Users Worldwide."

36. Smeltz et al., *Rejecting Retreat*, 34.

37. Ibid.

38. See, e.g., McFaul et al., "Securing American Elections."

39. See Election Integrity Partnership, *Evaluating Platform Election-Related Speech Policies.*

40. See chapter 7 for a more detailed discussion of these issues.

41. See Miller et al., "Sockpuppets Spin COVID Yarns."

42. Gorwa, "Computational Propaganda in Poland."

43. Facebook, *Community Standards Enforcement Report* (August 2020), https://about .fb.com/news/2020/08/community-standards-enforcement-report-aug-2020/ (last visited September 6, 2021).

44. A recent Supreme Court decision arguably makes the registration system more vulnerable to a constitutional challenge. See *Americans for Prosperity Foundation v. Bonta*, 141 S. Ct. 2373 (2021).

45. See pp. 247–50.

CHAPTER TWO: RUSSIAN INFORMATION WARFARE
AND U.S. ELECTIONS

1. DiResta et al., "Tactics and Tropes," 86.

2. Special Counsel Robert S. Mueller, III, *Report on the Investigation into Russian Interference in the 2016 Presidential Election*, vol. I, p. 4 [hereinafter, "Mueller Report"].

3. *New York Times* Editorial Board, "They're Doing It."

4. See Rid, *Active Measures.*

5. *Disinformation: A Primer in Russian Active Measures and Influence Campaigns*, Hearing Before the Select Comm. on Intelligence, at 10–11 (March 30, 2017) [hereinafter, "Disinformation Hearing"] (statement of Roy Goodson, Emeritus Professor of Government at Georgetown University).

6. Intelligence Community Assessment, *Assessing Russian Activities and Intentions in Recent U.S. Elections*, ICA 2017-01D, at ii (January 6, 2017) [hereinafter, "ICA Report"].

7. Ibid.

8. DiResta et al., "Tactics and Tropes," 4.

9. Howard et al., "IRA, Social Media and Political Polarization," 3.

10. See United States v. Elena Alekseevna Khusyaynova, *Affidavit in Support of a Criminal Complaint*, ¶ 15 (E.D. Va., September 28, 2018) [hereinafter "Khusyaynova Complaint"].

11. Mueller Report, vol. I, p. 1.

12. Ibid., 15.

13. Khusyaynova Complaint, ¶ 15.

14. Mueller Report, vol. I, p. 4.

15. ICA Report, i.

16. Disinformation Hearing, 28 (testimony of Eugene Rumer, Senior Fellow and Director, Russia and Eurasia Program, Carnegie Endowment for International Peace).

17. ICA Report, ii, 1.

18. See Mueller Report, vol. I, pp. 36–51.

19. DiResta et al., "Tactics and Tropes," 76–77.

20. ICA Report, ii.

21. DiResta et al., "Tactics and Tropes," 9, 76.

22. Mueller Report, vol. I, p. 36.

23. Ibid., 36–37.

24. Ibid., 41–42.

25. United States of America v. Viktor Borisovich Netysho et al. (D.D.C. July 13, 2018), ¶ 40.

26. Ibid., ¶¶ 40–45.

27. Mueller Report, vol. I, p. 43.

28. Ibid., 44.

29. Ibid., 44–47.

30. Ibid., 48.

31. Shane and Mazzetti, "Inside a 3-Year Russian Campaign."

32. DiResta et al., "Tactics and Tropes," 6.

33. Shuster and Ifraimova, "A Former Russian Troll."

34. United States of America v. Internet Research Agency, et al. (D.D.C. Feb. 16, 2018) [hereinafter, "IRA Indictment"].

35. Ibid., ¶ 30.

36. Ibid., ¶ 31.

37. Howard et al., "IRA, Social Media and Political Polarization," 3.

38. Ibid., 7.

39. DiResta et al., "Tactics and Tropes," 16, 18, 21, 26.

40. Ibid., 32.

41. Ibid., 6–7.

42. Mueller Report, vol. 1, p. 15.

43. IRA Indictment, ¶ 32.

44. See DiResta et al., "Tactics and Tropes," 85; IRA Indictment, ¶ 76.

45. See Howard et al., "IRA, Social Media and Political Polarization," 32, 35.

46. DiResta et al., "Tactics and Tropes," 27.

47. Ibid., 85.

48. See ibid., 85–87.

49. See IRA Indictment, ¶¶ 70–80.

50. Mueller Report, vol. 1, p. 22.

51. Ibid., 33–34.

52. DiResta et al., "Tactics and Tropes," 85.

53. Ibid., 86.

54. Ibid., 88.

55. Ibid., 90.

56. Howard et al., "IRA, Social Media and Political Polarization," 40.

57. Costa-Roberts, "How to Spot a Russian Bot."

58. Twitter Trends FAQs, https://help.twitter.com/en/using-twitter/twitter-trending
-faqs (last visited September 6, 2021).

59. Shane, "The Fake Americans."

60. Wells and McMillan, "Scrutiny over Fake Accounts."

61. See Silverman, "People Are Renting Out Their Facebook Accounts."

62. Shane and Mazzetti, "Inside a 3-Year Russian Campaign."

63. Shane, "The Fake Americans."

64. See IRA Indictment, ¶¶ 70, 89–90.

65. DiResta et al., "Tactics and Tropes," 70.

66. Silverman, "This Analysis Shows."

67. Langin, "Fake News Spreads Faster."

68. Howard et al., "IRA, Social Media and Political Polarization," 3.

69. Ibid., 39.

70. Ibid., 35.

71. Ibid., 39.

72. Ibid., 3.

73. DiResta et al., "Tactics and Tropes," 89.

74. Ibid., 21.

75. Ibid., 85.

76. Ibid., 90.

77. Ibid., 8.

78. Ibid., 81.

79. Ibid., 88.

80. Ibid., 82.

81. IRA Indictment, ¶ 46.
82. DiResta et al., "Tactics and Tropes," 9.
83. IRA Indictment, ¶ 46.
84. DiResta et al., "Tactics and Tropes," 17.
85. Ibid., 86.
86. Howard et al., "IRA, Social Media and Political Polarization," 39.
87. Mueller Report, vol. 1, pp. 29–31.
88. Ibid., 35.
89. Ruck et al., "Internet Research Agency Twitter Activity."
90. Ibid.
91. Jamieson, *Cyber-War*.
92. Ibid., 40.
93. Ibid., 154–55.
94. Ibid., 60–61.
95. Ibid., 180.
96. Ibid., 234–37.
97. Ibid., 51–52.
98. Ibid., 57.
99. Ibid., 61.
100. Ruck et al., "Internet Research Agency Twitter Activity."
101. Jamieson, *Cyber-War*, 62.
102. See DiResta et al., "Tactics and Tropes," 79.
103. Jamieson, *Cyber-War*, 227–29.
104. Ibid., 38–39.
105. Ibid., 63.
106. Ibid., 39.
107. Ibid., 48.
108. Ibid., 103.
109. Ibid., 104.
110. Ibid., 109.
111. Ibid., 114.
112. Ibid., 115.
113. Pew Research Center, "Partisan Antipathy," 5.
114. Jones, "Trump Job Approval."
115. Pew Research Center, "Partisan Antipathy."
116. Barnes and Goldman, "Russian Trying to Stoke U.S. Racial Tensions."
117. Polyakova, "Kremlin's Plot against Democracy," 141.
118. Karpf, "On Digital Misinformation and Democratic Myths."
119. Stubbs, "Russian Operatives Sacrifice Followers."
120. Dwoskin and Timberg, "Facebook Takes Down Russian Operation."
121. Ibid.
122. Kim, "New Evidence Shows."
123. Ibid.
124. Dwoskin and Timberg, "Facebook Takes Down Russian Operation."
125. Ibid.
126. Rosenberg and Barnes, "A Bible Burning."

127. Ibid.

128. Ibid.

129. Perlroth, "A Conspiracy Made in America."

130. Ibid.

131. Ibid.

CHAPTER THREE: RUSSIAN INFLUENCE OPERATIONS IN EUROPE

1. Polyakova, "Introduction," 3.

2. See Casey and Way, "Russian Electoral Interventions"; Martin and Shapiro, *Trends in Online Foreign Influence Efforts*; Senate Foreign Relations Comm., Minority Staff Report (2018); Mazarr et al., *Hostile Social Manipulation.*

3. See Satariano, "Russia Sought to Use Social Media"; EUvsDisinfo, *EU Elections Update.*

4. EUvsDisinfo, *EU Elections Update.*

5. Polyakova, "Introduction," 6.

6. European Council, *EU Restrictive Measures in Response to the Crisis in Ukraine.*

7. Rudolph and Morley, "Covert Foreign Money."

8. Barnett, "United Kingdom: Vulnerable but Resistant."

9. See, e.g., Mazarr et al., *Hostile Social Manipulation*, 187–92; Narayanan et al., "Russian Involvement and Junk News."

10. Sabbagh, Harding, and Roth, "Russia Report Reveals UK Government Failed."

11. Persily, Metzger, and Krowitz, "Confronting Efforts at Election Manipulation," 35.

12. Association for International Broadcasting, "RT Weekly TV Audience Grows."

13. Dearden, "RT Could be Banned from Broadcasting."

14. Sputnik, "About Us," https://sputniknews.com/docs/about/index.html (last visited September 6, 2021).

15. Nimmo, "Putin's Media Are Pushing Britain."

16. 89up, "Putin's Brexit."

17. Ibid., slide 10.

18. Waterson, "RT Fined £200,000."

19. Mazarr et al., *Hostile Social Manipulation*, 188–89.

20. Davies, "Amid Brexit Uncertainty and Allegations."

21. 89up, "Putin's Brexit," slide 65. The report expresses the values in British pounds. I converted those figures into dollars using a rate of 1.45 USD to GBP, which—according to 89up—was the average conversion rate for the period from January 1 to June 22, 2016.

22. Ibid., slide 9.

23. See Howard, *Lie Machines*, at 125–26. The Electoral Commission found that Vote Leave spent an extra £449,079. Howard's analysis uses a conversion rate of 1.4795 USD to GBP.

24. Ibid., 117–36.

25. Ibid., 133.

26. Ibid., 134.

27. 89up, "Putin's Brexit," slide 24.

28. Persily, Metzger, and Krowitz, "Confronting Efforts at Election Manipulation," 36.

29. 89up, "Putin's Brexit," slides 36–37.

30. See ibid., slide 13.

31. Ibid., slide 12.

32. DiResta et al., "Tactics and Tropes," 22 (chart).

33. Ball, "A Suspected Network of 13,000 Twitter Bots."

34. Ibid.

35. O'Sullivan, "Russian Trolls Pushed Pro-Brexit Spin."

36. Burgess, "Here's the First Evidence Russia Used Twitter."

37. Adam and Booth, "Rising Alarm in Britain."

38. Ibid.

39. Narayanan et al., "Russian Involvement and Junk News."

40. Neudert, Howard, and Kollanyi, "Sourcing and Automation of Political News."

41. Narayanan et al., "Russian Involvement and Junk News."

42. United Kingdom, Intelligence and Security Committee of Parliament (2020).

43. Ibid., 13.

44. Ibid., 14.

45. Sabbagh, Harding, and Roth, "Russia Report Reveals UK Government Failed."

46. Rudolph and Morley, "Covert Foreign Money," 80.

47. Caesar, "The Chaotic Triumph of Arron Banks."

48. British Social Attitudes, *The Vote to Leave the EU.*

49. Davies, "Amid Brexit Uncertainty and Allegations."

50. Ibid.

51. United Kingdom, House of Commons, Digital, Culture, Media and Sport Committee, *Disinformation and Fake News,* 74.

52. Rudolph and Morley, "Covert Foreign Money," 80.

53. United Kingdom, Electoral Commission, *Investigation into Payments.*

54. United Kingdom, National Crime Agency, *Public Statement on NCA Investigation.*

55. Rudolph and Morley, "Covert Foreign Money," 81.

56. Ibid.

57. British Social Attitudes, *The Vote to Leave the EU,* 15–17.

58. Ibid., 17.

59. Polyakova, "Introduction," 4.

60. Laruelle, "France: Mainstreaming Russian Influence," 9.

61. Ibid., 8.

62. Ibid., 8–10.

63. Rudolph and Morley, "Covert Foreign Money," 74.

64. Laruelle, "France: Mainstreaming Russian Influence," 9.

65. Ibid., 8.

66. Clarke and Holder, "French Presidential Election."

67. Willsher, "Penelopegate."

68. See Vilmer, "The 'Macron Leaks' Operation," 4–9.

69. Ibid., 6.

70. Ibid., 42.

71. Senate Foreign Relations Comm., Minority Staff Report, *Putin's Asymmetric Assault on Democracy,* 121.

72. Daniels, "How Russia Hacked the French Election."

73. Rose and Dyomkin, "After Talks, France's Macron Hits Out."

74. McAuley, "French President Macron Blasts Russian State-Owned Media."

75. Menn, "Exclusive: Russia Used Facebook."

76. Senate Foreign Relations Comm., Minority Staff Report, *Putin's Asymmetric Assault on Democracy*, 123.

77. Ibid., 123–24.

78. Auchard and Bate, "French Candidate Macron Claims Massive Hack."

79. Vilmer, "The 'Macron Leaks' Operation," 11.

80. Ibid., 12.

81. Volz, "U.S. Far-Right Activists."

82. Vilmer, "The 'Macron Leaks' Operation," 13.

83. Ibid., 13–14.

84. See Mohan, "Macron Leaks."

85. Vilmer, "The 'Macron Leaks' Operation," 19.

86. Ibid.

87. Ibid., 20.

88. Ibid.

89. U.S. Department of Justice, "Six Russian GRU Officers Charged."

90. Vilmer, "The 'Macron Leaks' Operation," 27.

91. See Benoit, "France's Le Pen Gains Ground."

92. Vilmer, "The 'Macron Leaks' Operation," 26.

93. Senate Foreign Relations Comm., Minority Staff Report, *Putin's Asymmetric Assault on Democracy*, 125.

94. Ibid., 126.

95. Ferrara, "Disinformation and Social Bot Operations."

96. Howard et al., "Junk News and Bots" (2017b).

97. Desigaud et al., "Junk News and Bots."

98. Bakamo, "French Election Social Media Landscape," 167.

99. Ferrara, "Disinformation and Social Bot Operations," 15.

100. Howard et al., "Junk News and Bots" (2017b), 3.

101. Desigaud et al., Junk News and Bots," 3.

102. Bakamo, "French Election Social Media Landscape," 5.

103. Bakamo, "Role and Impact of Non-Traditional Publishers," 4–6. The language quoted in the text that describes the different categories is taken from the first preliminary report, cited in this endnote. However, the percentages are taken from the final report: Bakamo, "French Election Social Media Landscape." The first report covered the period from November 1, 2016 to April 4, 2017. The final report covered the period from November 1, 2016 to May 22, 2017.

104. Additionally, the definitions of the corresponding categories are not identical.

105. See Howard et al., "Junk News and Bots" (2017b), 4; Desigaud et al., "Junk News and Bots," 4.

106. Desigaud et al., "Junk News and Bots," 4.

107. Howard et al., "Junk News and Bots" (2017a).

108. Bakamo, "Role and Impact of Non-Traditional Publishers," 7.

109. Ibid., 7–8.

110. Bakamo, "Patterns of Disinformation," 5.

111. See Benkler, Faris, and Roberts, *Network Propaganda*.

112. See ibid.

113. See Central Intelligence Agency, *The World Factbook: Sweden*, https://www.cia.gov/the-world-factbook/countries/sweden/ (last visited September 6, 2021).

114. Cederberg, *Catching Swedish Phish*, 7.

115. Berzina, "Sweden—Preparing for the Wolf."

116. See North Atlantic Treaty Organization, *Partnership Interoperability Initiative.*

117. Kragh and Asberg, "Russia's Strategy for Influence," 10.

118. Berzina, "Sweden—Preparing for the Wolf."

119. Kragh and Asberg, "Russia's Strategy for Influence," 9–12.

120. Cederberg, *Catching Swedish Phish*, 8.

121. Berzina, "Sweden—Preparing for the Wolf."

122. Cederberg, *Catching Swedish Phish*, 5.

123. EUvsDisinfo, *Sweden's Feminist Government Orders.*

124. Cederberg, *Catching Swedish Phish*, 9.

125. Ibid., 6.

126. Chalfant, "Denmark, Sweden Team Up."

127. See Alliance for Securing Democracy, "Authoritarian Interference Tracker," https://securingdemocracy.gmfus.org/toolbox/authoritarian-interference-tracker/ (last visited September 6, 2021).

128. Kragh and Asberg, "Russia's Strategy for Influence," 17.

129. Cederberg, *Catching Swedish Phish*, 6.

130. Berzina, "Sweden—Preparing for the Wolf."

131. Kragh and Asberg, "Russia's Strategy for Influence," 18–25.

132. Ibid., 21.

133. Ibid., 18–19.

134. Ibid., 25.

135. Ibid., 26.

136. Berzina, "Sweden—Preparing for the Wolf."

137. Ibid.

138. Hedman et al., "News and Political Information Consumption."

139. Neudert, Howard, and Kollanyi, "Sourcing and Automation of Political News."

140. Hedman et al., "News and Political Information Consumption."

141. Kragh and Asberg, "Russia's Strategy for Influence," 7.

142. See Cederberg, *Catching Swedish Phish.*

143. See ibid. See also Berzina, "Sweden—Preparing for the Wolf"; Senate Foreign Relations Comm., Minority Staff Report, *Putin's Asymmetric Assault on Democracy,* 109–12.

144. Duxbury, "Sweden Gets New Government."

145. Ibid.

146. Cederberg, *Catching Swedish Phish*, 30.

147. Ibid.

CHAPTER FOUR: CHINA'S GLOBAL INFORMATION OPERATIONS

1. Kania, "The Right to Speak."

2. Schrader, "Friends and Enemies."

3. United Nations Human Rights Council, *Cross-regional Statement on Hong Kong and Xinjiang* (June 30, 2020).

4. United Nations Human Rights Council, *Joint Statement Delivered by Permanent Mission of Cuba* (June 30, 2020).

5. Ibid.

6. Charter of the United Nations, arts. 55, 56.

7. Ibid., art. 2(7).

8. DiResta et al., "Telling China's Story."

9. Campbell and Rapp-Hooper, "China Is Done Biding Its Time."

10. Ibid.

11. See Pei, "Chinese Diplomats Behaving Badly."

12. Lippman, "Trump National Security Adviser."

13. McFaul, "Xi Jinping Is Not Stalin."

14. Ibid.

15. Pompeo, "Communist China and the Free World's Future."

16. Weiss, "Ideological Contest in U.S.-China Relations?"

17. Friedberg, "An Answer to Aggression," 152.

18. See ibid. See also Ginsburg, "Authoritarian International Law?"

19. Thompson, "The TikTok War."

20. Weiss, "Ideological Contest in U.S.-China Relations?"

21. Vilmer and Charon, "Russia as a Hurricane" (quoting Rob Joyce, senior cybersecurity advisor to the National Security Agency).

22. See Cave et al., "Mapping China's Technology Giants."

23. Joske, "The Party Speaks for You," 3.

24. Mantesso and Zhou, "China's Multi-Billion-Dollar Media Campaign."

25. China Global Television Network, "About Us," https://www.cgtn.com/about-us.

26. Mantesso and Zhou, "China's Multi-Billion-Dollar Media Campaign."

27. "About China Daily Group," https://www.chinadaily.com.cn/static_e/2011about
.html.

28. "Introduction to People's Daily," http://en.people.cn/other/about.shtml.

29. Cook, "Beijing's Global Megaphone," 5.

30. "About the Global Times," http://www.globaltimes.cn/about-us/.

31. China Plus, "Who We Are," http://chinaplus.cri.cn/aboutus/aboutcri/62/
20170216/393.html.

32. China Plus, http://chinaplus.cri.cn/aboutus/abouttheengiishservice/61/20170216/
389.html.

33. Xinhua News Agency, http://english.visitbeijing.com.cn/a1/a-XAHSGGC3D36037
CD215DD7.

34. Mantesso and Zhou, "China's Multi-Billion-Dollar Media Campaign."

35. China News, "About Us," https://www.chinanews.com/common/footer/aboutus
.shtml.

36. Yan, "Seeing Double?"

37. Hernandez, "As Protests Engulf the United States."

38. Cave et al., "Mapping China's Technology Giants," 7.

39. Ibid.

40. Ibid.

41. Ibid., 8.

42. Shahbaz, "Freedom on the Net 2018," 1–2.

43. Cave et al., "Mapping China's Technology Giants," 9.

44. Ibid., 10.

45. Ibid.

46. See Kendall-Taylor, Frantz, and Wright, "The Digital Dictators."

47. In 2019, Zimbabwe ranked 158 out of 198 countries on Transparency International's Corruption Perceptions Index.

48. Cave et al., "Mapping China's Technology Giants," 11.

49. Ibid.

50. Kliman et al., "Grading China's Belt and Road."

51. Ibid.

52. *The Economist*, "The Big Unfriending."

53. Ibid.

54. TenCent, *TenCent Announces 2020 First Quarter Results*.

55. See Culpan, "The World's Most Powerful App" (stating that approximately 20 percent of WeChat users are outside of China).

56. TikTok has 800 million monthly active users, with 57 percent of the user base in China. See Iqbal, October 30, 2020. If 43 percent of users are outside China, that would be 344 million users outside of China.

57. Thompson, "The TikTok War."

58. Ibid.

59. Ibid.

60. See Exec. Order No. 13,942; Exec. Order No. 13,943.

61. See, e.g., Marland v. Trump, 2020 WL 6381397 (E.D. Pa. Oct. 30, 2020) (granting preliminary injunction to block enforcement of the TikTok ban); U.S. WeChat Users All. v. Trump, 2020 WL 6891820 (N.D. Cal. Nov. 24, 2020) (affirming preliminary injunction to block enforcement of the WeChat ban).

62. See Davis, "Biden Administration Still Weighing TikTok and WeChat Bans."

63. Joske, "The Party Speaks for You," 6.

64. Ibid., 7.

65. Ibid., 10.

66. Yoshihara and Bianchi, "Uncovering China's Influence in Europe," 8.

67. Ibid.

68. Ibid.

69. Joske, "The Party Speaks for You," 26.

70. Ibid.

71. Ibid., 27.

72. Ibid.

73. Ibid., 12.

74. Ibid.

75. Eko, Kumar, and Yao, "Google This."

76. King, Pan, and Roberts, "How the Chinese Government Fabricates Social Media Posts," 484.

77. Ibid.

78. Ibid., 485.

79. Cook, "Beijing's Global Megaphone," 6.

80. The data on likes and followers may include a small number of people inside China who are using virtual private networks (VPNs) to circumvent the "great firewall" to access Facebook and/or Twitter.

81. Molter and DiResta, "Pandemics & Propaganda."

82. Schechter, "China Launches New Twitter Accounts."

83. See DiResta et al., "Telling China's Story," 13.

84. Lin, "Digital News Report: Taiwan."

85. See Horton, "Specter of Meddling by Beijing"; Huang, "Chinese Cyber-Operatives."

86. DiResta et al., "Telling China's Story," 26.

87. Bradshaw and Howard, *The Global Disinformation Order*, 2.

88. Wallis et al., "Retweeting through the Great Firewall," 19.

89. DiResta et al., "Telling China's Story," 19.

90. Ibid., 25.

91. Ibid., 20.

92. Twitter Safety, "Information Operations."

93. Gleicher, "Removing Coordinated Inauthentic Behavior from China."

94. Welch, "YouTube Disabled 210 Accounts."

95. DiResta et al., "Telling China's Story," 20.

96. Ibid., 21.

97. Wallis et al., "Retweeting through the Great Firewall," 23.

98. Ibid., 4.

99. DiResta et al., "Telling China's Story," 23.

100. Wallis et al., "Retweeting through the Great Firewall," 5.

101. DiResta et al., "Telling China's Story," 23.

102. Ibid., 33.

103. Insikt Group, "Chinese State Media Seeks to Influence," 2.

104. Ibid., 3.

105. Schechter, "China Launches New Twitter Accounts."

106. Molter and DiResta, "Pandemics & Propaganda," 14.

107. Ibid., 15.

108. Ibid., 14.

109. Ibid., 14.

110. Twitter Safety, "Disclosing Networks of State-Linked Operations."

111. Miller et al. "Sockpuppets Spin COVID Yarns," 5.

112. Ibid., 17.

113. Thomas and Zhang, "COVID-19 Attracts Patriotic Troll Campaigns."

114. Ibid.

115. Wallis et al., "Retweeting through the Great Firewall," 5. See also Molter and DiResta, "Pandemics & Propaganda," 5–10.

116. Wallis et al., "Retweeting through the Great Firewall," 12.

117. See ibid., 13–17.

118. See Insikt Group, "Chinese State Media Seeks to Influence," 11–12.

119. See Schechter, "China Launches New Twitter Accounts."

120. See Wallis et al., "Retweeting through the Great Firewall," 4, 7.

121. See Molter and DiResta, "Pandemics & Propaganda," 14.

122. Schechter, "China Launches New Twitter Accounts."

123. Miller et al., "Sockpuppets Spin COVID Yarns," 6, 10.

124. Schechter, "China Launches New Twitter Accounts."

125. Rosenberger, "China's Coronavirus Information Offensive."

126. See Haass, "Foreign Policy"; Abrams, "American Leadership."

127. O'Connor et al., "Cyber-Enabled Foreign Interference."

128. V-Dem Institute, "Democracy Facing Global Challenges," 34.

129. DiResta et al., "Telling China's Story," 28.

130. Ibid.

131. See Green and Medeiros, "Is Taiwan the Next Hong Kong?"

132. See Kurlantzick, "How China Is Interfering in Taiwan's Election."

133. Ibid.

134. Doshi, "China Steps Up Its Information War." See also Schmitt and Mazza, "Blinding the Enemy."

135. See Greene, "Chinese Spy Wang Liqiang"; Joske, "Wang Liqiang."

136. DiResta et al., "Telling China's Story," 26.

137. Schmitt and Mazza, "Blinding the Enemy," 9.

138. Doshi, "China Steps Up Its Information War."

139. Schmitt and Mazza, "Blinding the Enemy," 9.

140. DiResta et al., "Telling China's Story," 27.

141. Ibid., 28.

142. Ibid., 29–30.

143. Ibid., 30.

144. Ibid.

145. Ibid.

146. Ibid., 31.

147. Ibid., 31.

148. Ibid.

149. Knockel et al., "We Chat, They Watch," 7–10.

150. Ibid., 5.

151. Ibid.

152. Feng, "China Intercepts WeChat Texts."

153. Ibid.

154. Cook, "Beijing's Global Megaphone," 19.

155. Feng, "China Intercepts WeChat Texts."

156. Ibid.

157. Cave et al., "Mapping China's Technology Giants," 15.

158. Walsh and Xiao, "Uncharted Territory."

159. Ibid.

160. Cave et al., "Mapping China's Technology Giants," 15.

161. Cook, "Beijing's Global Megaphone," 8.

162. Ibid.

163. Mantesso and Zhou, "China's Multi-Billion-Dollar Media Campaign."

164. Ibid.

165. Ross, "*Washington Post* and *Wall Street Journal.*"

166. Ibid.

167. Mantesso and Zhou, "China's Multi-Billion-Dollar Media Campaign."

168. Cook, "Beijing's Global Megaphone," 8.
169. Feldstein, "When It Comes to Digital Authoritarianism."
170. Kendall-Taylor, Frantz, and Wright, "The Digital Dictators," 109.
171. Barma, Durbin, and Kendall-Taylor, "Digital Authoritarianism."
172. Feldstein, "When It Comes to Digital Authoritarianism."
173. Shahbaz and Funk, "Freedom on the Net 2019," 18.
174. Kendall-Taylor, Frantz, and Wright, "The Digital Dictators," 112.
175. Ibid.
176. Andersen, "The Panopticon Is Already Here."
177. Weiss, "Understanding and Rolling Back Digital Authoritarianism."
178. Zuboff, *The Age of Surveillance Capitalism.*
179. Shahbaz and Funk, "Freedom on the Net 2019," 12.
180. Ibid., 16.
181. Ibid., 13.
182. Gallagher, "Middle East Dictators Buy Spy Tech."
183. Ibid.
184. O'Neill, "Chinese Surveillance Giant Knowlesys."
185. Ibid.
186. Franceschi-Bicchierai, "Hackers Leak Alleged Internal Files."
187. Ibid.
188. Mantesso and Zhou, "China's Multi-Billion-Dollar Media Campaign."
189. Cave et al., "Mapping China's Technology Giants," 3.
190. Shahbaz, "Freedom on the Net 2018," 8–9.
191. Ibid., 10.
192. Cook, "Beijing's Global Megaphone," 16–17.
193. Mantesso and Zhou, "China's Multi-Billion-Dollar Media Campaign."
194. Ibid.
195. Cook, "Beijing's Global Megaphone," 8.
196. Ibid., 8.
197. Ibid., 17.
198. Ibid.
199. Australian Strategic Policy Institute, "Covid-19 Disinformation."
200. Cook, "Beijing's Global Megaphone," 17.
201. Mantesso and Zhou, "China's Multi-Billion-Dollar Media Campaign."
202. Ibid.

CHAPTER FIVE: AN UNEVEN PLAYING FIELD
1. Kreps, *Social Media and International Relations.*
2. Kendall-Taylor, Frantz, and Wright, "The Digital Dictators."
3. The V-Dem database and codebook are available at https://www.v-dem.net/en/data/data-version-10/.
4. See Freedom House, "Freedom in the World 2020."
5. Goodman and Jinks, *Socializing States,* 53–54.
6. See Simmons, *Mobilizing for Human Rights,* 88–96.
7. See, e.g., Pariser, *The Filter Bubble;* Sunstein, *#Republic;* Settle, *Frenemies.*
8. See, e.g., Kreps, *Social Media and International Relations;* Howard, *Lie Machines.*

9. Brazil, Croatia, and Suriname were never "liberal democracies" based on the v2x_ regime variable at any time in the past twenty years. The Czech Republic, Poland, and South Africa all dropped from liberal democracies to electoral democracies (according to the v2x_ regime variable) within the past decade. Hungary dropped from a liberal democracy to an electoral autocracy between 2009 and 2018.

10. Bradshaw and Howard, *The Global Disinformation Order*.

11. The Oxford disinformation report presents data in five tables for all seventy countries covered in the report. Tables 1–4, in the aggregate, provide basic yes/no answers for nineteen separate questions related to OSM activities. I assigned 1 point for each "yes" answer. Table 5 divides all seventy countries into four groups based on their "cyber troop capacities." I assigned 4 points for high capacity, 3 points for medium capacity, 2 points for low capacity, and 1 point for minimal capacity. Hence, the maximum possible score for any particular country is 23 points.

12. I thank my friend Wayne Sandholtz for his help in preparing the scatterplot in figure 4.

13. See European Commission, *Rule of Law*.

14. Freedom House, "Freedom in the World 2020," Poland, sec. D1.

15. Gorwa, "Computational Propaganda in Poland," 4.

16. Ibid., 8.

17. Ibid., 16.

18. Ibid.

19. Howard, *Lie Machines*, 87.

20. Gorwa, "Computational Propaganda in Poland," 17–18.

21. Ibid., 16.

22. Ibid., 10.

23. Ibid., 8.

24. Ibid., 25.

25. This definition is adapted from Howard, *Lie Machines*, 172–73.

26. O'Connor and Weatherall, *The Misinformation Age*, 148.

27. Ibid., 149.

28. Ibid., 147.

29. Howard, *Lie Machines*, 84.

30. For a good explanation of how to make things go viral on social media, see Marantz, *Anti-Social*, 84–98.

31. Rovetta, Suchacka, and Masulli, "Bot Recognition in a Web Store."

32. See Howard, *Lie Machines*, 54–81.

33. Ibid., 173–74.

34. Ibid., 54.

35. See ibid., 82–107.

36. Ibid., 107.

37. Ibid., 113.

38. Ibid., 122.

39. See ibid., 117–36.

40. Kreps, *Social Media and International Relations*, 3.

41. See Pew Research Center, "The Partisan Divide."

42. Benkler, Faris, and Roberts, *Network Propaganda*.

43. Klein, *Why We're Polarized*.

44. Chua, "Divided We Fall," 160.

45. Pariser, *The Filter Bubble*, 5.

46. See ibid. See also Sunstein, *#Republic*.

47. Pew Research Center, "How Americans See Climate Change."

48. Settle, *Frenemies*, 3.

49. Ibid., 3.

50. Ibid., 6.

51. MacKinnon, "Liberation Technology," 33.

52. Ibid.

53. Freedom House, "Freedom on the Net 2019," Russia, sec. A3.

54. Freedom House, "Freedom on the Net 2019," China, sec. A3.

55. Kerr, "Russian Model of Digital Control," 67.

56. Freedom House, "Freedom on the Net 2019," China, sec. C5.

57. MacKinnon, "Liberation Technology," 41.

58. Freedom House, "Freedom on the Net 2019," Russia, sec. B4.

59. Freedom House, "Freedom on the Net 2019," China, sec. B4.

60. Kerr, "Russian Model of Digital Control," 66.

61. MacKinnon, "Liberation Technology," 38.

62. Kerr, "Russian Model of Digital Control," 65–66.

63. King, Pan, and Roberts, "How the Chinese Government Fabricates Social Media Posts," 484.

64. Kerr, "Russian Model of Digital Control," 67–68.

65. Freedom House, "Freedom on the Net 2019, Internet Freedom Scores."

66. Eko, Kumar, and Yao, "Google This," 5.

67. Chen, Lin, and Liu, "Rule of Trust," 10.

68. Ibid., 9.

69. Ibid., 14.

70. Ibid., 12.

71. Kendall-Taylor, Frantz, and Wright, "The Digital Dictators," 109.

72. Chen, Lin, and Liu, "Rule of Trust," 26.

73. Hyun and Kim, "The Role of New Media."

74. Kreps, *Social Media and International Relations*, 3.

75. See Linos, *Democratic Foundations of Policy Diffusion*.

76. Cooley and Nexon, "How Hegemony Ends," 146.

77. Bradshaw and Howard, *The Global Disinformation Order*.

78. Pearce and Kendzior, "Networked Authoritarianism," 286.

79. Ibid.

80. Ibid., 287.

81. Kerr, "Information, Security, and Authoritarian Stability," 3814.

82. Ibid., 3819–27.

83. Ibid., 3820.

84. Ibid., 3820.

85. Ibid., 3821.

86. Ibid., 3822.

87. Ibid., 3823–24.

88. Ibid., 3823.

89. Ibid., 3828.

90. See Tufekci, *Twitter and Tear Gas.*

91. See Yerkes, "The Tunisia Model in Crisis."

92. Gleicher, ""Removing Coordinated Inauthentic Behavior in UAE."

93. Twitter Safety, "Disclosing New Data."

94. Walsh and Rashwan, "We're at War."

95. See Bradshaw and Howard, *The Global Disinformation Order.*

96. See Al Jazeera, "Qatar Blockade."

97. See Bradshaw and Howard, *Case Studies.*

98. Perez and Prokupecz, "US Suspects Russian Hackers."

99. See Bradshaw and Howard, *The Global Disinformation Order.*

100. Shahbaz, "Freedom on the Net 2018," 8.

101. Ibid., 8–9.

102. See Freedom House, "Freedom on the Net 2019," Country Reports for Bahrain, Egypt, Saudi Arabia, Syria, and UAE, secs. B1 and B2.

103. See Freedom House, "Freedom on the Net 2019," Sudan, secs. B1 and B2.

104. U.S. Department of State, *2019 Country Reports on Human Rights Practices,* Qatar.

105. See Freedom House, "Freedom on the Net 2019," Country Reports for Bahrain, Egypt, Saudi Arabia, Sudan, Syria, and UAE, secs. C5 and C6.

106. Freedom House, "Freedom on the Net 2019," Bahrain, sec. C6.

107. Freedom House, "Freedom in the World 2020," Qatar, sec. D4.

108. See Freedom House, "Freedom on the Net 2019," Country Reports for Bahrain, Egypt, Saudi Arabia, Sudan, Syria, and UAE, secs. B4, C2, C3, and C7; "Freedom in the World 2020," Qatar, sec. D4.

109. Freedom House, "Freedom on the Net 2019," Sudan, sec. C3.

110. This paragraph is based on Bradshaw and Howard, *The Global Disinformation Order.*

111. Kendall-Taylor, Frantz, and Wright, "The Digital Dictators," 112.

112. Ibid.

CHAPTER SIX: A PROPOSAL FOR TRANSNATIONAL REGULATION

1. See chapter 2.

2. See Wallis et al., "Retweeting through the Great Firewall," 10–11.

3. See ibid.

4. See Silverman, "People Are Renting Out Their Facebook Accounts."

5. Rovetta et al., "Bot Recognition in a Web Store," 1.

6. See chapters 2 and 3.

7. See chapter 4, pp. 86–87.

8. VKontakte (VK) is the Russian equivalent of Facebook. It has 97 million monthly active users. See VK.com., "About Us," https://vk.com/about (last visited September 6, 2021). As of June 2020, 79 percent of its monthly active users are inside Russia. See Similarweb, "VK.com: June 2020 Traffic Overview." Thus, VK has about 20 million monthly active users outside Russia. Sina Weibo is the Chinese equivalent of Twitter. It has 550 million monthly active users. See Statista, "Number of Monthly Active Users of Sina Weibo." According to Sina Weibo's 2018 annual report, only 8 percent of its monthly active users are

outside China. See Sina Weibo, "Annual Report 2018." Thus, Sina Weibo has about 44 million monthly active users outside of China.

9. As of March 31, 2020, WeChat had about 1.2 billion monthly active users. See Ten-Cent, *TenCent Announces 2020 First Quarter Results*. Approximately 20 percent of WeChat users are outside of China. See Culpan, "The World's Most Powerful App." Thus, WeChat has about 240 million monthly active users outside of China.

10. Nuclear Suppliers Group, "About the NSG," https://www.nuclearsuppliersgroup .org/en/ (last visited September 6, 2021).

11. Nuclear Nonproliferation Act of 1978, Pub. L. No. 95-242, 92 Stat. 120 (codified as amended in scattered sections of 22 and 42 U.S.C.).

12. For a list of OECD member states, see https://www.oecd.org/about/members -and-partners/.

13. The government effectiveness indicator measures "the quality of public services, the quality of the civil service and the degree of its independence from political pressures, the quality of policy formulation and implementation, and the credibility of the government's commitment to such policies." See World Bank, "Worldwide Governance Indicators," http://info.worldbank.org/governance/wgi/ (last visited September 6, 2021).

14. From 2014 to 2018, Mexico received scores of .20, .21, .13, −.03, and −.15.

15. They are Australia, Austria, Belgium, Canada, Chile, Czech Republic, Denmark, Estonia, Finland, France, Germany, Greece, Hungary, Iceland, Ireland, Israel, Italy, Japan, Latvia, Lithuania, Luxembourg, Netherlands, New Zealand, Norway, Poland, Portugal, Slovakia, Slovenia, South Korea, Spain, Sweden, Switzerland, the United Kingdom, and the United States.

16. The V-Dem database is available at https://www.v-dem.net/en/.

17. For an international law analysis of Taiwanese statehood, see Roth, "Entity That Dare Not Speak Its Name."

18. See the appendix for proposed definitions of "social media platform" and "public communication." The definitions of these terms should be substantially identical in all Alliance member states.

19. This provision is adapted from the definition of "electioneering communication" in 52 U.S.C. § 30104(f). The specific limitation of "120 days before" an election is somewhat arbitrary, but some such time limitation may be required under the First Amendment.

20. This definition is substantially identical to the existing statutory definition of "clearly identified" in 52 U.S.C. § 30101.

21. Anderson et al., "From Warning to Wallpaper."

22. Bradshaw and Howard, *The Global Disinformation Order*, i.

23. See Mozur, "A Genocide Incited on Facebook."

24. The transnational regulatory system is designed to apply to social media platforms with more than 50 million monthly active users outside of China and Russia. Both China and Russia have other platforms that are used primarily for internal communications. These include VK (the Russian equivalent of Facebook) and Sina Weibo (the Chinese equivalent of Twitter). Those platforms would not be covered by the transnational regulatory system because they fall below the 50 million threshold. See note 8.

25. Bradshaw and Howard, *The Global Disinformation Order*, i.

26. See International Law Commission, *Responsibility of States for Internationally Wrongful Acts*.

27. United Nations Security Council, S.C. Res. 1373, para. 1(c) (September 28, 2001).

28. See United Nations Security Council, "Counter-Terrorism Committee," https://www.un.org/sc/ctc/ (last visited September 6, 2021).

29. See note 8.

30. Open Technology Fund, "About," https://www.opentech.fund/about/ (last visited September 6, 2021).

31. Verma and Wong, "Trump's Pick Criticized."

32. Some tools developed by the Open Technology Fund operate in conjunction with social media platforms. Other tools operate independently. See generally Open Technology Fund, *FY 2018 Annual Report.*

33. See note 9.

34. See Allyn, "Biden Drops Trump's Ban."

35. See Borak, "ByteDance Says TikTok and Douyin Are Different."

36. United States v. Curtiss-Wright Export Corp., 299 U.S. 304 (1936).

37. Exec. Order No. 13,456, sec. 6(b). See generally https://home.treasury.gov/policy-issues/international/the-committee-on-foreign-investment-in-the-united-states-cfius.

38. See Chinen, "Presidential Certifications."

39. Agency for International Development v. Alliance for Open Society International, Inc., 140 S. Ct. 2082 (2020).

40. See Instagram, "Getting Started," https://business.instagram.com/getting-started/#get-a-business-profile (last visited September 6, 2021). See also Instagram, "Adding Accounts," https://help.instagram.com/589697191199472/?helpref=hc_fnav&bc[0]=Instagram%20Help&bc[1]=Managing%20Your%20Account (last visited September 6, 2021).

41. Roth, "Automation and the Use of Multiple Accounts."

42. See REAL ID Act of 2005, § 202(d)(6), 119 Stat. 311, 314.

43. See Twitter, "About Public and Protected Tweets," https://help.twitter.com/en/safety-and-security/public-and-protected-tweets (last visited September 6, 2021); Instagram, "Controlling Your Visibility," https://help.instagram.com/116024195217477 (last visited September 6, 2021).

44. Facebook allows users to control the audience for posts they make on their own profiles. However, when a user posts to another user's profile, or to a separate page, that user or the page's administrator controls the audience. See Facebook, "Basic Privacy Settings & Tools," https://www.facebook.com/help/325807937506242 (last visited September 6, 2021).

45. Facebook, "Create an Account," https://www.facebook.com/help/345121355559712 (last visited September 6, 2021).

46. Twitter, "Signing Up with Twitter," https://help.twitter.com/en/create-twitter-account (last visited September 6, 2021); see also Twitter, "Help with Username Registration," https://help.twitter.com/en/managing-your-account/twitter-username-rules (last visited September 6, 2021).

47. See Children's Online Privacy Protection Act of 1998, Pub. L. No. 105-277, §§ 1301–1308, 112 Stat. 2681 (codified at 15 U.S.C. §§ 6501–6506).

48. See Children's Online Privacy Protection Rule, 16 C.F.R. Part 312, §§ 312.1–312.13.

49. Krajewska, *Documenting Americans*, 2.

50. See REAL ID Act of 2005, 119 Stat. 311-16.

51. U.S. Department of Homeland Security, "All U.S. States Now Compliant."

52. See REAL ID Act of 2005, § 202(d)(12,13), 119 Stat. 311, 315.

53. See, e.g., American Civil Liberties Union, "Real ID," https://www.aclu.org/issues/privacy-technology/national-id/real-id (last visited September 6, 2021).

54. Companies will need to exercise some discretionary judgment in classifying accounts as duplicates or nonduplicates. For example, suppose John Smith creates a new account with the same email address as an existing "John Smith" account but with a slightly different passport number. Is it the same person who provided mistaken information about the passport number for one account? Or are they two different people, one of whom provided an incorrect email address? Or is it a foreign agent trying to register as John Smith to evade the statutory requirements for foreign users? Other information (such as birth date) may provide clues about which scenario is more likely.

55. This could happen, for example, if a person who does not understand the rules about master accounts and subsidiary accounts mistakenly tries to create a second master account instead of creating a new subsidiary account.

56. See Gressin, "The Equifax Data Breach."

57. European Union, General Data Protection Regulation, Regulation 2016/679.

58. Irick, "Data Hashing and Encryption."

59. See, e.g., Clapper v. Amnesty Int'l USA, 568 U.S. 398, 417–18 (2013).

60. Facebook, "Community Standard on Misrepresentation," https://www.facebook.com/communitystandards/integrity_authenticity (last visited September 6, 2021).

61. Facebook, *Community Standards Enforcement Report* (May 2020), https://about.fb.com/news/2020/05/community-standards-enforcement-report-may-2020/ (last visited September 6, 2021).

62. Ibid.

63. See Rovetta et al., "Bot Recognition in a Web Store."

64. California Business and Professions Code, § 17941.

65. See Stieglitz et al., "Do Social Bots Dream of Electric Sheep?"

CHAPTER SEVEN: POLICY ANALYSIS

1. Sunstein, *#Republic*, 200.

2. See Barlow, "A Declaration."

3. Telecommunications Act of 1996, Pub. L. No. 104-104, Sec. 509, 110 Stat. 137-39.

4. See 47 U.S.C. § 230.

5. See Goldman, "An Overview."

6. Goldsmith and Woods, "Internet Speech."

7. See Facebook, "Community Standards," https://www.facebook.com/communitystandards/ (last visited September 6, 2021).

8. See Twitter, "Rules and Policies," https://help.twitter.com/en/rules-and-policies (last visited September 6, 2021).

9. See YouTube Creator Academy, "YouTube's Community Guidelines," https://creatoracademy.youtube.com/page/course/community-guidelines (last visited September 6, 2021).

10. See Klonick, "The New Governors"; Balkin, "Free Speech Is a Triangle."

11. For a good survey of issues related to "platform law," see the symposium in the *Berkeley Journal of Law and Technology* 32 (2017): 713–1299.

12. See New York Stock Exchange, *Corporate Governance Guide.*

13. U.S. Constitution, Preamble.

14. Goldsmith and Woods, "Internet Speech."

15. Murphy, "Inside Facebook's Information Warfare Team."

16. Ibid.

17. See chapter 1, pp. 18–20.

18. See Isaac and Browning, "Fact-Checked on Facebook and Twitter."

19. Howard et al., "IRA, Social Media and Political Polarization," 3.

20. See U.S. Department of Justice, "DOJ Criminal Cases against Chinese."

21. Exec. Order No. 13,757.

22. Ibid., sec. 1.

23. See Countering America's Adversaries Through Sanctions Act, Pub. L. No. 115-44, 131 Stat. 886 (2017).

24. Howard et al., "IRA, Social Media and Political Polarization," 3.

25. Ibid., 3.

26. Mueller Report, vol. 1, p. 174.

27. Ibid.

28. Ibid., 175.

29. United States of America v. Paul J. Manafort, Jr. and Konstantin Kilimnik, *Superseding Indictment* (D.D.C. June 8, 2018).

30. Pecorin, "What You Need to Know."

31. See Bering, "The Prohibition on Annexation"; Daugirdis and Mortenson, "Contemporary Practice."

32. See chapter 3.

33. See BBC News, "Navalny Novichok Poisoning."

34. See Countering America's Adversaries Through Sanctions Act, Pub. L. No. 115-44, 131 Stat. 886 (2017).

35. See Congresswoman Anna G. Eshoo, "Rep. Eshoo Introduces Bill."

36. Honest Ads Act, S.1989, 115th Cong., 1st Sess. (Oct. 19, 2017).

37. See Senator Amy Klobuchar, "Klobuchar, Graham, Warner Introduce Legislation."

38. Honest Ads Act, sec. 2.

39. Ibid., sec. 3(5).

40. Ibid., sec. 3(4).

41. DiResta et al., "Tactics and Tropes," 6.

42. Howard et al., "IRA, Social Media and Political Polarization," 6–7.

43. Ibid., 7.

44. Ibid., 3.

45. Silverman and Mac, "Facebook Knows."

46. See Federal Cigarette Labeling and Advertising Act, Pub. L. No. 89-92, § 2, 79 Stat. 282 (1965).

47. Goodman, "Visual Gut Punch," 532 (quoting FTC Report).

48. Cornell, "The Aesthetic Toll of Nudging," 849.

49. Anderson, "From Warning to Wallpaper."

50. See chapter 6, pp. 147–50.

51. Facebook, *Community Standards Enforcement Report* (August 2020).

52. Ibid.

53. See Sloss, "Corporate Defenses."

54. Facebook, *Community Standards Enforcement Report* (August 2020).

55. See Krajewska, *Documenting Americans*, 2–3.

56. Wallis et al., "Retweeting through the Great Firewall," 10–11.

57. Ibid.

58. See chapter 6, pp. 173–75.

59. See chapter 6, pp. 160–62.

60. See chapter 6, pp. 179–80.

61. See Aratani, "Tsunami of Untruths."

62. See *The Economist*, "Democracy Index 2016."

63. Fessler, "American Distrust of the Voting Process."

64. See Polyakova, "Putinism and the European Far-Right."

65. See chapter 3, pp. 49–53.

66. British Social Attitudes, *The Vote to Leave the EU*, 17.

67. See chapter 4, pp. 103–5.

68. Krajewska, *Documenting Americans*, 2–3.

69. See Carpenter et al., *License to Work*.

70. Ibid.

71. Howard, *Lie Machines*, 96.

72. King, Pan, and Roberts, "How the Chinese Government Fabricates Social Media Posts."

73. DiResta et al., "Tactics and Tropes," 6.

74. *India Today*, "Over 125 Crore People."

75. See Cederberg, *Catching Swedish Phish*, 28–29.

76. See Benkler, Faris, and Roberts, *Network Propaganda*.

77. See Election Integrity Partnership, *Evaluating Platform Election-Related Speech Policies*.

78. Facebook, *Community Standards Enforcement Report* (August 2020).

79. See Rudolph and Morley, "Covert Foreign Money."

80. See Sloss, "Best Way to Regulate Disinformation."

81. Krajewska, *Documenting Americans*, 2.

82. See chapter 6, pp. 154–56.

83. REAL ID Act of 2005, § 202(d) (12, 13).

84. U.S. Department of Homeland Security, "All U.S. States Now Compliant."

85. See chapter 6, pp. 173–75.

86. 52 U.S.C. § 30101.

87. See Roberts, *Behind the Screen*.

88. Klayman v. Obama, 957 F.Supp.2d 1, 10 (D.D.C. 2013).

89. Rosenberg, Confessore, and Cadwalladr, "How Trump Consultants Exploited."

90. Thompson and Warzel, "12 Million Phones."

91. Al Jazeera, "US Military Buys Location Data."

92. Koreh, "CBP's New Social Media Surveillance."

93. Biddle, "Police Surveilled George Floyd Protests."

94. See Granick and Gorski, "How to Address Newly Revealed Abuses."

95. McIntyre v. Ohio Elections Comm'n, 514 U.S. 334, 342 (1995).

96. See Instagram, "How Do I Create an Instagram Account?" https://help.instagram.com/155940534568753 (last visited September 6, 2021).

97. See chapter 6, p. 177.

98. See Zuboff, *The Age of Surveillance Capitalism*.

99. Dance, LaForgia, and Confessore, "As Facebook Raised a Privacy Wall."

100. 18 U.S.C. § 2511.

101. 18 U.S.C. § 2701.

102. See American Civil Liberties Union, "Real ID."

103. 18 U.S.C. § 2721(a).

104. 18 U.S.C. § 2721(b)(1).

105. See Associated Press, "Trump Administration Takes Aim."

106. REAL ID Act of 2005, § 202(d)(11).

107. See Associated Press, "Trump Administration Takes Aim."

108. Murphy, "Inside Facebook's Information Warfare Team."

CHAPTER EIGHT: THE FIRST AMENDMENT

1. For the purpose of this chapter, I will disregard the specific proposals to address bots, rental accounts, and fake foreign national accounts. See chapter 6, pp. 177–81. The proposals on rental accounts and fake foreign national accounts do not raise significant First Amendment issues. The proposal on bots is potentially vulnerable to a First Amendment challenge, but this chapter focuses on the First Amendment implications of the proposed rules involving the ban, the disclaimer requirement, and the registration system.

2. Cass Sunstein distinguishes between the "Madisonian First Amendment" and the "free market view" of the First Amendment. See Sunstein, *Democracy and the Problem*, xvi–xx, 17–20. I prefer the term "libertarian" to "free market," but the First Amendment analysis in this chapter is heavily influenced by Sunstein's work.

3. Nat'l Federation of Independent Business v. Sebelius, 567 U.S. 519, 538 (2012).

4. Post, *Citizens Divided*, 8.

5. Bhagwat, *Our Democratic First Amendment*, 9.

6. Schauer, *Free Speech*, 86.

7. Barnett, *Our Republican Constitution*, 36.

8. Madison, Federalist No. 10, at 126 (Isaac Kramnick, ed., 1987).

9. See generally Barnett, *Our Republican Constitution*.

10. See Whittington, *Constitutional Construction*.

11. See Alexander and Schauer, "On Extrajudicial Constitutional Interpretation"; Alexander and Schauer, "Defending Judicial Supremacy."

12. Madison, *The Report of 1800*, 8.

13. See Kramer, *The People Themselves*.

14. There is some tension in this respect between Madison's view, as expressed in the preceding quotation, and Kramer's theory of popular constitutionalism. When Madison suggested that the "parties to the constitution" have the right to determine whether the judiciary has violated the Constitution, he was referring to the states as the "parties." He did not necessarily envision a mechanism for "We the People" to act as a check on judicial power, other than by acting through the states. See Madison, *The Report of 1800*, 7–8.

15. See Kramer, "The Interest of Man."

16. Bethune-Hill v. Virginia State Bd. of Elections, 137 S. Ct. 788, 801 (2017).

17. United States v. Windsor, 570 U.S. 744, 812 (2013) (Alito, J., dissenting).

18. Box v. Planned Parenthood of Indiana and Kentucky, Inc., 139 S. Ct. 1780, 1781–82 (2019).

19. See Barnett, *Our Republican Constitution*, 222–45.

20. See, e.g., Post, *Citizens Divided*, 66–94.

21. Abrams v. United States, 250 U.S. 616, 630 (1919) (Holmes, J., dissenting).

22. See Lochner v. New York, 198 U.S. 45, 74–76 (Holmes, J., dissenting).

23. See, e.g., Shanor, "The New Lochner"; Bagenstos, "The Unrelenting Libertarian Challenge."

24. See, e.g., Sunstein, *Democracy and the Problem*, 17–51.

25. In re Ross, 140 U.S. 453, 464 (1891).

26. Reid v. Covert, 354 U.S. 1 (1957) (plurality opinion).

27. Agency for Int'l Development v. Alliance for Open Society Int'l, Inc., 140 S. Ct. 2082 (2020).

28. Boumediene v. Bush, 553 U.S. 723 (2008).

29. See generally Thai, "Right to Receive Foreign Speech."

30. Stanley v. Georgia, 394 U.S. 557, 564 (1969).

31. Lamont v. Postmaster General of U.S., 381 U.S. 301 (1965).

32. See Kleindienst v. Mandel, 408 U.S. 753 (1972).

33. 52 U.S.C. § 30101(18).

34. Janus v. American Fed'n of State, County, and Municipal Employees, 138 S. Ct. 2448, 2463 (2018).

35. Issacharoff et al., *The Law of Democracy*, 386.

36. Citizens United v. Federal Election Commission, 558 U.S. 310 (2010).

37. Bipartisan Campaign Reform Act, Pub. L. No. 107-155, 116 Stat. 81 (2002).

38. Ibid., § 201, 116 Stat. 81, 88 (2002) (codified at 52 U.S.C. 30104(f)).

39. Ibid., § 311, 116 Stat. 81, 105 (2002) (codified at 52 U.S.C. 30120).

40. *Citizens United*, 558 U.S. at 366–71.

41. Buckley v. Valeo, 424 U.S. 1 (1976).

42. Ibid., 60.

43. Ibid., 64–66.

44. See *Citizens United*, 558 U.S. at 366–67.

45. *Buckley*, 424 U.S. at 74–75 (quoting 2 U.S.C. § 434(e)). In 2014, election-related provisions in Title 2 of the U.S. Code were transferred to a new Title 52. See Editorial Reclassification, Title 52, United States Code, available at https://uscode.house.gov/editorialreclassification/t52/index.html. After reclassification, 2 U.S.C. § 434 became 52 U.S.C. § 30104.

46. *Buckley*, 424 U.S. at 76–77.

47. Ibid., 77.

48. Ibid., 80 (emphasis added).

49. Bipartisan Campaign Reform Act, Pub. L. No. 107-155, § 201(a), 116 Stat. 81, 89 (2002) (codified at 52 U.S.C. § 30104(f)(3)).

50. McConnell v. Federal Election Commission, 540 U.S. 93, 190 (2003).

51. Ibid., 191–92.

52. Ibid., 193.

53. Election Campaign Act Amendments, Pub. L. No. 94-283, 90 Stat. 475 (1976).

54. Ibid., § 323, 90 Stat. 493 (1976).

55. *McConnell*, 540 U.S. at 230–31.

56. Ibid., 231.

57. *Citizens United*, 558 U.S. 310.

58. *McConnell*, 540 U.S. at 204. See ibid., 203–11 (presenting the Court's constitutional analysis).

59. *Citizens United*, 558 U.S. at 336–66.

60. Ibid., 366–71.

61. Ibid., 368 (citing and quoting both *McConnell* and *Buckley*).

62. Ibid., 371.

63. See 52 U.S.C. § 30120.

64. See chapter 7, pp. 191–92.

65. See 52 U.S.C. § 30120.

66. Washington Post v. McManus, 944 F.3d 506, 516 (4th Cir. 2019).

67. See, e.g., DiResta et al., "Tactics and Tropes."

68. See chapter 2, pp. 37–42.

69. *Citizens United*, 558 U.S. at 366 (quoting both *Buckley* and *McConnell*).

70. 52 U.S.C. § 30104(f)(3)(A).

71. 52 U.S.C. § 30104(f)(3)(A).

72. 52 U.S.C. § 30104(f)(3)(C).

73. 52 U.S.C. § 30104(f)(3)(A)(II).

74. McIntyre v. Ohio Elections Commission, 514 U.S. 334 (1995).

75. Ibid., 342.

76. For example, Facebook has a "real name policy," which requires users to use "the name they go by in everyday life. This makes it so that you always know who you're connecting with." Facebook, "What Names Are Allowed on Facebook?" https://www.facebook .com/help/112146705538576 (last visited September 6, 2021).

77. *Buckley*, 424 U.S. at 66.

78. National Association for Advancement of Colored People v. Alabama, 357 U.S. 449, 450 (1958).

79. Ibid., 462.

80. *Buckley*, 424 U.S. at 68–69.

81. Ibid., 64–66. See *also Citizens United*, 558 U.S. at 366–67.

82. *Buckley*, 424 U.S. at 66.

83. Ibid., 67–68.

84. Ibid., 71.

85. Ibid., 71–72.

86. Brown v. Socialist Workers '74 Campaign Committee, 459 U.S. 87 (1982).

87. Ibid., 88.

88. Ibid., 88 (quoting *Buckley*).

89. Ibid., 91.

90. Ibid., 102.

91. Doe v. Reed, 561 U.S. 186, 200–202 (2010).

92. *Buckley*, 424 U.S. at 67–68.

93. Ibid., 66.

94. *Brown*, 459 U.S. at 88.

95. *Buckley*, 424 U.S. at 70.

96. Eisen, Painter, and Tribe, "The Emoluments Clause," 2.

97. Hamilton, Federalist No. 22, at 181 (Isaac Kramnick, ed., 1987).

98. George Washington, Farewell Address (September 17, 1796), in Finley, *American Democracy*, 18.

99. Zivotofsky ex rel. Zivotofsky v. Clinton, 566 U.S. 189, 214 (Breyer, J., dissenting).

100. The analysis in this section was written before the Supreme Court decided *Americans for Prosperity Foundation v. Bonta*, 141 S. Ct. 2373 (2021). The Court's decision in that case clearly strengthens the libertarian argument against the registration system, but does not fundamentally alter the analysis.

101. See Gellman and Poitras, "U.S., British Intelligence Mining Data."

102. Biddle, "Police Surveilled George Floyd Protests."

103. *Buckley*, 424 U.S. at 65.

104. *Packingham v. North Carolina*, 137 S.Ct. 1730, 1735 (2017).

105. See Dep't of Commerce v. New York, 139 S. Ct. 2551 (2019).

106. Ibid., 2562.

107. See European Union, General Data Protection Regulation, Regulation 2016/679.

108. See Thai, "Right to Receive Foreign Speech."

109. Schauer, *Free Speech*, 86.

110. *Buckley*, 424 U.S. at 67–68.

111. *Brown*, 459 U.S. at 88. See also *Doe*, 561 U.S. at 200.

112. Meese v. Keene, 481 U.S. 465 (1987).

113. Foreign Agents Registration Act, Pub L. No. 75-583, 52 Stat. 631 (codified at 22 U.S.C. § 611 et seq.).

114. *Meese*, 481 U.S. at 465.

115. Ibid., 478.

116. See Voice of America, "Record Number of Americans."

117. *Citizens United*, 558 U.S. at 354.

118. Ibid., 340.

119. Ibid., 362.

120. See Chemerinsky, *Constitutional Law*, 1036–77.

121. Miller v. California, 413 U.S. 15, 24 (1973).

122. See Post, *Citizens Divided*, 7–16.

123. See chapter 2.

124. New York v. Ferber, 458 U.S. 747, 763 (1982) (declaring that child pornography is "a category of material outside the protection of the First Amendment").

125. See Brown v. Entertainment Merchants Ass'n, 564 U.S. 786 (2011) (rejecting argument that violent video games qualify as unprotected speech); United States v. Stevens, 559 U.S. 460 (2010) (rejecting argument that depictions of animal cruelty should be treated as unprotected speech).

126. 137 S.Ct. 1730, 1735 (2017).

127. *Citizens United*, 558 U.S. at 366–67.

128. Ibid., 340.

129. Eisen, Painter, and Tribe, "The Emoluments Clause."

130. See, e.g., Trump v. Hawaii, 138 S. Ct. 2392, 2409 (2018) (discussing "the deference traditionally accorded the President" in matters pertaining to international affairs); Ku and Yoo, "*Hamden v. Rumsfeld*."

131. Sitaraman and Wuerth, "Normalization of Foreign Relations Law."

132. See, e.g., Bradley, "Foreign Relations Law"; Vladeck, "Exceptionalism of Foreign Relations Normalization."

133. See Sullivan and Gunther, *Constitutional Law*, 763–66.

134. See Schauer, *Free Speech*, 85–86.

135. *Holder*, 561 U.S. 1 (2010).

136. Ibid., 8 (quoting 18 U.S.C. § 2339B).

137. Ibid., 25–28.

138. Gunther, "Foreword: In Search of Evolving Doctrine, 8.

139. Adarand Constructors, Inc. v. Pena, 515 U.S. 200, 237 (1995).

140. Williams-Yulee v. Florida Bar, 575 U.S. 433 (2015) (applying strict scrutiny and upholding validity of state judicial conduct rule that prohibited judicial candidates from personally soliciting campaign funds).

141. *Holder*, 561 U.S. 1 (applying strict scrutiny and upholding validity of federal criminal law banning material support to foreign terrorist organizations).

142. Ibid., 29.

143. Ibid., 33.

144. Ibid.

145. *Citizens United*, 558 U.S. at 362.

146. See, e.g., *Citizens United*, 558 U.S. 310 (affirming validity of disclaimer provisions in the Bipartisan Campaign Reform Act, but invalidating the ban on corporate electoral speech); *Buckley*, 424 U.S. 1 (upholding validity of disclaimer provisions in the Federal Election Campaign Act, but invalidating ban on campaign expenditures in excess of statutory limits).

147. See, e.g., Holder v. Humanitarian Law Project, 561 U.S. 1, 29 (2010) (quoting with approval a specific congressional finding that foreign terrorist organizations "are so tainted by their criminal conduct that any contribution to such an organization facilitates that conduct").

148. Anderson, "From Warning to Wallpaper."

149. See ibid.

150. Bluman v. Federal Election Commission, 800 F.Supp.2d 281 (D.D.C. 2011).

151. Ibid., 284.

152. Ibid., 285–86.

153. Bluman v. Federal Election Commission, 565 U.S. 1104 (Mem.) (2012).

154. See *Bluman*, 800 F.Supp.2d at 284–85.

155. Ibid., 288.

BIBLIOGRAPHY

BOOKS, ARTICLES, REPORTS, BLOGS

89up. 2018. "Putin's Brexit?: The Influence of Kremlin Media and Bots during the 2016 UK EU Referendum." February. https://www.89up.org/russia-report

Abrams, Stacey. 2020. "American Leadership Begins at Home: The Global Imperative to Rebuild Governance and Restore Democracy." *Foreign Affairs*, May 1.

Adam, Karla, and William Booth. 2017. "Rising Alarm in Britain over Russian Meddling in Brexit Vote." *Washington Post*, November 17.

Akram, Susan M., and Kevin R. Johnson. 2002. "Race, Civil Rights, and Immigration Law after September 11, 2001: The Targeting of Arabs and Muslims." 58 *NYU Annual Survey of American Law* 295.

Al Jazeera. 2020. "Qatar Blockade: Five Things to Know about the Gulf Crisis." June 5.

Al Jazeera. 2020. "US Military Buys Location Data of Popular Muslim Apps." November 17.

Alexander, Larry, and Frederick Schauer. 1997. "On Extrajudicial Constitutional Interpretation." 110 *Harvard Law Review* 1359.

Alexander, Larry, and Frederick Schauer. 2000. "Defending Judicial Supremacy: A Reply." 17 *Constitutional Commentary* 455.

Allyn, Bobby. 2021. "Biden Drops Trump's Ban on TikTok and WeChat—But Will Continue the Scrutiny." National Public Radio, June 9.

American Civil Liberties Union, Real ID, https://www.aclu.org/issues/privacy-technology/national-id/real-id

Andersen, Ross. 2020. "The Panopticon Is Already Here." *The Atlantic*, September.

Anderson, Bonnie, et al. 2016. "From Warning to Wallpaper: Why the Brain Habituates to Security Warnings and What Can be Done about It." *Journal of Management Information Systems* 33(3): 713–43.

Aratani, Lauren. 2020. "Tsunami of Untruths: Trump Has Made 20,000 False or Misleading Claims." *The Guardian*, July 13.

Associated Press. 2019. "Trump Administration Takes Aim at Laws Allowing Undocumented Immigrants to Obtain Driver's Licenses." NBC News, December 31.

Association for International Broadcasting. 2018. "RT Weekly TV Audience Grows." April 3. https://aib.org.uk/rt-weekly-tv-audience-grows-by-more-than-a-third-now-100-mln-ipsos/

Auchard, Eric, and Felix Bate. 2017. "French Candidate Macron Claims Massive Hack as Emails Leaked." Reuters, May 5.

Australian Strategic Policy Institute. 2020. "Covid-19 Disinformation and Social Media Manipulation." October 27.

Bagenstos, Samuel R. 2014. "The Unrelenting Libertarian Challenge to Public Accommodations Law." 66 Stanford Law Review 1205.

Bakamo. 2017a. "The Role and Impact of Non-Traditional Publishers in the French Elections." https://www.bakamosocial.com/frenchelection

Bakamo. 2017b. "Patterns of Disinformation in the 2017 French Presidential Election." https://www.bakamosocial.com/frenchelection

Bakamo. 2017c. "French Election Social Media Landscape: Final Report." https://www.bakamosocial.com/frenchelection

Balkin, Jack M. 2018. "Free Speech Is a Triangle." 118 Columbia Law Review 2011.

Ball, James. 2017. "A Suspected Network of 13,000 Twitter Bots Pumped Out Pro-Brexit Messages in the Run-Up to the EU Vote." BuzzFeed News, October 20.

Barlow, John Perry. 1996. "A Declaration of the Independence of Cyberspace." Electronic Frontier Foundation, February 8. https://www.eff.org/cyberspace-independence

Barma, Naazneen, Brent Durbin, and Andrea Kendall-Taylor. 2020. "Digital Authoritarianism: Finding Our Way Out of the Darkness." Center for a New American Security, February 10. https://www.cnas.org/publications/commentary/digital-authoritarianism-finding-our-way-out-of-the-darkness

Barnes, Julian E., and Adam Goldman. 2020. "Russia Trying to Stoke U.S. Racial Tensions before Election, Officials Say." New York Times, March 10.

Barnett, Neil. 2016. "United Kingdom: Vulnerable but Resistant." In Alina Polyakova et al., Russian Influence in France, Germany, and the United Kingdom. Atlantic Council: Dinu Patriciu's Eurasia Center, November 15.

Barnett, Randy E. 2016. Our Republican Constitution: Securing the Liberty and Sovereignty of We the People. New York: Broadside Books.

BBC News. 2020. "Navalny Novichok Poisoning: EU Sanctions Hit Top Russians." October 15.

Benkler, Yochai, Robert Faris, and Hal Roberts. 2018. Network Propaganda: Manipulation, Disinformation, and Radicalization in American Politics. New York: Oxford University Press.

Benoit, Angeline. 2021. "France's Le Pen Gains Ground for 2022 Elections, Poll Shows." Bloomberg, April 11.

Bering, Juergen. 2017. "The Prohibition on Annexation: Lessons from Crimea." 49 NYU Journal of International Law and Politics 747.

Berkes, Anna. 2010. "Eternal Vigilance." Monticello.org (blog), August 22. https://www.monticello.org/site/blog-and-community/posts/eternal-vigilance

Berzina, Kristine. 2018. "Sweden—Preparing for the Wolf, not Crying Wolf: Anticipating and Tracking Influence Operations in Advance of Sweden's 2018 General Elections." German Marshall Fund of the United States.org (blog), September 7. https://www.gmfus.org/blog/2018/09/07/sweden-preparing-wolf-not-crying-wolf-anticipating-and-tracking-influence

Bhagwat, Ashutosh. 2020. Our Democratic First Amendment. Cambridge: Cambridge University Press.

Biddle, Sam. 2020. "Police Surveilled George Floyd Protests with Help from Twitter-Affiliated Startup Dataminr." *The Intercept*, July 9.

Borak, Masha. 2019. "ByteDance Says TikTok and Douyin Are Different, but They Face Similar Criticisms." *Abacus*, December 2. https://www.scmp.com/abacus/tech/article/3040147/bytedance-says-tiktok-and-douyin-are-different-they-face-similar

Bradley, Curtis A. 2015. "Foreign Relations Law and the Purported Shift Away from Exceptionalism." 128 *Harvard Law Review Forum* 294.

Bradshaw, Samantha, and Philip N. Howard. 2019a. *The Global Disinformation Order: 2019 Inventory of Organized Social Media Manipulation*. Oxford Internet Institute, University of Oxford. https://demtech.oii.ox.ac.uk/wp-content/uploads/sites/93/2019/09/CyberTroop-Report19.pdf

Bradshaw, Samantha, and Philip N. Howard. 2019b. *Case Studies*. Oxford Internet Institute, University of Oxford. https://comprop.oii.ox.ac.uk/wp-content/uploads/sites/93/2019/09/Case-Studies-Collated-NOV-2019-1.pdf

British Social Attitudes. 2016. *The Vote to Leave the EU: Litmus Test or Lightning Rod?* https://www.bsa.natcen.ac.uk/media/39149/bsa34_brexit_final.pdf

Burgess, Matt. 2017. "Here's the First Evidence Russia Used Twitter to Influence Brexit." *Wired*, November 10.

Caesar, Ed. 2019. "The Chaotic Triumph of Arron Banks, The Bad Boy of Brexit." *New Yorker*, March 25.

Campbell, Kurt M., and Mira Rapp-Hooper. 2020. "China Is Done Biding Its Time: The End of Beijing's Foreign Policy Restraint?" *Foreign Affairs*, July 15.

Carpenter, Dick M., et al. 2017. *License to Work: A National Study of Burdens from Occupational Licensing*, 2nd ed. Arlington, VA: Institute for Justice. www.ij.org

Casey, Adam, and Lucan A. Way. 2017. "Russian Electoral Interventions, 1991–2017." https://dataverse.scholarsportal.info/dataset.xhtml?persistentId=doi:10.5683/SP/BYRQQS

Cave, Danielle, et al. 2019. "Mapping China's Technology Giants." Australian Strategic Policy Institute, International Cyber Policy Centre, April.

Cederberg, Gabriel. 2018. *Catching Swedish Phish: How Sweden Is Protecting Its 2018 Elections*. Harvard Kennedy School: Belfer Center for Science and International Affairs, September 7.

Chalfant, Morgan. 2017. "Denmark, Sweden Team Up to Counter Russian Fake News." *The Hill*, August 31.

Chemerinsky, Erwin. 2015. *Constitutional Law: Principles and Policies*, 5th ed. Wolters Kluwer.

Chen, Yu-Jie, Ching-Fu Lin, and Han-Wei Liu. 2018. "Rule of Trust: The Power and Perils of China's Social Credit Megaproject." 32 *Columbia Journal of Asian Law* 1.

Chinen, Mark A. 1999. "Presidential Certifications in U.S. Foreign Policy Legislation." 31 *NYU Journal of International Law and Politics* 217.

Chua, Amy. 2020. "Divided We Fall: What Is Tearing America Apart?" *Foreign Affairs*, July–August.

Clarke, Sean, and Josh Holder. 2017. "French Presidential Election: First Round Results in Charts and Maps." *The Guardian*, April 23.

Cook, Sarah. 2020. "Beijing's Global Megaphone: The Expansion of Chinese Communist Party Media Influence since 2017." Freedom House, January.

Cooley, Alexander, and Daniel H. Nexon. 2020. "How Hegemony Ends: The Unraveling of American Power." *Foreign Affairs*, July–August.

Cornell, Nicolas. 2016. "The Aesthetic Toll of Nudging." 14 *Georgetown Journal of Law and Public Policy* 841.

Costa-Roberts, Daniel. 2018. "How to Spot a Russian Bot." *Mother Jones*, August 1.

Culpan, Tim. 2018. "The World's Most Powerful App Is Squandering Its Lead." Bloomberg, July 22.

Dance, Gabriel J. X., Michael LaForgia, and Nicholas Confessore. 2018. "As Facebook Raised a Privacy Wall, It Carved an Opening for Tech Giants." *New York Times*, December 18.

Daniels, Laura. 2017. "How Russia Hacked the French Election." *Politico*, April 23.

Daugirdis, Kristina, and Julian D. Mortenson, eds. 2014. "Contemporary Practice of the United States Relating to International Law." 108 *American Journal of International Law* 784.

Davies, Guy. 2019. "Amid Brexit Uncertainty and Allegations, UK Lawmakers Consider Mueller-Like Inquiry." ABC News, April 28.

Davis, Wendy. 2021. "Biden Administration Still Weighing TikTok and WeChat Bans." Digital News, April 14. https://www.mediapost.com/publications/article/362342/biden-administration-still-weighing-tiktok-and-wec.html

Dearden, Lizzie. 2018. "RT Could be Banned from Broadcasting in UK for Breaching Impartiality Rules." *The Independent*, December 20.

Desigaud, Clementine, et al. 2017. "Junk News and Bots during the French Presidential Election: What Are French Voters Sharing over Twitter in Round Two?" Oxford Internet Institute, University of Oxford, May.

DiResta, Renee, et al. 2018. "The Tactics and Tropes of the Internet Research Agency." Homeland Security Digital Library, December. https://www.hsdl.org/c/tactics-and-tropes-of-the-internet-research-agency/

DiResta, Renee, et al. 2020. "Telling China's Story: The Chinese Communist Party's Campaign to Shape Global Narratives." Stanford Internet Observatory, Cyber Policy Center.

Doshi, Rush. 2020. "China Steps Up Its Information War in Taiwan." *Foreign Affairs*, January 9.

Douek, Evelyn. 2021. "The Free Speech Blind Spot: Foreign Election Interference on Social Media." In *Defending Democracies: Combating Election in a Digital Age*, edited by Duncan B. Hollis and Jens David Ohlin (Oxford University Press).

Duxbury, Charlie. 2019. "Sweden Gets New Government after Weeks of Coalition Wrangling." *Politico*, January 18.

Dwoskin, Elizabeth, and Craig Timberg. 2020. "Facebook Takes Down Russian Operation That Recruited U.S. Journalists, Amid Rising Concerns about Election Misinformation." *Washington Post*, September 1.

Dwoskin, Elizabeth, and Craig Timberg. 2020. "The Unseen Machine Pushing Trump's Social Media Megaphone into Overdrive." *Washington Post*, October 30.

Eisen, Norman L., Richard Painter, and Laurence H. Tribe. 2016. "The Emoluments Clause: Its Text, Meaning, and Application to Donald J. Trump." Washington, DC: Brookings Institution.

Eko, Lyombe, Anup Kumar, and Qingjiang Yao. 2011. "Google This: The Great Firewall of China, The IT Wheel of India, Google, Inc., and Internet Regulation." 15 *Journal of Internet Law* 3.

Election Integrity Partnership. 2020. *Evaluating Platform Election-Related Speech Policies.* https://static1.squarespace.com/static/5f19d72fae0908591b9feccb/t/5f99b20b9261b 014f0dac468/1603908112824/3_EIP_Platform_Policy_Comparison.docx+-+Google +Docs.pdf

Facebook, *Community Standards Enforcement Report* (Aug. 2020), https://about.fb.com/news/2020/08/community-standards-enforcement-report-aug-2020/

Fearnow, Benjamin. 2020. "82 Percent of Trump Voters Say Biden's Win Not Legitimate: CBS News Poll." *Newsweek*, December 13.

Feldstein, Steven. 2020. "When It Comes to Digital Authoritarianism, China Is a Challenge— But Not the Only Challenge." War on the Rocks, February 12. https://warontherocks .com/2020/02/when-it-comes-to-digital-authoritarianism-china-is-a-challenge-but -not-the-only-challenge/

Feng, Emily. 2019. "China Intercepts WeChat Texts from U.S. and Abroad, Researchers Say." National Public Radio, August 29.

Ferrara, Emilio. 2017. "Disinformation and Social Bot Operations in the Run Up to the 2017 French Presidential Election." *First Monday* 22(8). https://doi.org/10.5210/fm.v22i8 .8005

Fessler, Pam. 2020. "American Distrust of the Voting Process Is Widespread, NPR Poll Finds." National Public Radio, January 21.

Finley, John H., ed. 1925. *American Democracy from Washington to Wilson: Addresses and State Papers.* Repr. 2017, Forgotten Books.

Franceschi-Bicchierai, Lorenzo. 2020. "Hackers Leak Alleged Internal Files of Chinese Social Media Monitoring Firms." *Vice*, August 21.

Freedom House. 2019. "Freedom on the Net 2019: Internet Freedom Scores." https:// freedomhouse.org/countries/freedom-net/scores

Freedom House. 2020. "Freedom in the World 2020: Global Freedom Scores." https:// freedomhouse.org/countries/freedom-world/scores

Friedberg, Aaron L. 2020. "An Answer to Aggression: How to Push Back against Beijing." *Foreign Affairs*, September–October.

Fukuyama, Francis. 1992. *The End of History and the Last Man.* New York: Free Press.

Gallagher, Ryan. 2019. "Middle East Dictators Buy Spy Tech from Company Linked to IBM and Google." *The Intercept*, July 12.

Gellman, Barton, and Laura Poitras. 2013. "U.S., British Intelligence Mining Data from Nine U.S. Internet Companies in Broad Secret Program." *Washington Post*, June 7.

Ginsburg, Tom. 2020. "Authoritarian International Law?" 114 *American Journal of International Law* 221.

Gleicher, Nathaniel. 2019a. "Removing Coordinated Inauthentic Behavior in UAE, Egypt, and Saudi Arabia." Facebook, August 1.

Gleicher, Nathaniel. 2019b. "Removing Coordinated Inauthentic Behavior from China." Facebook, August 19.

Goldman, Eric. 2019. "An Overview of the United States' Section 230 Internet Immunity." In *The Oxford Handbook of Online Intermediary Liability.* https://papers.ssrn.com/sol3/papers.cfm?abstract_id=3306737

Goldsmith, Jack, and Andrew Keane Woods. 2020. "Internet Speech Will Never Go Back to Normal." *The Atlantic*, April 25.

Goodman, Ellen P. 2014. "Visual Gut Punch: Persuasion, Emotion, and the Constitutional Meaning of Graphic Disclosure." 99 *Cornell Law Review* 513.

Goodman, Ryan, and Derek Jinks. 2013. *Socializing States: Promoting Human Rights through International Law.* New York: Oxford University Press.

Goodyear, Michael P. 2021. "Priam's Folly: United States v. Alvarez and the Fake News Trojan Horse." 73 *Stanford Law Review Online* (September).

Gorwa, Robert. 2017. "Computational Propaganda in Poland: False Amplifiers and the Digital Public Sphere." Oxford Internet Institute, University of Oxford, June.

Granick, Jennifer Stisa, and Ashley Gorski. 2019. "How to Address Newly Revealed Abuses of Section 702 Surveillance." Just Security, October 18.

Gray, Christine. 2018. *International Law and the Use of Force*, 4th ed. New York: Oxford University Press.

Green, Michael, and Evan Medeiros. 2020. "Is Taiwan the Next Hong Kong? China Tests the Limits of Impunity." *Foreign Affairs*, July 8.

Greene, Andrew. 2019. "Chinese Spy Wang Liqiang Alleges Beijing Ordered Overseas Murders, Including in Australia." Australian Broadcasting Corp., November 22.

Gressin, Seena. 2017. "The Equifax Data Breach: What to Do." *FTC Consumer Information* (blog), September 8. https://www.consumer.ftc.gov/blog/2017/09/equifax-data-breach-what-do

Gunther, Gerald. 1972. "Foreword: In Search of Evolving Doctrine on a Changing Court: A Model for a Newer Equal Protection." 86 *Harvard Law Review* 1.

Haass, Richard. 2020. "Foreign Policy by Example: Crisis at Home Makes the United States Vulnerable Abroad." *Foreign Affairs*, June 5.

Hamilton, Clive, and Mareike Ohlberg. 2020. *Hidden Hand: Exposing How the Chinese Communist Party Is Reshaping the World.* Toronto: Optimum Publishing International.

Hedman, Freja, et al. 2018. "News and Political Information Consumption in Sweden: Mapping the 2018 Swedish General Election on Twitter." Oxford Internet Institute, University of Oxford, September.

Hernandez, Javier C. 2020. "As Protests Engulf the United States, China Revels in the Unrest." *New York Times*, June 2.

Horton, Chris. 2018. "Specter of Meddling by Beijing Looms over Taiwan's Elections." *New York Times*, November 22.

Howard, Philip N., et al. 2017a. "Junk News and Bots during the U.S. Election: What Were Michigan Voters Sharing over Twitter?" Oxford Internet Institute, University of Oxford, March.

Howard, Phillip N., et al. 2017b. "Junk News and Bots during the French Presidential Election: What Are French Voters Sharing over Twitter?" Oxford Internet Institute, University of Oxford, April.

Howard, Philip N., et al. 2018. "The IRA, Social Media and Political Polarization in the United States." Oxford Internet Institute, University of Oxford, December.

Howard, Philip N. 2020. *Lie Machines: How to Save Democracy from Troll Armies, Deceitful Robots, Junk News Operations, and Political Operatives.* New Haven, CT: Yale University Press.

Huang, Paul. 2019. "Chinese Cyber-Operatives Boosted Taiwan's Insurgent Candidate." *Foreign Policy*, June 26.

Hyun, Ki Deuk, and Jinhee Kim. 2015. "The Role of New Media in Sustaining the Status Quo: Online Political Expression, Nationalism, and System Support in China." *Information, Communication, and Society* 18(7): 766–81.

India Today. 2019. "Over 125 Crore People Now Have Aadhaar Cards." December 27. https://www.indiatoday.in/india/story/over-125-crore-people-now-have-aadhaar-cards-government-1631952-2019-12-27

Insikt Group. 2020. "Chinese State Media Seeks to Influence International Perceptions of COVID-19 Pandemic." Recorded Future, March. https://www.recordedfuture.com/covid-19-chinese-media-influence/

Iqbal, Mansoor. 2020. "TikTok Revenue and Usage Statistics." Business of Apps, October 30. https://www.businessofapps.com/data/tik-tok-statistics/

Irick, Miker. 2020. "Data Hashing and Encryption and How They Enhance Security." Sand-Storm[IT], May 11. https://sandstormit.com/data-hashing-and-encryption-and-how-they-enhance-security/

Isaac, Mike, and Kellen Browning. 2020. "Fact-Checked on Facebook and Twitter, Conservatives Switch Their Apps." *New York Times*, November 11.

Issacharoff, Samuel, et al. 2016. *The Law of Democracy: Legal Structure of the Political Process*, 5th ed. St. Paul, MN: Foundation Press.

Jamieson, Kathleen Hall. 2018. *Cyber-War: How Russian Hackers and Trolls Helped Elect a President.* New York: Oxford University Press.

Jones, Jeffrey M. 2019. "Trump Job Approval Sets New Record for Polarization." Gallup, January 16.

Joske, Alex. 2019. "Wang Liqiang: Analysing Wang Liqiang's Claims about China's Military Networks." Australian Strategic Policy Institute, December 12.

Joske, Alex. 2020. "The Party Speaks for You: Foreign Interference and the Chinese Communist Party's United Front System." Australian Strategic Policy Institute, International Cyber Policy Centre, June.

Kania, Elsa. 2018. "The Right to Speak: Discourse Power and Chinese Power." Center for Advanced China Research, November 27.

Karpf, David. 2019. "On Digital Disinformation and Democratic Myths." Social Science Research Council: Mediawell, December 10. https://mediawell.ssrc.org/expert-reflections/on-digital-disinformation-and-democratic-myths/

Kendall-Taylor, Andrea, Erica Frantz, and Joseph Wright. 2020. "The Digital Dictators: How Technology Strengthens Autocracy." *Foreign Affairs*, March–April.

Kerr, Jaclyn A. 2018. "Information, Security, and Authoritarian Stability: Internet Policy Diffusion and Coordination in the Former Soviet Region." *International Journal of Communication* 12: 3814–34.

Kerr, Jaclyn. 2019. "The Russian Model of Digital Control and Its Significance." In *Artificial Intelligence, China, Russia, and the Global Order*, edited by Nicholas D. Wright. Maxwell Air Force Base, AL: Air University Press.

Kim, Young Mie. 2020. "New Evidence Shows How Russia's Election Interference Has Gotten More Brazen." Brennan Center on Election Interference, March.

King, Gary, Jennifer Pan, and Margaret E. Roberts. 2017. "How the Chinese Government Fabricates Social Media Posts for Strategic Distraction, not Engaged Argument." *American Political Science Review* 111(3): 484–501.

Klein, Ezra. 2020. *Why We're Polarized*. New York: Simon & Schuster.

Kliman, Daniel, et al. 2019. "Grading China's Belt and Road." Center for a New American Security, April 8.

Klonick, Kate. 2018. "The New Governors: The People, Rules, and Processes Governing Online Speech." 131 *Harvard Law Review* 1598.

Knockel, Jeffrey, et al. 2020. "We Chat, They Watch." The Citizen Lab, University of Toronto, May.

Koreh, Raya. 2019. "CBP's New Social Media Surveillance: A Threat to Free Speech and Privacy." Just Security, April 26.

Kragh, Martin, and Sebastian Asberg. 2017. "Russia's Strategy for Influence through Public Diplomacy and Active Measures: The Swedish Case." *Journal of Strategic Studies* 40(6): 773–816.

Krajewska, Magdalena. 2017. *Documenting Americans: A Political History of National ID Card Proposals in the United States*. New York: Cambridge University Press.

Kramer, Larry D. 2004. *The People Themselves: Popular Constitutionalism and Judicial Review*. New York: Oxford University Press.

Kramer, Larry D. 2006. "The Interest of Man: James Madison, Popular Constitutionalism, and the Theory of Deliberative Democracy." 41 *Valparaiso University Law Review* 697.

Kreps, Sarah. 2020. *Social Media and International Relations*. Cambridge: Cambridge University Press.

Ku, Julian, and John Yoo. 2006. "*Hamdan v. Rumsfeld*: The Functional Case for Foreign Affairs Deference to the Executive Branch." 23 *Constitutional Commentary* 179.

Kundnani, Hans. 2020. "Foreign Interference Starts at Home." *Foreign Policy*, February 24.

Kurlantzick, Joshua. 2019. "How China Is Interfering in Taiwan's Election." Council on Foreign Relations, November 7.

Langin, Katie. 2018. "Fake News Spreads Faster Than True News on Twitter—Thanks to People, not Bots." *Science Magazine*, March 1.

Laruelle, Marlene. 2016. "France: Mainstreaming Russian Influence." In Alina Polyakova et al., *Russian Influence in France, Germany, and the United Kingdom*. Atlantic Council: Dinu Patriciu's Eurasia Center, November 15.

Lin, Lihyun. 2018. "Digital News Report: Taiwan (2018)." http://www.digitalnewsreport .org/survey/2018/taiwan-2018/

Linos, Katerina. 2013. *The Democratic Foundations of Policy Diffusion: How Health, Family, and Employment Laws Spread across Countries*. New York: Oxford University Press.

Lippman, Daniel. 2020. "Trump National Security Adviser Compares Xi Jinping to Josef Stalin." *Politico*, June 24.

Lührmann, Anna, Marcus Tannenberg, and Staffan I. Lindberg. 2018. "Regimes of the World (RoW): Opening New Avenues for the Comparative Study of Political Regimes." *Politics and Governance* 6(1). https://doi.org/10.17645/pag.v6i1.1214

MacKinnon, Rebecca. 2011. "Liberation Technology: China's Networked Authoritarianism." *Journal of Democracy* 22(2): 32–46.

Madison, James. 1800. *The Report of 1800*. Available from Founders Online, https://founders .archives.gov/documents/Madison/01-17-02-0202

Madison, James, Alexander Hamilton, and John Jay. [1788] 1987. *The Federalist Papers*. Edited by Isaac Kramnick. New York: Penguin Classics.

Mantesso, Sean, and Christina Zhou. 2019. "China's Multi-Billion-Dollar Media Campaign a Major Threat for Democracies around the World." Australia Broadcasting Corp., February 7.

Marantz, Andrew. 2019. *Anti-Social: Online Extremists, Techno-Utopians, and the Hijacking of the American Conversation*. New York: Viking.

Martin, Diego A., and Jacob N. Shapiro. 2019. *Trends in Online Foreign Influence Efforts, Version 1.2*. https://scholar.princeton.edu/sites/default/files/jns/files/trends_in _foreign_influence_efforts_2019jul08_0.pdf

Mazarr, Michael J., et al. 2019. *Hostile Social Manipulation: Present Realities and Emerging Trends*. Santa Monica, CA: Rand Corporation.

McAuley, James. 2017. "French President Macron Blasts Russian State-Owned Media as Propaganda." *Washington Post*, May 29.

McFaul, Michael, et al. 2019. "Securing American Elections: Prescriptions for Enhancing the Integrity and Independence of the 2020 U.S. Presidential Election and Beyond." Stanford Cyber Policy Center, Stanford University, June.

McFaul, Michael. 2020. "Xi Jinping Is Not Stalin: How a Lazy Historical Analogy Derailed Washington's China Strategy." *Foreign Affairs*, August 10.

Menn, Joseph. 2017. "Exclusive: Russia Used Facebook to Try to Spy on Macron Campaign." Reuters, July 26.

Menn, Joseph. 2020. "QAnon Received Earlier Boost from Russian Accounts on Twitter, Archives Show." Reuters, November 2.

Miller, Carly, et al. 2020. "Sockpuppets Spin COVID Yarns: An Analysis of PRC-Attributed June 2020 Twitter Takedown." Stanford Cyber Policy Center, Stanford University, June.

Mohan, Megha. 2017. "Macron Leaks: The Anatomy of a Hack." BBC, May 9.

Molter, Vanessa, and Renee DiResta. 2020. "Pandemics & Propaganda: How Chinese State Media Creates and Propagates CCP Coronavirus Narratives." Harvard Kennedy School: Misinformation Review, June.

Morozov, Evgeny. 2011. *The Net Delusion: The Dark Side of Internet Freedom*. New York: PublicAffairs.

Mozur, Paul. 2018. "A Genocide Incited on Facebook with Posts from Myanmar's Military." *New York Times*, October 15.

Murphy, Hannah. 2019. "Inside Facebook's Information Warfare Team." *Financial Times*, July 5.

Narayanan, Vidya, et al. 2017. "Russian Involvement and Junk News during Brexit." Oxford Internet Institute, University of Oxford, December.

Neudert, Lisa-Maria, Philip Howard, and Bence Kollanyi. 2019. "Sourcing and Automation of Political News and Information during Three European Elections." *Social Media and Society*, July–September.

New York Stock Exchange. 2014. *Corporate Governance Guide*. https://www.nyse.com/ publicdocs/nyse/listing/NYSE_Corporate_Governance_Guide.pdf

New York Times Editorial Board. 2019. "They're Doing It as We Sit Here." July 24.

Newton, Casey. 2020. "The Interface with Casey Newton." *The Verge*, no. 522, June 8. https://www.getrevue.co/profile/caseynewton/issues/how-content-moderation-can -empower-racists-254325?

Nimmo, Ben. 2016. "Putin's Media Are Pushing Britain for the Brexit." *The Interpreter*, February 12.

O'Connor, Cailin, and James Owen Weatherall. 2019. *The Misinformation Age: How False Beliefs Spread*. New Haven, CT: Yale University Press.

O'Connor, Sarah, et al. 2020. "Cyber-Enabled Foreign Interference in Elections and Referendums." Australian Strategic Policy Institute, October.

O'Neill, Patrick Howell. 2017. "Chinese Surveillance Giant Knowlesys Pushes Further into International Market." CyberScoop, April 6.

O'Sullivan, Donie. 2017. "Russian Trolls Pushed Pro-Brexit Spin on Day of Referendum." CNN, November 10.

Open Technology Fund. 2018. *FY 2018 Annual Report*. https://public.opentech.fund/documents/OTF_FY2018_Annual_Report_FINAL.pdf

Pariser, Eli. 2011. *The Filter Bubble: What the Internet Is Hiding from You*. New York: Penguin.

Pearce, Katy E., and Sarah Kendzior. 2012. "Networked Authoritarianism and Social Media in Azerbaijan." *Journal of Communication* 62(2): 283–98.

Pecorin, Allison. 2019. "What You Need to Know about the Indictments against Konstantin Kilimnik." ABC News, February 20.

Pei, Minxin. 2020. "Chinese Diplomats Behaving Badly." Project Syndicate, June 9. https://www.project-syndicate.org/commentary/china-reputation-wolf-warrior-diplomacy-covid19-by-minxin-pei-2020-06?barrier=accesspaylog

Perez, Evan, and Shimon Prokupecz. 2017. "US Suspects Russian Hackers Planted Fake News behind Qatar Crisis." CNN, June 7.

Perlroth, Nicole. 2020. "A Conspiracy Made in America May Have Been Spread by Russia." *New York Times*, June 15.

Persily, Nate, Megan Metzger, and Zachary Krowitz. 2019. "Confronting Efforts at Election Manipulation from Foreign Media Organizations." In "Securing American Elections: Prescriptions for Enhancing the Integrity and Independence of the 2020 U.S. Presidential Election and Beyond," edited by Michael McFaul et al. Stanford Cyber Policy Center, Stanford University, June.

Pew Research Center. 2017. "The Partisan Divide on Political Values Grows Even Wider." October 5.

Pew Research Center. 2019a. "Public Trust in Government: 1958–2019." April.

Pew Research Center. 2019b. "Partisan Antipathy: More Intense, More Personal." October.

Pew Research Center. 2020. "How Americans See Climate Change and the Environment in 7 Charts." April.

Polyakova, Alina. 2015. "Putinism and the European Far-Right." Atlantic Council, November.

Polyakova, Alina, et al. 2016. *The Kremlin's Trojan Horses: Russian Influence in France, Germany, and the United Kingdom*. Atlantic Council: Dinu Patriciu's Eurasia Center, November 15.

Polyakova, Alina. 2016. "Introduction: The Kremlin's Toolkit of Influence in Europe." In Polyakova et al., *The Kremlin's Trojan Horses: Russian Influence in France, Germany, and the United Kingdom*. Atlantic Council: Dinu Patriciu's Eurasia Center, November 15.

Polyakova, Alina. 2020. "The Kremlin's Plot against Democracy: How Russia Updated Its 2016 Playbook for 2020." *Foreign Affairs*, September–October.

Post, Robert C. 2014. *Citizens Divided: Campaign Finance Reform and the Constitution*. Cambridge, MA: Harvard University Press.

Rid, Thomas. 2020. *Active Measures: The Secret History of Disinformation and Political Warfare*. New York: Farrar, Straus and Giroux.

Roberts, Sarah T. 2019. *Behind the Screen: Content Moderation in the Shadows of Social Media*. New Haven, CT: Yale University Press.

Rose, Michel, and Denis Dyomkin. 2017. "After Talks, France's Macron Hits Out at Russian Media, Putin Denies Hacking." Reuters, May 28.

Rosenberg, Matthew, and Julian E. Barnes. 2020. "A Bible Burning, a Russian News Agency and a Story Too Good to Check Out." *New York Times*, August 11.

Rosenberg, Matthew, Nicholas Confessore, and Carole Cadwalladr. 2018. "How Trump Consultants Exploited the Facebook Data of Millions." *New York Times*, March 17.

Rosenberger, Laura. 2020a. "China's Coronavirus Information Offensive." *Foreign Affairs*, April 22.

Rosenberger, Laura. 2020b. "Making Cyberspace Safe for Democracy: The New Landscape of Information Competition." *Foreign Affairs*, May–June.

Ross, Chuck. 2020. "*Washington Post* and *Wall Street Journal* Took Millions from Chinese Communist Party Newspaper." *National Interest*, June 10.

Roth, Brad R. 2009. "The Entity That Dare Not Speak Its Name: Unrecognized Taiwan as a Right-Bearer in the International Legal Order." 4 *East Asia Law Review* 91.

Roth, Yoel. 2018. "Automation and the Use of Multiple Accounts." Twitter, February 21. https://blog.twitter.com/developer/en_us/topics/tips/2018/automation-and-the -use-of-multiple-accounts.html

Rovetta, Stefano, Grazyna Suchacka, and Francesco Masulli. 2020. "Bot Recognition in a Web Store: An Approach Based on Unsupervised Learning." *Journal of Network and Computer Applications* 157(May 1). https://doi.org/10.1016/j.jnca.2020.102577

Ruck, Damian J., et al. 2019. "Internet Research Agency Twitter Activity Predicted 2016 U.S. Election Polls." *First Monday* 24(7). https://doi.org/10.5210/fm.v24i7.10107

Rudolph, Josh, and Thomas Morley. 2020. "Covert Foreign Money: Financial Loopholes Exploited by Authoritarians to Fund Political Interference in Democracies." Alliance for Securing Democracy, August 18.

Sabbagh, Dan, Luke Harding, and Andrew Roth. 2020. "Russia Report Reveals UK Government Failed to Investigate Kremlin Interference." *The Guardian*, July 21.

Satariano, Adam. 2019. "Russia Sought to Use Social Media to Influence E.U. Vote, Report Finds." *New York Times*, June 14.

Schauer, Frederick. 1982. *Free Speech: A Philosophical Enquiry*. Cambridge: Cambridge University Press.

Schechter, Anna. 2020. "China Launches New Twitter Accounts, 90,000 Tweets in Covid-19 Info War." NBC News, May 20.

Schmitt, Gary, and Michael Mazza. 2019. "Blinding the Enemy: CCP Interference in Taiwan's Democracy." Global Taiwan Institute, October.

Schrader, Matt. 2020. "Friends and Enemies: A Framework for Understanding Chinese Political Interference in Democratic Countries." Alliance for Securing Democracy, April.

Settle, Jaime E. 2018. *Frenemies: How Social Media Polarizes America*. Cambridge: Cambridge University Press.

Shahbaz, Adrian. 2018. "Freedom on the Net 2018: The Rise of Digital Authoritarianism." Freedom House, October.

Shahbaz, Adrian, and Allie Funk. 2019. "Freedom on the Net 2019: The Crisis of Social Media." Freedom House.

Shane, Scott. 2017. "The Fake Americans Russia Created to Influence the Election." *New York Times*, September 7.

Shane, Scott, and Mark Mazzetti. 2018. "Inside a 3-Year Russian Campaign to Influence U.S. Votes." *New York Times*, February 16.

Shanor, Amanda. 2016. "The New Lochner." 2016 *Wisconsin Law Review* 133.

Shuster, Simon, and Sandra Ifraimova. 2018. "A Former Russian Troll Explains How to Spread Fake News." *Time*, March 14.

Silverman, Craig. 2016. "This Analysis Shows How Viral Fake Election News Stories Outperformed Real News on Facebook." BuzzFeed News, November 16.

Silverman, Craig. 2019. "People Are Renting Out Their Facebook Accounts in Exchange for Cash and Free Laptops." BuzzFeed News, January 18.

Silverman, Craig and Ryan Mac. 2020. "Facebook Knows That Adding Labels to Trump's False Claims Does Little to Stop Their Spread." BuzzFeed News, November 16.

Similarweb. 2020. "VK.com: June 2020 Traffic Overview." https://www.similarweb.com/website/vk.com/

Simmons, Beth A. 2009. *Mobilizing for Human Rights: International Law in Domestic Politics*. New York: Cambridge University Press.

Sina Weibo. 2018. "Annual Report, 2018." https://data.weibo.com/report/reportDetail?id=433

Sitaraman, Ganesh, and Ingrid Wuerth. 2015. "The Normalization of Foreign Relations Law." 128 *Harvard Law Review* 1897.

Sloss, David L. 2019. "Corporate Defenses against Information Warfare." Just Security, August 20.

Sloss, David L. 2020. "The Best Way to Regulate Disinformation." Opinio Juris, October 29.

Smeltz, Dina, et al. 2019. *Rejecting Retreat: Americans Support US Engagement in Global Affairs*. Chicago Council on Global Affairs, September. https://www.thechicagocouncil.org/sites/default/files/2020-11/report_ccs19_rejecting-retreat_20190909.pdf

Snyder, Timothy. 2021. "The American Abyss: Trump, the Mob and What Comes Next." *New York Times Magazine*, January 17.

Statista. 2020a. "Number of Monthly Active Facebook Users Worldwide as of Second Quarter 2020." https://www.statista.com/statistics/264810/number-of-monthly-active-facebook-users-worldwide/

Statista. 2020b. "Number of Monthly Active Users of Sina Weibo Q4 2017-Q2 2020." https://www.statista.com/statistics/795303/china-mau-of-sina-weibo/

Stieglitz, Stefan, et al. 2017. "Do Social Bots Dream of Electric Sheep?: A Categorisation of Social Media Bot Accounts." Australasian Conference on Information Systems, October. https://arxiv.org/abs/1710.04044

Stubbs, Jack. 2019. "Russian Operatives Sacrifice Followers to Stay under Cover on Facebook." Reuters, October 24.

Sullivan, Andrew. 2009. "The Revolution Will be Twittered." *The Atlantic*, June 13.

Sullivan, Kathleen M., and Gerald Gunther. 2010. *Constitutional Law*, 17th ed. St. Paul, MN: Foundation Press.

Sunstein, Cass R. 1995. *Democracy and the Problem of Free Speech*. New York: Free Press.

Sunstein, Cass R. 2017. *#Republic: Divided Democracy in the Age of Social Media*. Princeton, NJ: Princeton University Press.

TenCent. 2020. *TenCent Announces 2020 First Quarter Results*. May 13. https://
cdc-tencent-com-1258344706.image.myqcloud.com/uploads/2020/05/18/
13009f73ecab16501df9062e43e47e67.pdf

Thai, Joseph. 2018. "The Right to Receive Foreign Speech." 71 *Oklahoma Law Review* 269.

The Economist. 2017. "Democracy Index 2016: Revenge of the Deplorables." Intelligence Unit.

The Economist. 2020. "The Big Unfriending: Donald Trump Has Caused Panic among Millions of WeChat Users." August 13.

Thomas, Elise, and Albert Zhang. 2020. "COVID-19 Attracts Patriotic Troll Campaigns in Support of China's Geopolitical Interests." Australian Strategic Policy Institute, International Cyber Policy Center, April.

Thompson, Ben. 2020. "The TikTok War." Stratechery, July 14.

Thompson, Stuart A., and Charlie Warzel. 2020. "12 Million Phones, One Dataset, Zero Privacy." *New York Times*, January 26.

Tufekci, Zeynep. 2017. *Twitter and Tear Gas: The Power and Fragility of Networked Protest*. New Haven, CT: Yale University Press.

Twitter Safety. 2019a. "Disclosing New Data to Our Archive of Information Operations." September 20.

Twitter Safety. 2019b. "Information Operations Directed at Hong Kong." August 19.

Twitter Safety. 2020. "Disclosing Networks of State-Linked Information Operations We've Removed." June 12.

V-Dem Institute. 2019. "Democracy Facing Global Challenges: V-Dem Annual Democracy Report." May 21.

V-Dem Institute. 2020a. "Autocratization Surges—Resistance Grows: V-Dem Annual Democracy Report."

V-Dem Institute. 2020b. "V-Dem Codebook, version 10." March.

V-Dem Institute. 2021. *Autocratization Turns Viral: Democracy Report 2021*. https://www.v-dem.net/files/25/DR%202021.pdf

Verma, Pranshu, and Edward Wong. 2020. "Trump's Pick Criticized at Global Internet Fund." *New York Times*, July 5.

Vilmer, Jean-Baptiste Jeangène. 2019. "The 'Macron Leaks' Operation: A Post-Mortem." Atlantic Council, June.

Vilmer, Jean-Baptiste Jeangène, and Paul Charon. 2020. "Russia as a Hurricane, China as Climate Change: Different Ways of Information Warfare." War on the Rocks, January 21. https://warontherocks.com/2020/01/russia-as-a-hurricane-china-as-climate-change-different-ways-of-information-warfare/

Vladeck, Stephen I. 2015. "The Exceptionalism of Foreign Relations Normalization." 128 *Harvard Law Review Forum* 322.

Voice of America. 2018. "Record Number of Americans Hold Passports." January 18. https://blogs.voanews.com/all-about-america/2018/01/18/record-number-of-americans-hold-passports/

Volz, Dustin. 2017. "U.S. Far-Right Activists, WikiLeaks and Bots Help Amplify Macron Leaks." Reuters, May 6.

Wallis, Jacob, et al. 2020. "Retweeting through the Great Firewall: A Persistent and Undeterred Threat Actor." Australian Strategic Policy Institute, International Cyber Policy Center, June.

Walsh, Declan, and Nada Rashwan. 2019. "We're at War: A Covert Social Media Campaign Boosts Military Rulers." *New York Times*, September 6.

Walsh, Michael, and Bang Xiao. 2019. "Uncharted Territory: WeChat's New Role in Australian Public Life Raises Difficult Questions." Australian Broadcasting Corp., April 18.

Washington Post Staff. 2020. "Mapping the Worldwide Spread of the Virus." https://www.washingtonpost.com/graphics/2020/world/mapping-spread-new-coronavirus/

Waterson, Jim. 2019. "RT Fined £200,000 for Breaching Impartiality Rules." *The Guardian*, July 26.

Weiss, Jessica Chen. 2021. "An Ideological Contest in U.S.-China Relations? Assessing China's Defense of Autocracy." In *After Engagement: Dilemmas in U.S.-China Security Relations*, edited by Avery Goldstein and Jacques deLisle. Brookings Institution Press.

Weiss, Jessica Chen. 2020. "Understanding and Rolling Back Digital Authoritarianism." War on the Rocks, February 17. https://warontherocks.com/2020/02/understanding-and-rolling-back-digital-authoritarianism/

Welch, Chris. 2019. "YouTube Disabled 210 Accounts for Spreading Disinformation about Hong Kong Protests." *The Verge*, August 22.

Wells, Georgia, and Robert McMillan. 2017. "Scrutiny over Fake Accounts Turns from Facebook to Twitter." *Wall Street Journal*, October 2.

Whittington, Keith E. 1999. *Constitutional Construction: Divided Powers and Constitutional Meaning*. Cambridge, MA: Harvard University Press.

Willsher, Kim. 2017. "Penelopegate: My Part in the François Fillon Scandal." *The Guardian*, February 2.

Yan, Alice. 2018. "Seeing Double? Chinese Newspapers Use Identical Front Pages for African Summit Coverage." *South China Morning Post*, September 3.

Yerkes, Sarah E. 2021. "The Tunisia Model in Crisis: The President's Power Grab Risks an Authoritarian Regression." *Foreign Affairs*, August 6.

Yoshihara, Toshi, and Jack Bianchi. 2020. "Uncovering China's Influence in Europe: How Friendship Groups Coopt European Elites." Center for Strategic and Budgetary Assessments, July.

Zuboff, Shoshana. 2019. *The Age of Surveillance Capitalism: The Fight for a Human Future at the New Frontier of Power*. New York: PublicAffairs.

U.S. STATUTES AND REGULATIONS

18 U.S.C. § 2339B.

18 U.S.C. § 2511.

18 U.S.C. § 2701.

18 U.S.C. § 2721.

47 U.S.C. § 230.

52 U.S.C. § 30101.

52 U.S.C. § 30104.

52 U.S.C. § 30120.

Bipartisan Campaign Reform Act, Pub. L. No. 107-155, 116 Stat. 81 (2002).

California Business and Professions Code, § 17941.

Children's Online Privacy Protection Act, Pub. L. No. 105-277, §§ 1301–1308, 112 Stat. 2681 (1998).

Children's Online Privacy Protection Rule, 16 C.F.R. Part 312, §§ 312.1–312.13.

Countering America's Adversaries through Sanctions Act, Pub. L. No. 115-44, 131 Stat. 886 (2017).

Election Campaign Act Amendments, Pub. L. No. 94-283, 90 Stat. 475 (1976).

Federal Cigarette Labeling and Advertising Act, Pub. L. No. 89-92, 79 Stat. 282 (1965).

Federal Election Campaign Act Amendments, Pub. L. No. 94-283, 90 Stat. 475 (1976).

Foreign Agents Registration Act, Pub. L. No. 75-583, 52 Stat. 631 (1938).

Honest Ads Act, S.1989, 115th Cong., 1st Sess. (Oct. 19, 2017).

Nuclear Nonproliferation Act, Pub. L. No. 95-242, 92 Stat. 120 (1978).

REAL ID Act, Pub. L. No. 109-13, Div. B, Title II, 119 Stat. 311 (2005).

Telecommunications Act, Pub. L. No. 104-104, 110 Stat. 56 (1996).

JUDICIAL DECISIONS

Abrams v. United States, 250 U.S. 616 (1919).

Adarand Constructors, Inc. v. Pena, 515 U.S. 200 (1995).

Agency for International Development v. Alliance for Open Society International, Inc., 140 S. Ct. 2082 (2020).

Bethune-Hill v. Virginia State Bd. of Elections, 137 S. Ct. 788 (2017).

Bluman v. Federal Election Commission, 800 F.Supp.2d 281 (D.D.C. 2011).

Bluman v. Federal Election Commission, 565 U.S. 1104 (Mem.) (2012).

Boumediene v. Bush, 553 U.S. 723 (2008).

Box v. Planned Parenthood of Indiana and Kentucky, Inc., 139 S. Ct. 1780 (2019).

Brown v. Entertainment Merchants Ass'n, 564 U.S. 786 (2011).

Brown v. Socialist Workers '74 Campaign Committee, 459 U.S. 87 (1982).

Buckley v. Valeo, 424 U.S. 1 (1976).

Citizens United v. Federal Election Commission, 558 U.S. 310 (2010).

Clapper v. Amnesty Int'l USA, 568 U.S. 398 (2013).

Dep't of Commerce v. New York, 139 S. Ct. 2551 (2019).

Doe v. Reed, 561 U.S. 186 (2010).

Holder v. Humanitarian Law Project, 561 U.S. 1 (2010).

In re Ross, 140 U.S. 453 (1891).

Janus v. American Federation of State, County, and Municipal Employees, 138 S. Ct. 2448 (2018).

Klayman v. Obama, 957 F.Supp.2d 1 (D.D.C. 2013).

Kleindienst v. Mandel, 408 U.S. 753 (1972).

Lamont v. Postmaster General of U. S., 381 U.S. 301 (1965).

Lochner v. New York, 198 U.S. 45 (1905).

Marland v. Trump, 2020 WL 6381397 (E.D. Pa. Oct. 30, 2020).

McConnell v. Federal Election Commission, 540 U.S. 93 (2003).

McIntyre v. Ohio Elections Commission, 514 U.S. 334 (1995).

Miller v. California, 413 U.S. 15 (1973).

Meese v. Keene, 481 U.S. 465 (1987).

National Association for Advancement of Colored People v. Alabama, 357 U.S. 449 (1958).

National Federation of Independent Business v. Sebelius, 567 U.S. 519 (2012).

New York v. Ferber, 458 U.S. 747 (1982).

Packingham v. North Carolina, 137 S. Ct. 1730 (2017).

Reid v. Covert, 354 U.S. 1 (1957).

Stanley v. Georgia, 394 U.S. 557 (1969).

Trump v. Hawaii, 138 S. Ct. 2392 (2018).

U.S. WeChat Users All. v. Trump, 2020 WL 6891820 (N.D. Cal. Nov. 24, 2020).

United States v. Alvarez, 567 U.S. 709 (2012).

United States v. Curtiss-Wright Export Corp., 299 U.S. 304 (1936).

United States v. Stevens, 559 U.S. 460 (2010).

United States v. Windsor, 570 U.S. 744 (2013).

Washington Post v. McManus, 944 F.3d 506 (4th Cir. 2019).

Williams-Yulee v. Florida Bar, 575 U.S. 433 (2015).

Zivotofsky ex rel. Zivotofsky v. Clinton, 566 U.S. 189 (2012).

OTHER U.S. GOVERNMENT DOCUMENTS

Congresswoman Anna G. Eshoo. 2020. "Rep. Eshoo Introduces Bill to Ban Microtargeted Political Ads." Press release, May 26.

Disinformation: A Primer in Russian Active Measures and Influence Campaigns. Hearing Before the Senate Select Comm. on Intelligence, S. Hrg. 115-40 (March 30, 2017).

Exec. Order No. 13,456. *Further Amendment of Executive Order 11858 Concerning Foreign Investment in the United States.* 73 Fed. Reg. 4677 (January 25, 2008).

Exec. Order No. 13,757. *Taking Additional Steps to Address the National Emergency with Respect to Significant Malicious Cyber-Enabled Activities.* 82 Fed. Reg. 1 (January 3, 2017).

Exec. Order No. 13,942. *Addressing the Threat Posed by TikTok, and Taking Additional Steps to Address the National Emergency with Respect to the Information and Communications Technology and Services Supply Chain.* 85 Fed. Reg. 48637 (August 11, 2020).

Exec. Order No. 13,943. *Addressing the Threat Posed by WeChat, and Taking Additional Steps to Address the National Emergency with Respect to the Information and Communications Technology and Services Supply Chain.* 85 Fed. Reg. 48641 (August 11, 2020).

Intelligence Community Assessment. 2017. *Assessing Russian Activities and Intentions in Recent U.S. Elections.* ICA 2017-01D (January 6).

Pompeo, Michael R. 2020. "Communist China and the Free World's Future." U.S. Department of State. Speech delivered at Richard Nixon Presidential Library, Yorba Linda, CA, July 23.

Sen. Foreign Relations Comm., Minority Staff Report, 115th Cong. *Putin's Asymmetric Assault on Democracy in Russia and Europe: Implications for U.S. National Security* (January 10, 2018).

Senator Amy Klobuchar. 2019. "Klobuchar, Graham, Warner Introduce Legislation to Improve National Security and Protect Integrity of U.S. Elections by Bringing Transparency and Accountability to Online Political Ads." Press release, May 8.

Special Counsel Robert S. Mueller, III. 2019. *Report on the Investigation into Russian Interference in the 2016 Presidential Election* ["Mueller Report"].

U.S. Department of Homeland Security. 2020. "All U.S. States Now Compliant Ahead of REAL ID Deadline." Press release, September 10.

U.S. Department of Justice. 2017. "DOJ Criminal Cases against Chinese during the Trump Administration." https://multimedia.scmp.com/widgets/us/doj/.

U.S. Department of Justice. 2020. "Six Russian GRU Officers Charged in Connection with Worldwide Deployment of Destructive Malware and Other Disruptive Actions in Cyberspace." Press release, October 19.

U.S. Department of State, Bureau of Democracy, Human Rights, and Labor. 2020. *2019 Country Reports on Human Rights Practices*, March 11.

United States of America v. Elena Alekseevna Khusyaynova, *Affidavit in Support of a Criminal Complaint* (E.D. Va., September 28, 2018).

United States of America v. Internet Research Agency et al., *Indictment* (D.D.C. February 16, 2018).

United States of America v. Viktor Borisovich Netyksho et al., *Indictment* (D.D.C. July 13, 2018).

United States of America v. Paul J. Manafort, Jr. and Konstantin Kilimnik, *Superseding Indictment* (D.D.C. June 8, 2018).

FOREIGN AND INTERNATIONAL DOCUMENTS

Charter of the United Nations, *multilateral*, October 24, 1945, 1 UNTS 16.

European Commission. 2020. "Rule of Law: European Commission Launches Infringement Procedure to Safeguard the Independence of Judges in Poland." April 29. https://ec.europa.eu/commission/presscorner/detail/en/ip_20_772

European Council. 2021. "EU Restrictive Measures in Response to the Crisis in Ukraine." https://www.consilium.europa.eu/en/policies/sanctions/ukraine-crisis/.

European Union. 2016. "General Data Protection Regulation, Regulation 2016/679."

EUvsDisinfo. 2019a. "Disinfo: Sweden's Feminist Government Orders not to Investigate Rapes to Protect the Immigrants that Committed Them." February 14. https://euvsdisinfo.eu/report/swedens-feminist-government-orders-not-to-investigate-rapings-to-protect-the-immigrants-that-committed-them/

EUvsDisinfo. 2019b. "EU Elections Update: Reaping What Was Sown." May 23. https://euvsdisinfo.eu/eu-elections-update-reaping-what-was-sown/

International Law Commission. 2001. *Responsibility of States for Internationally Wrongful Acts*. https://legal.un.org/ilc/texts/instruments/english/draft_articles/9_6_2001.pdf

North Atlantic Treaty Organization. 2020. "Partnership Interoperability Initiative." November 3. https://www.nato.int/cps/em/natohq/topics_132726.htm

United Kingdom, Electoral Commission. 2018. "Investigation into Payments Made to Better for the Country and Leave.EU." November 1. https://www.electoralcommission.org.uk/who-we-are-and-what-we-do/our-enforcement-work/investigations/investigation-payments-made-better-country-and-leaveeu

United Kingdom, Intelligence and Security Committee of Parliament. 2020. *Russia*. July 21.

United Kingdom, House of Commons, Digital, Culture, Media and Sport Committee. 2019. *Disinformation and Fake News: Final Report*. February 14.

United Kingdom, National Crime Agency. 2019. "Public Statement on NCA Investigation Into Suspected EU Referendum Offences." September 24. https://www.nationalcrimeagency.gov.uk/news/public-statement-on-nca-investigation-into-suspected-eu-referendum-offences

United Nations Human Rights Council. 2020. "Cross-regional Statement on Hong Kong and Xinjiang." June 30. https://www.gov.uk/government/speeches/un-human-rights-council-44-cross-regional-statement-on-hong-kong-and-xinjiang

United Nations Human Rights Council. 2020. "Joint Statement Delivered by Permanent Mission of Cuba." June 30. http://www.china-un.ch/eng/hom/t1793804.htm

United Nations Security Council, S.C. Res. 1373 (September 28, 2001).

INDEX

Note: page numbers followed by *f* and *t* refer to figures and tables respectively. Those followed by n refer to notes, with note number.

tent by Trump campaign officials, 33; stolen accounts, 34; types used, 32–34; voter suppression messages, 36

Russian interference in 2016 U.S. election, likely impact of: responsibility for Trump victory, 26, 38–42, 199; studies on, 37–42; success in increasing polarization, 42

Salvini, Matteo, 126–27

sanctions in regulation of social media, 188–91; expressive value of, 188; ineffectiveness of, 188–91, 203

Sanders campaign: Russian impostor account mimicking, 43–44; Russian support for, to undermine Clinton, 36; spread of misinformation by supporters of, 45

Saudi Arabia: and digital authoritarianism, 137–41; and information warfare, 13–14

self-regulation of social media: as government by unelected rulers, 7; as inadequate, 3, 4, 6, 114

Semptian, 109

September 11th terrorist attacks, restrictions on US Muslims following, 14

Settle, Jaime, 128

shared reference points based on accurate information: erosion through cognitive polarization, 127; erosion through OSM, 129; as necessary for democracy, 126

Shorten, Bill, 105

Sina Weibo: number of users, 275n8; transnational regulatory system and, 151, 162, 276n24; use within China, 5

Sitaraman, Ganesh, 244

smart city technologies, 85, 86

Snowden, Edward, 209, 235

social media: autocratic rulers' use for surveillance purposes, 108–9; banning of Alex Jones from, 124; and China's state-run media, followers of, 90–91, 91t; companies selling technology to monitor users on, 108–9; dominance of US platforms, as potential strategic advantage, 6; and election of 2020, claimed Democrat voter fraud in, ix; facilitation of authoritarian government by, 134; fake accounts, types of, 31–32; and filter bubbles, 127; government regulation of, as potential strategic advantage, 6; information warfare on, 5; political communication on, exacerbation of polarization by, 127–29; unrestricted access by Russia and China, as problematic, 5

social media, undermining of democracy by: scholarship on, 117; through increased polarization, 117; through increased spread of misinformation and disinformation, 117, 123–24

social media companies: costs imposed on, by transnational regulatory system, 21–22, 207–9; current reactive regulation system, problems with, 187, 204; and fake accounts, inability to detect, 178–79; legal immunity regarding user content, 184; regulation of internet speech, 184–85; and surveillance capitalism, 108; Type A and B platforms, 168, 208; violations of privacy and anonymity, protections against in

STANFORD STUDIES IN LAW AND POLITICS
Edited by Keith J. Bybee

CPSIA information can be obtained
at www.ICGtesting.com
Printed in the USA
LVHW041027180222
711437LV00001B/1/J